DAKEN
DARK WOLVERINE

THE PRIDE COMES
BEFORE THE FALL

DAKEN: DARK WOLVERINE — THE PRIDE COMES BEFORE THE FALL. Contains material originally published in magazine form as DAKEN: DARK WOLVERINE #13-19. First printing 2012. Hardcover ISBN# 978-0-7851-5235-4. Softcover ISBN# 978-0-7851-5236-1. Published by MARVEL WORLDWIDE, INC., a subsidiary of MARVEL ENTERTAINMENT, LLC. OFFICE OF PUBLICATION: 135 West 50th Street, New York, NY 10020. Copyright © 2011 and 2012 Marvel Characters, Inc. All rights reserved. Hardcover: $19.99 per copy in the U.S. and $21.99 in Canada (GST #R127032852). Softcover: $15.99 per copy in the U.S. and $17.99 in Canada (GST #R127032852). Canadian Agreement #40668537. All characters featured in this issue and the distinctive names and likenesses thereof, and all related indicia are trademarks of Marvel Characters, Inc. No similarity between any of the names, characters, persons, and/or institutions in this magazine with those of any living or dead person or institution is intended, and any such similarity which may exist is purely coincidental. **Printed in the U.S.A.** ALAN FINE, EVP - Office of the President, Marvel Worldwide, Inc. and EVP & CMO Marvel Characters B.V.; DAN BUCKLEY, Publisher & President - Print, Animation & Digital Divisions; JOE QUESADA, Chief Creative Officer; DAVID BOGART, SVP of Business Affairs & Talent Management; TOM BREVOORT, SVP of Publishing; C.B. CEBULSKI, SVP of Creator & Content Development; DAVID GABRIEL, SVP of Publishing Sales & Circulation; MICHAEL PASCIULLO, SVP of Brand Planning & Communications; JIM O'KEEFE, VP of Operations & Logistics; DAN CARR, Executive Director of Publishing Technology; SUSAN CRESPI, Editorial Operations Manager; ALEX MORALES, Publishing Operations Manager; STAN LEE, Chairman Emeritus. For information regarding advertising in Marvel Comics or on Marvel.com, please contact John Dokes, SVP Integrated Sales and Marketing, at jdokes@marvel.com. For Marvel subscription inquiries, please call 800-217-9158. **Manufactured between 12/26/2011 and 1/23/2012 (hardcover), and 12/26/2011 and 7/23/2012 (softcover), by R.R. DONNELLEY, INC., SALEM, VA, USA.**

10 9 8 7 6 5 4 3 2 1

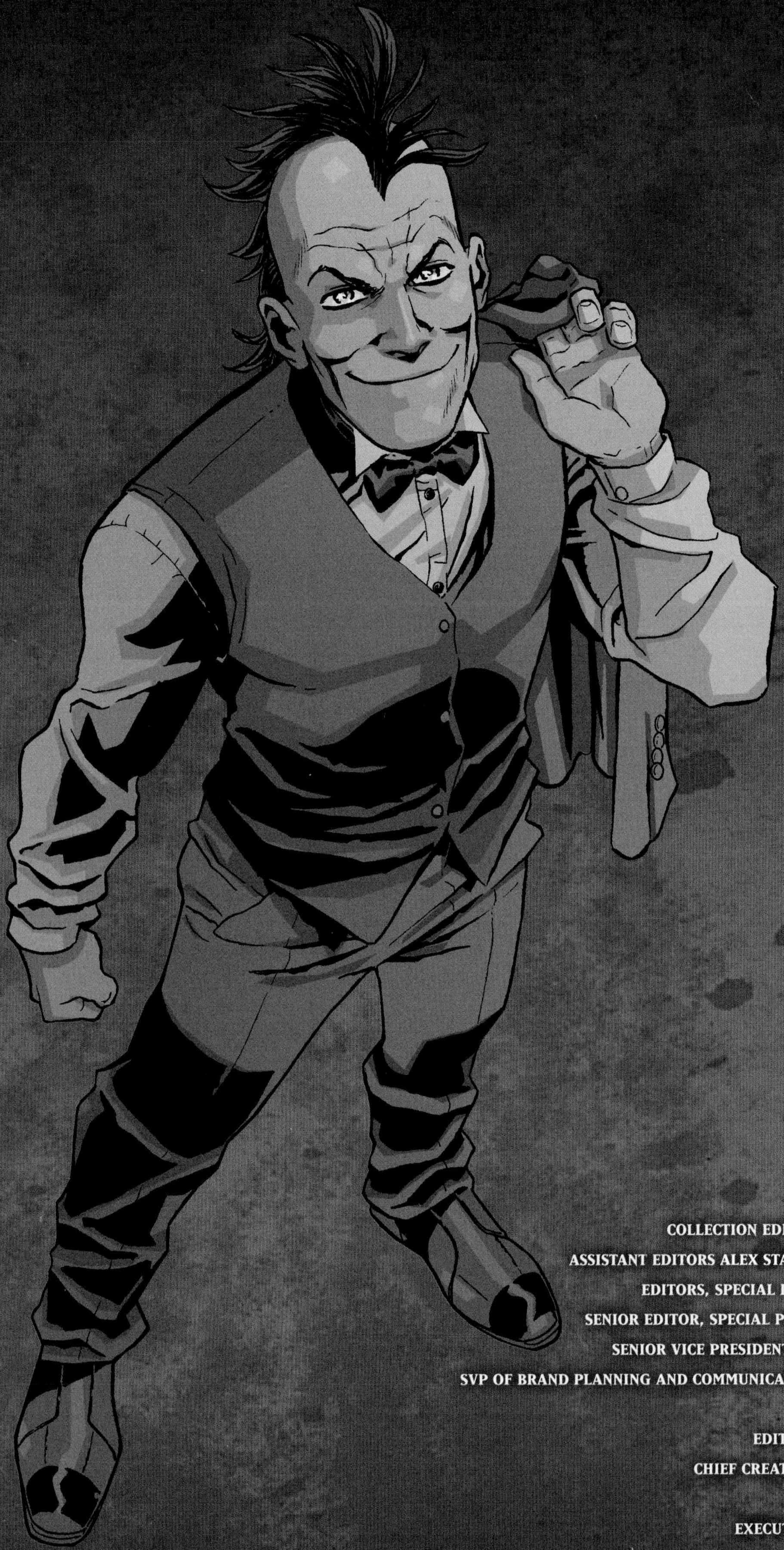

COLLECTION EDITOR JENNIFER GRÜNWALD
ASSISTANT EDITORS ALEX STARBUCK & NELSON RIBEIRO
EDITORS, SPECIAL PROJECT MARK D. BEAZLEY
SENIOR EDITOR, SPECIAL PROJECTS JEFF YOUNGQUIST
SENIOR VICE PRESIDENT OF SALES DAVID GABRIEL
SVP OF BRAND PLANNING AND COMMUNICATIONS MICHAEL PASCIULLO

EDITOR IN CHIEF AXEL ALONSO
CHIEF CREATIVE OFFICER JOE QUESADA
PUBLISHER DAN BUCKLEY
EXECUTIVE PRODUCER ALAN FINE

DAKEN
DARK WOLVERINE

THE PRIDE COMES BEFORE THE FALL

— WRITER —
ROB WILLIAMS

ISSUES #13-15
— PENCILS —
MICHELE BERTILORENZI

— INKS —
JOHN LUCAS & MICHELE BERTILORENZI

— COLORS —
CRIS PETER

— HEAT SEQUENCES —
RILEY ROSSMO

ISSUES #16-19
— PENCILS —
MATTEO BUFFAGNI
WITH MICHELE BERTILORENZI & ANDREA MUTTI (#18-19)

— INKS —
CRAIG YEUNG
WITH MICHELE BERTILORENZI & ANDREA MUTTI (#18-19)

— COLORS —
CRIS PETER
WITH RACHELLE ROSENBERG (#19)

— LETTERS —
VIRTUAL CALLIGRAPHY'S CORY PETIT

— COVER ART —
GIUSEPPE CAMUNCOLI
WITH FRANK MARTIN, MARTE GRACIA & JESSICA KHOLINE

ASSISTANT EDITORS
JODY LeHEUP & SEBASTIAN GIRNIR

— EDITOR —
JEANINE SCHAEFER

— GROUP EDITOR —
NICK LOWE

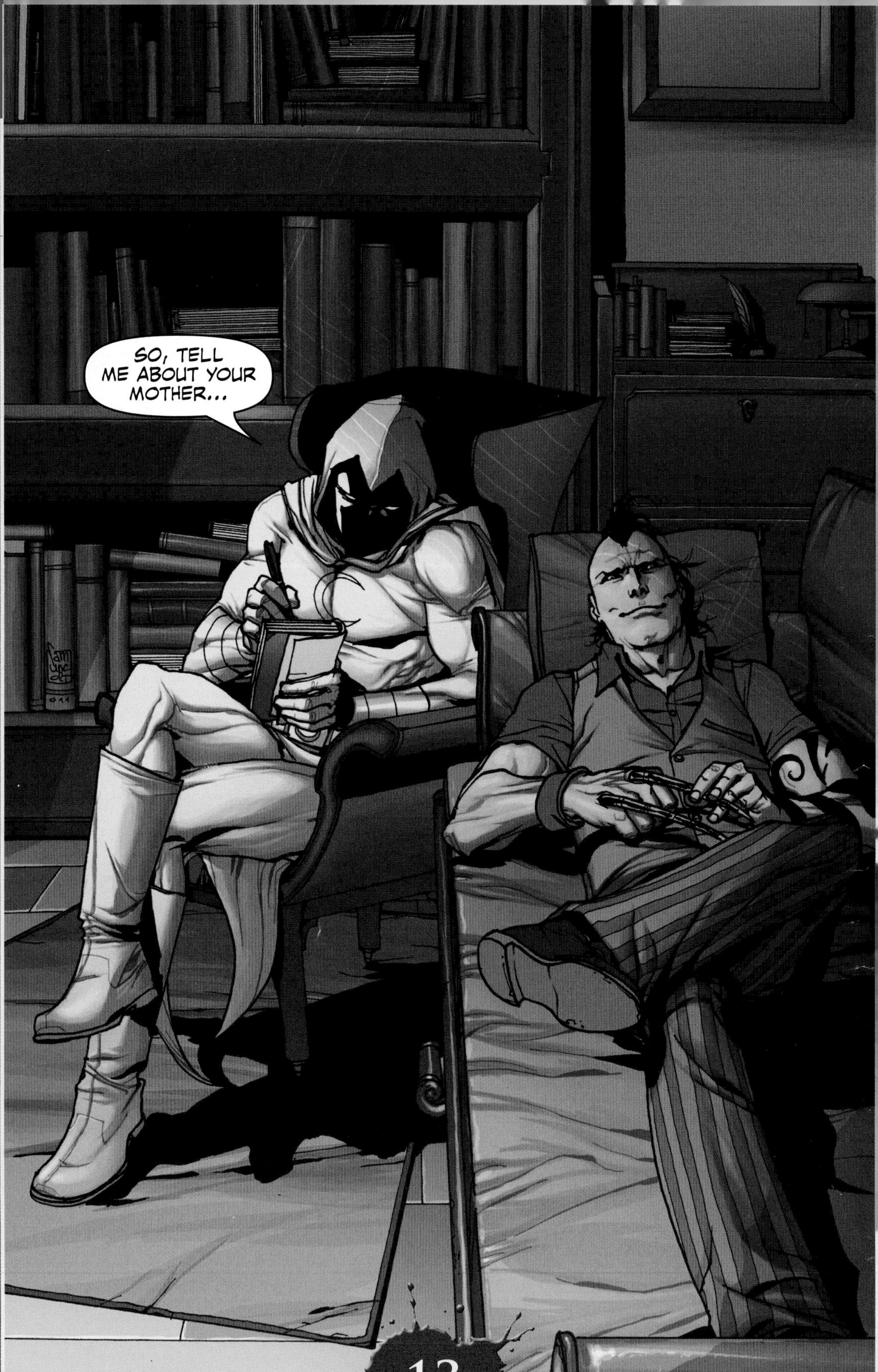
SO, TELL ME ABOUT YOUR MOTHER...

Years ago, the mutant known as Wolverine found peace in Japan and had a son with his wife, Itsu. The peace was short-lived--Itsu was murdered and Wolverine believed his son died with her...but the boy lived. The boy came to be known as Daken and grew up consumed with hatred for his father, wrongly blaming him for the death of his mother for much of his life. He discovered that he had the ability to manipulate the emotions of others, and like Wolverine, possessed a powerful healing factor and razor-sharp claws on each hand. But Daken walked a far different path than that of his father. Instead of righting the wrongs of the world, Daken wanted to set it on fire. He had become...

DAKEN DARK WOLVERINE

PREVIOUSLY...

Daken has emerged in Los Angeles, hoping to catch the attention of the city's mysterious Kingpin and eventually replace him as head of the criminal underworld. However, he's become distracted with the hedonistic lifestyle of the city's rich and famous and fallen into addiction via a mysterious designer drug called "Heat." The drug impedes Daken's healing factor and severely alters his perception, giving him either euphoric or nightmarish highs and causing him to black out for several hours. While attempting to steal millions of dollars from an armored car and secure his domination over several L.A. crime families, the Heat-addled Daken faces off against the car's bodyguard, the mercenary known as Taskmaster. Though he wins the battle and succeeds in pulling off the biggest cash robbery in U.S. history, he also sustains a serious injury that his weakened healing factor can't fix. Confused and in pain, Daken is cornered by F.B.I. agent Donna Kiel, who reveals that someone with claws has been murdering people all over the city at times that coincide with Daken's blackouts. Daken knocks out Agent Kiel and escapes, but the question remains: has Heat turned him into a thoughtless killing machine?

LOS ANGELES.

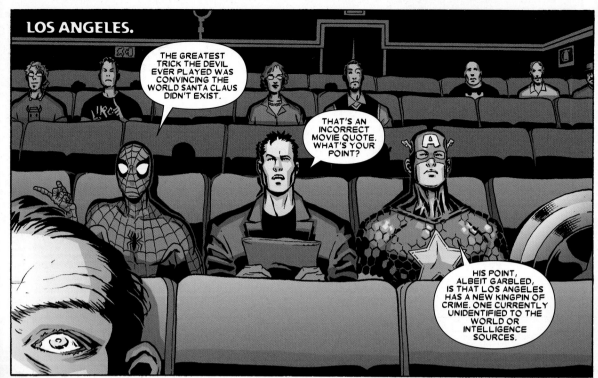

THE GREATEST TRICK THE DEVIL EVER PLAYED WAS CONVINCING THE WORLD SANTA CLAUS DIDN'T EXIST.

THAT'S AN INCORRECT MOVIE QUOTE. WHAT'S YOUR POINT?

HIS POINT, ALBEIT GARBLED, IS THAT LOS ANGELES HAS A NEW KINGPIN OF CRIME. ONE CURRENTLY UNIDENTIFIED TO THE WORLD OR INTELLIGENCE SOURCES.

PLUS THERE'S THIS SERIAL KILLER LOOSE IN HOLLYWOOD. "THE CLAWS KILLER."

AS THE AVENGER MOON KNIGHT YOU NEED TO FIND OUT THEIR IDENTITIES AND TAKE THEM DOWN.

AND I'M WORKING ON IT. BUT I'M ALSO MARK SPECTOR, HOLLYWOOD PRODUCER THESE DAYS. I HAVE TO DO SOME WORK.

BY THE WAY...

...WHY ISN'T HE SITTING WITH US?

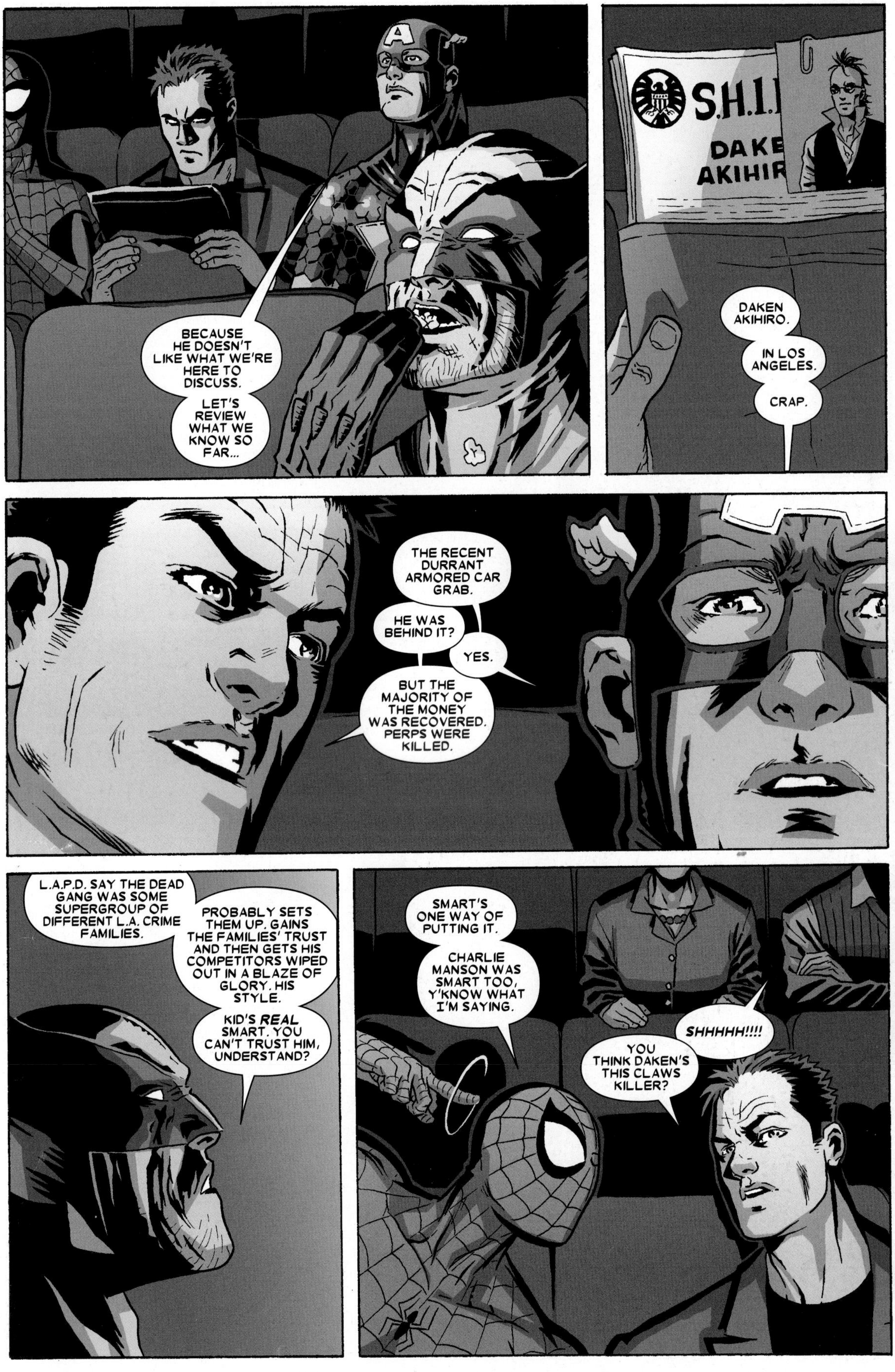
BECAUSE HE DOESN'T LIKE WHAT WE'RE HERE TO DISCUSS.
LET'S REVIEW WHAT WE KNOW SO FAR...
S.H.I.
DAKE
AKIHIR
DAKEN AKIHIRO.
IN LOS ANGELES.
CRAP.
THE RECENT DURRANT ARMORED CAR GRAB.
HE WAS BEHIND IT?
YES.
BUT THE MAJORITY OF THE MONEY WAS RECOVERED. PERPS WERE KILLED.
L.A.P.D. SAY THE DEAD GANG WAS SOME SUPERGROUP OF DIFFERENT L.A. CRIME FAMILIES.
PROBABLY SETS THEM UP. GAINS THE FAMILIES' TRUST AND THEN GETS HIS COMPETITORS WIPED OUT IN A BLAZE OF GLORY. HIS STYLE.
KID'S *REAL* SMART. YOU CAN'T TRUST HIM, UNDERSTAND?
SMART'S ONE WAY OF PUTTING IT.
CHARLIE MANSON WAS SMART TOO, Y'KNOW WHAT I'M SAYING.
SHHHHH!!!!
YOU THINK DAKEN'S THIS CLAWS KILLER?

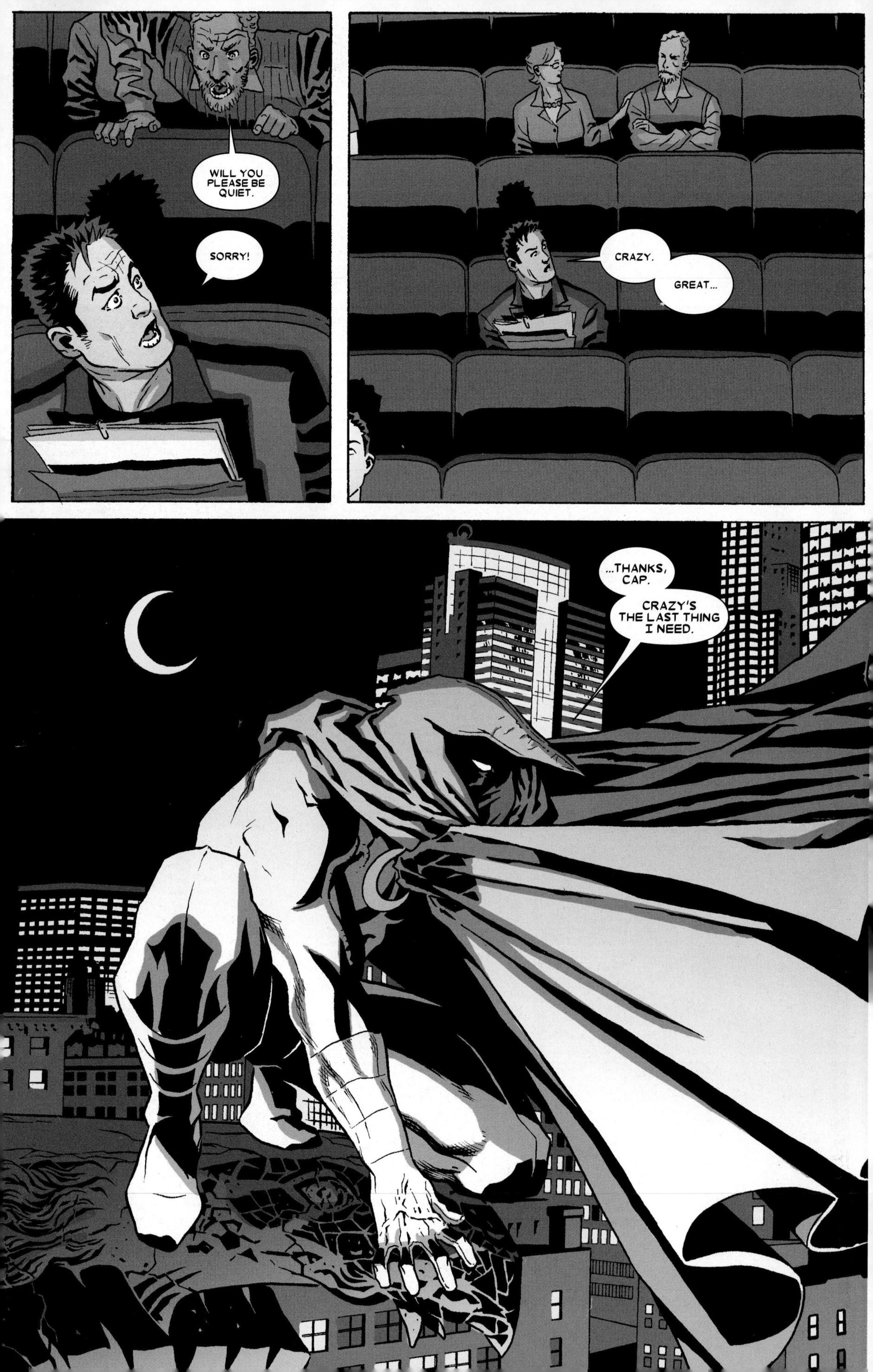
WILL YOU PLEASE BE QUIET.
SORRY!
CRAZY.
GREAT...
...THANKS, CAP.
CRAZY'S THE LAST THING I NEED.

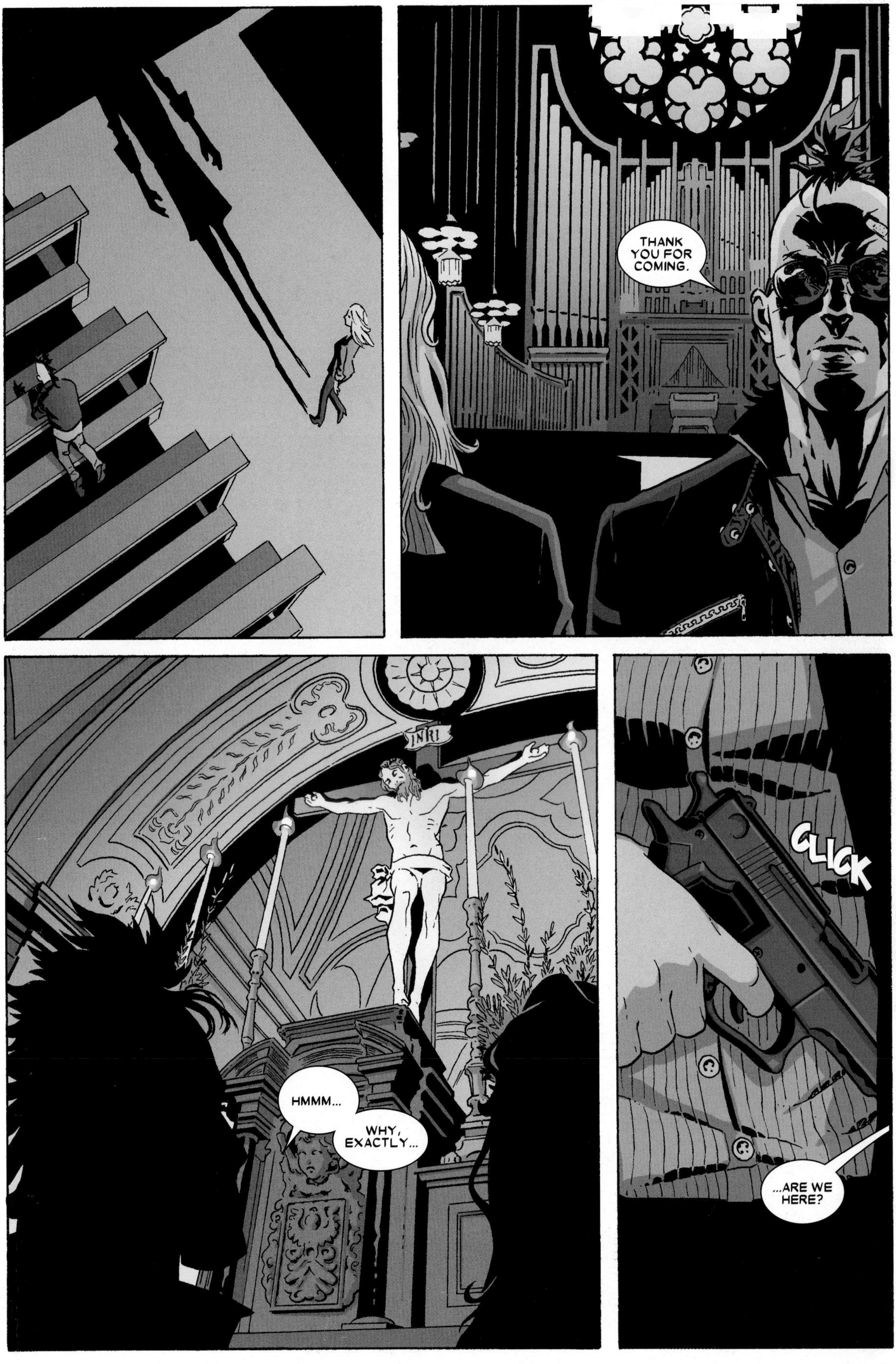
THANK YOU FOR COMING.
INRI
HMMM...
WHY, EXACTLY...
CLICK
...ARE WE HERE?

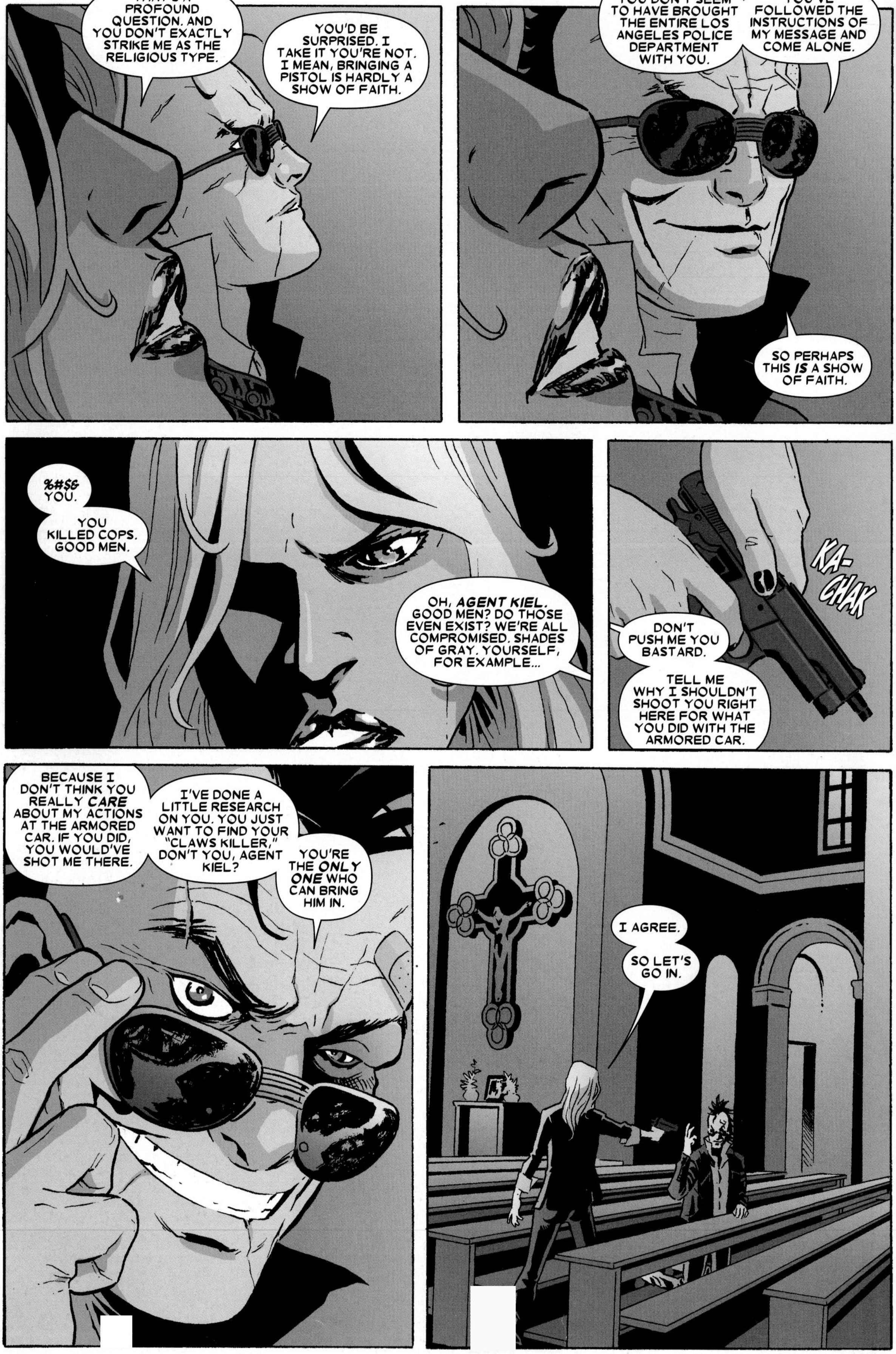
THAT'S A PROFOUND QUESTION. AND YOU DON'T EXACTLY STRIKE ME AS THE RELIGIOUS TYPE.
YOU'D BE SURPRISED. I TAKE IT YOU'RE NOT. I MEAN, BRINGING A PISTOL IS HARDLY A SHOW OF FAITH.
THEN AGAIN, YOU DON'T SEEM TO HAVE BROUGHT THE ENTIRE LOS ANGELES POLICE DEPARTMENT WITH YOU.
YOU'VE FOLLOWED THE INSTRUCTIONS OF MY MESSAGE AND COME ALONE.
SO PERHAPS THIS *IS* A SHOW OF FAITH.
%#$& YOU.
YOU KILLED COPS. GOOD MEN.
OH, *AGENT KIEL.* GOOD MEN? DO THOSE EVEN EXIST? WE'RE ALL COMPROMISED. SHADES OF GRAY. YOURSELF, FOR EXAMPLE...
KA-CHAK
DON'T PUSH ME YOU BASTARD.
TELL ME WHY I SHOULDN'T SHOOT YOU RIGHT HERE FOR WHAT YOU DID WITH THE ARMORED CAR.
BECAUSE I DON'T THINK YOU REALLY *CARE* ABOUT MY ACTIONS AT THE ARMORED CAR. IF YOU DID, YOU WOULD'VE SHOT ME THERE.
I'VE DONE A LITTLE RESEARCH ON YOU. YOU JUST WANT TO FIND YOUR "CLAWS KILLER," DON'T YOU, AGENT KIEL?
YOU'RE THE *ONLY ONE* WHO CAN BRING HIM IN.
I AGREE.
SO LET'S GO IN.

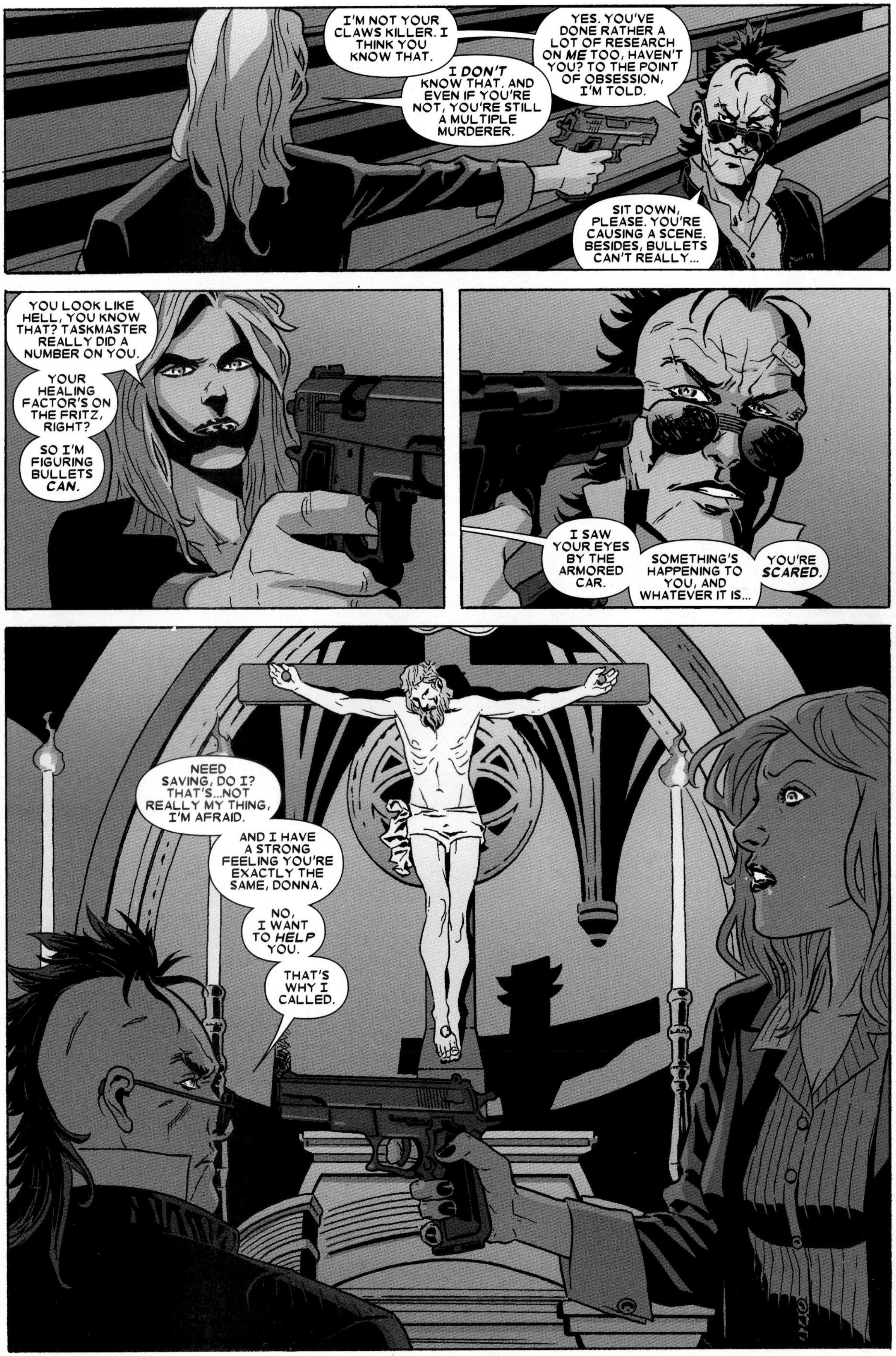
I'M NOT YOUR CLAWS KILLER. I THINK YOU KNOW THAT.
YES. YOU'VE DONE RATHER A LOT OF RESEARCH ON ME TOO, HAVEN'T YOU? TO THE POINT OF OBSESSION, I'M TOLD.
I DON'T KNOW THAT. AND EVEN IF YOU'RE NOT, YOU'RE STILL A MULTIPLE MURDERER.
SIT DOWN, PLEASE. YOU'RE CAUSING A SCENE. BESIDES, BULLETS CAN'T REALLY...
YOU LOOK LIKE HELL, YOU KNOW THAT? TASKMASTER REALLY DID A NUMBER ON YOU.
YOUR HEALING FACTOR'S ON THE FRITZ, RIGHT?
SO I'M FIGURING BULLETS CAN.
I SAW YOUR EYES BY THE ARMORED CAR.
SOMETHING'S HAPPENING TO YOU, AND WHATEVER IT IS...
YOU'RE SCARED.
NEED SAVING, DO I? THAT'S...NOT REALLY MY THING, I'M AFRAID.
AND I HAVE A STRONG FEELING YOU'RE EXACTLY THE SAME, DONNA.
NO, I WANT TO HELP YOU.
THAT'S WHY I CALLED.

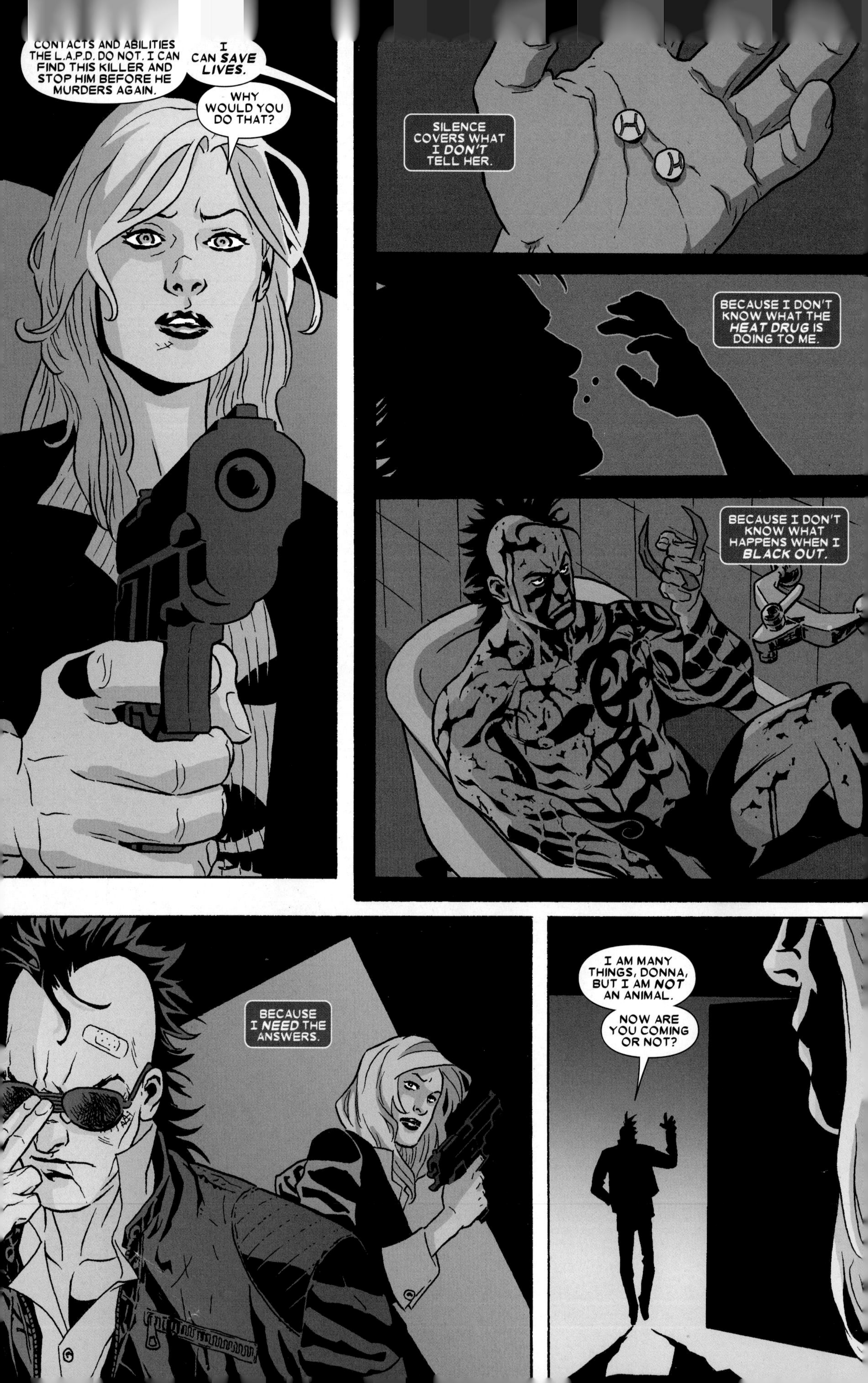
CONTACTS AND ABILITIES THE L.A.P.D. DO NOT. I CAN FIND THIS KILLER AND STOP HIM BEFORE HE MURDERS AGAIN.
I CAN SAVE LIVES.
WHY WOULD YOU DO THAT?
SILENCE COVERS WHAT I DON'T TELL HER.
BECAUSE I DON'T KNOW WHAT THE HEAT DRUG IS DOING TO ME.
BECAUSE I DON'T KNOW WHAT HAPPENS WHEN I BLACK OUT.
BECAUSE I NEED THE ANSWERS.
I AM MANY THINGS, DONNA, BUT I AM NOT AN ANIMAL.
NOW ARE YOU COMING OR NOT?

"THE LATEST VICTIM. TELL ME."

"TWO NIGHTS AGO. HAPPENED IN THE EARLY HOURS. ACTRESS AND SINGER. 22-YEAR-OLD. CAUCASIAN. PARTY TYPE.

"SAME PROFILE AS THE OTHER VICTIMS. ALL SHOWBIZ WANNABES. AUDITION FODDER. COUPLE OF UNINSPIRING, VERY SMALL TV PARTS, A FEW PLAYS..."

"HER NAME, DONNA.

"WHAT WAS HER NAME?"

"LUCILLE DAY.

"REAL NAME LUCIA ROMANOWSKI. SHE CHANGED IT WHEN SHE MOVED TO L.A. TO MAKE HERSELF MORE HIREABLE.

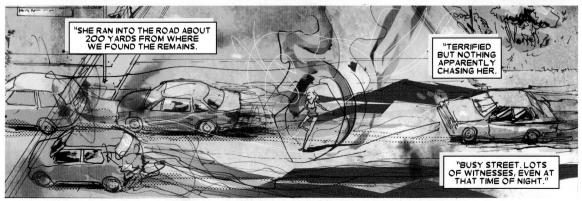

"SHE RAN INTO THE ROAD ABOUT 200 YARDS FROM WHERE WE FOUND THE REMAINS.

"TERRIFIED BUT NOTHING APPARENTLY CHASING HER.

"BUSY STREET. LOTS OF WITNESSES, EVEN AT THAT TIME OF NIGHT."

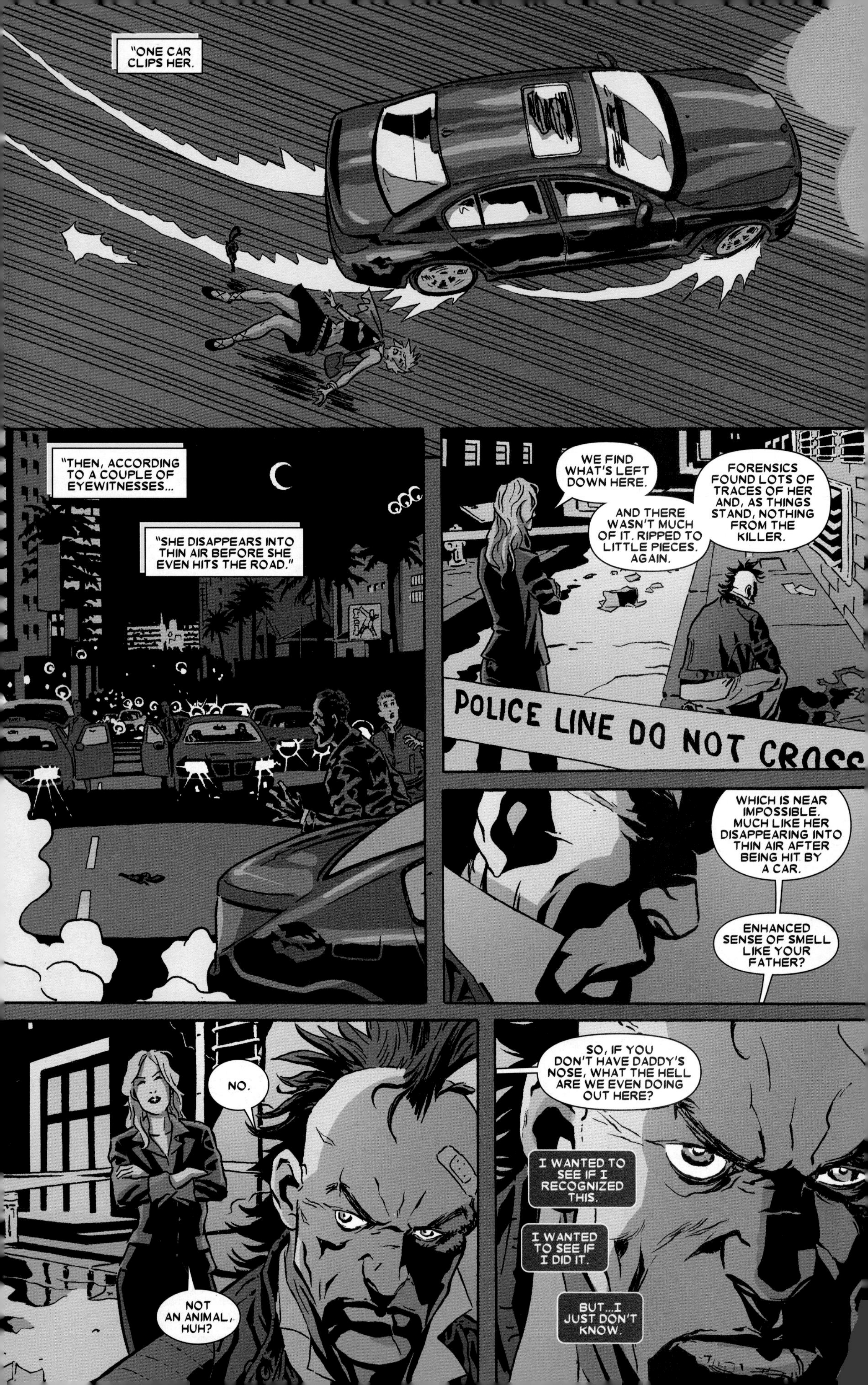
"ONE CAR CLIPS HER.
"THEN, ACCORDING TO A COUPLE OF EYEWITNESSES...
"SHE DISAPPEARS INTO THIN AIR BEFORE SHE EVEN HITS THE ROAD."
WE FIND WHAT'S LEFT DOWN HERE.
AND THERE WASN'T MUCH OF IT. RIPPED TO LITTLE PIECES. AGAIN.
FORENSICS FOUND LOTS OF TRACES OF HER AND, AS THINGS STAND, NOTHING FROM THE KILLER.
POLICE LINE DO NOT CROSS
WHICH IS NEAR IMPOSSIBLE. MUCH LIKE HER DISAPPEARING INTO THIN AIR AFTER BEING HIT BY A CAR.
ENHANCED SENSE OF SMELL LIKE YOUR FATHER?
NO.
NOT AN ANIMAL, HUH?
SO, IF YOU DON'T HAVE DADDY'S NOSE, WHAT THE HELL ARE WE EVEN DOING OUT HERE?
I WANTED TO SEE IF I RECOGNIZED THIS.
I WANTED TO SEE IF I DID IT.
BUT...I JUST DON'T KNOW.

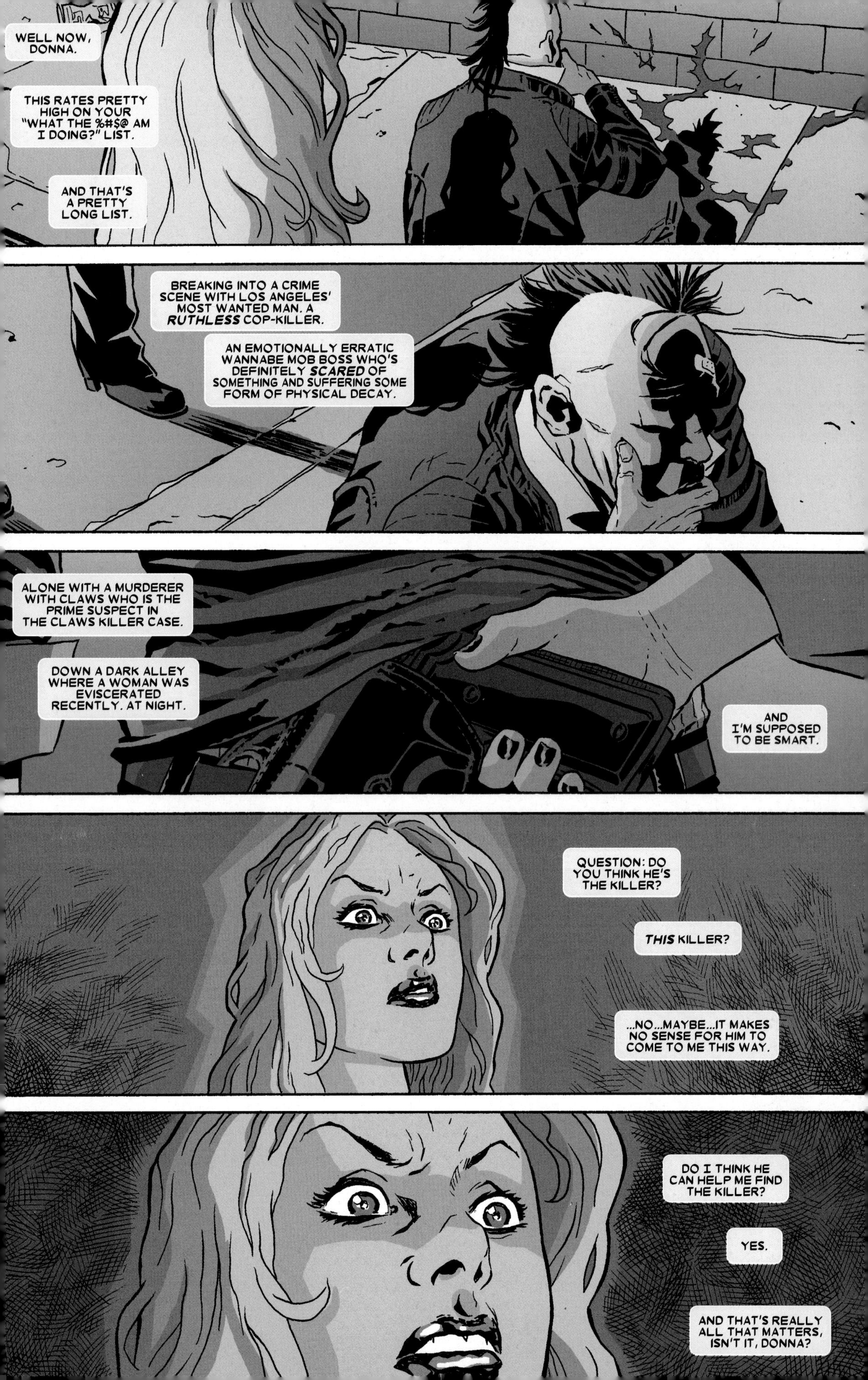
WELL NOW, DONNA.
THIS RATES PRETTY HIGH ON YOUR "WHAT THE %#$@ AM I DOING?" LIST.
AND THAT'S A PRETTY LONG LIST.
BREAKING INTO A CRIME SCENE WITH LOS ANGELES' MOST WANTED MAN. A RUTHLESS COP-KILLER.
AN EMOTIONALLY ERRATIC WANNABE MOB BOSS WHO'S DEFINITELY SCARED OF SOMETHING AND SUFFERING SOME FORM OF PHYSICAL DECAY.
ALONE WITH A MURDERER WITH CLAWS WHO IS THE PRIME SUSPECT IN THE CLAWS KILLER CASE.
DOWN A DARK ALLEY WHERE A WOMAN WAS EVISCERATED RECENTLY. AT NIGHT.
AND I'M SUPPOSED TO BE SMART.
QUESTION: DO YOU THINK HE'S THE KILLER?
THIS KILLER?
...NO...MAYBE...IT MAKES NO SENSE FOR HIM TO COME TO ME THIS WAY.
DO I THINK HE CAN HELP ME FIND THE KILLER?
YES.
AND THAT'S REALLY ALL THAT MATTERS, ISN'T IT, DONNA?

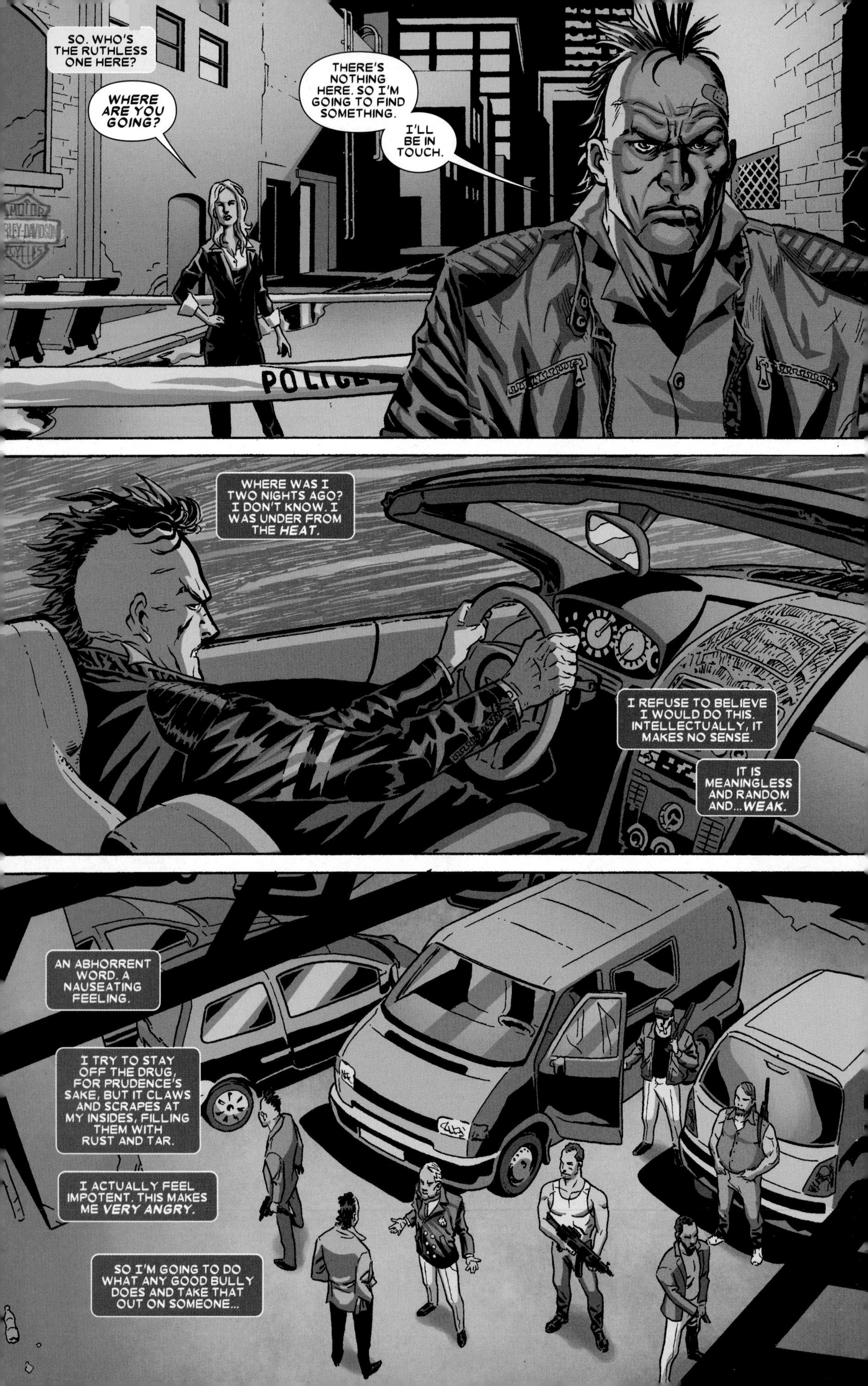
SO. WHO'S THE RUTHLESS ONE HERE?
WHERE ARE YOU GOING?
THERE'S NOTHING HERE. SO I'M GOING TO FIND SOMETHING.
I'LL BE IN TOUCH.
POLICE
WHERE WAS I TWO NIGHTS AGO? I DON'T KNOW. I WAS UNDER FROM THE HEAT.
I REFUSE TO BELIEVE I WOULD DO THIS. INTELLECTUALLY, IT MAKES NO SENSE.
IT IS MEANINGLESS AND RANDOM AND...WEAK.
AN ABHORRENT WORD. A NAUSEATING FEELING.
I TRY TO STAY OFF THE DRUG, FOR PRUDENCE'S SAKE, BUT IT CLAWS AND SCRAPES AT MY INSIDES, FILLING THEM WITH RUST AND TAR.
I ACTUALLY FEEL IMPOTENT. THIS MAKES ME VERY ANGRY.
SO I'M GOING TO DO WHAT ANY GOOD BULLY DOES AND TAKE THAT OUT ON SOMEONE...

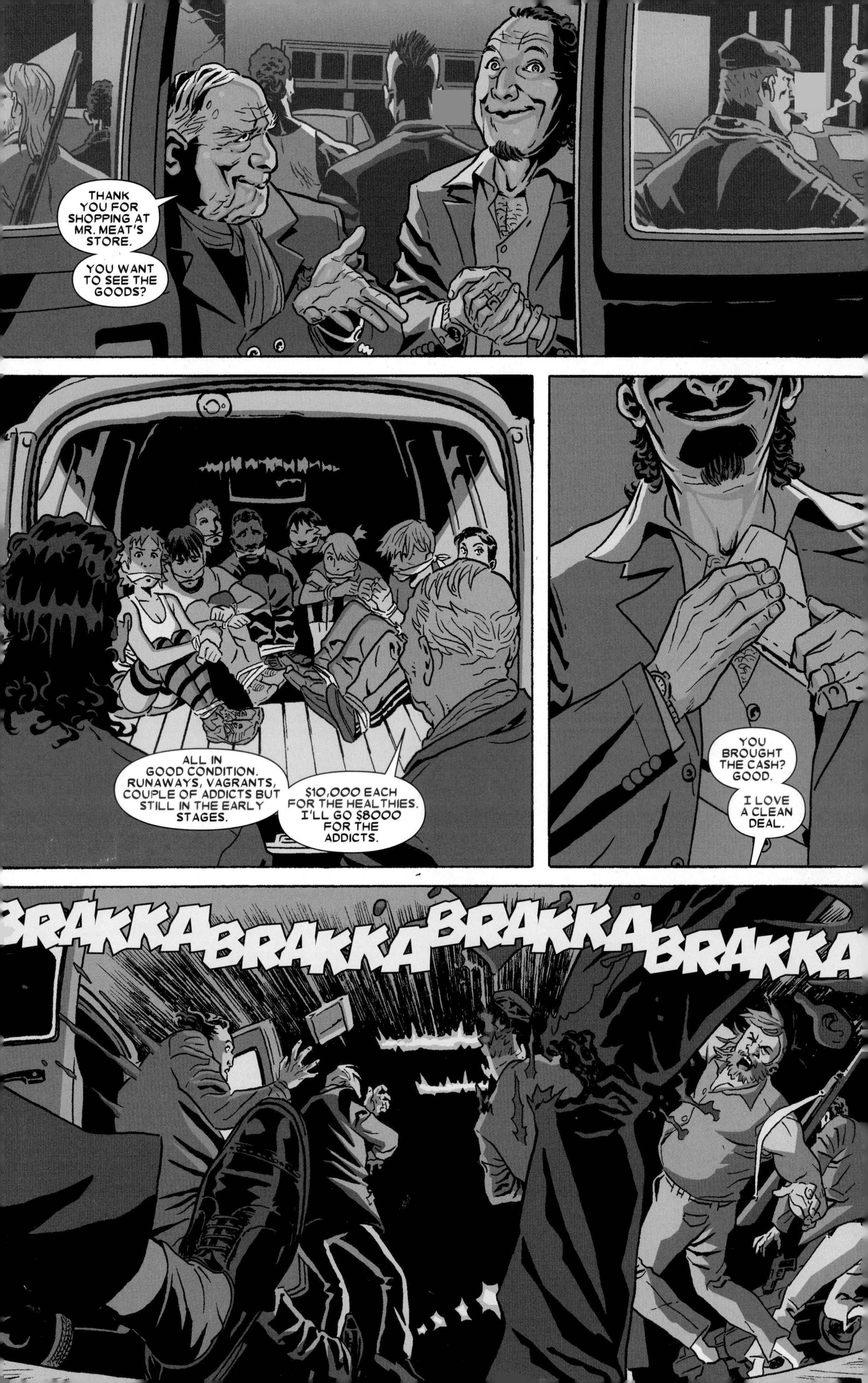
THANK YOU FOR SHOPPING AT MR. MEAT'S STORE.
YOU WANT TO SEE THE GOODS?
ALL IN GOOD CONDITION. RUNAWAYS, VAGRANTS, COUPLE OF ADDICTS BUT STILL IN THE EARLY STAGES.
$10,000 EACH FOR THE HEALTHIES. I'LL GO $8000 FOR THE ADDICTS.
YOU BROUGHT THE CASH? GOOD.
I LOVE A CLEAN DEAL.
BRAKKA BRAKKA BRAKKA BRAKKA

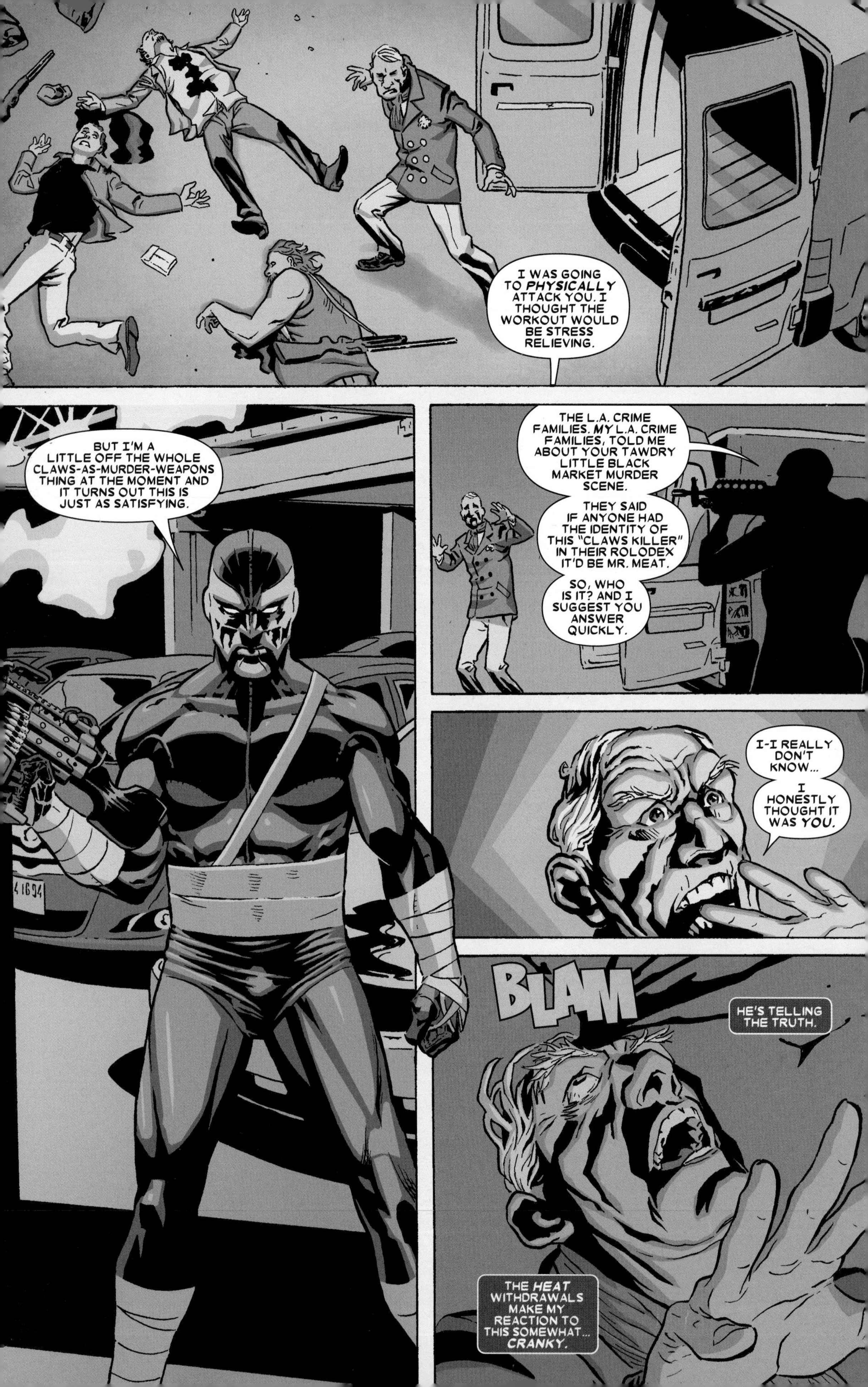
I WAS GOING TO PHYSICALLY ATTACK YOU. I THOUGHT THE WORKOUT WOULD BE STRESS RELIEVING.
BUT I'M A LITTLE OFF THE WHOLE CLAWS-AS-MURDER-WEAPONS THING AT THE MOMENT AND IT TURNS OUT THIS IS JUST AS SATISFYING.
THE L.A. CRIME FAMILIES. MY L.A. CRIME FAMILIES, TOLD ME ABOUT YOUR TAWDRY LITTLE BLACK MARKET MURDER SCENE.
THEY SAID IF ANYONE HAD THE IDENTITY OF THIS "CLAWS KILLER" IN THEIR ROLODEX IT'D BE MR. MEAT.
SO, WHO IS IT? AND I SUGGEST YOU ANSWER QUICKLY.
I-I REALLY DON'T KNOW...
I HONESTLY THOUGHT IT WAS YOU.
BLAM
HE'S TELLING THE TRUTH.
THE HEAT WITHDRAWALS MAKE MY REACTION TO THIS SOMEWHAT... CRANKY.

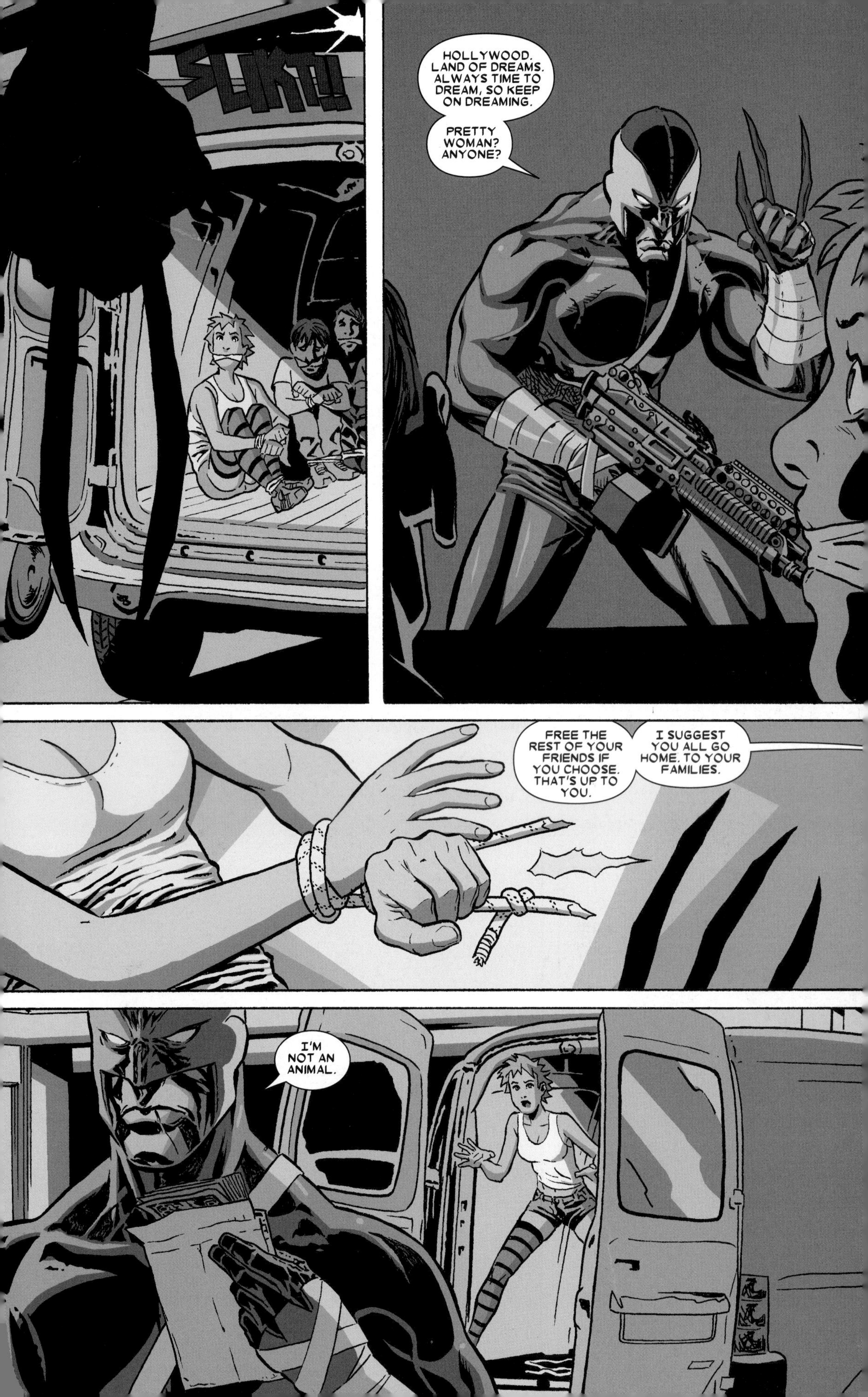
SLIKT!!
HOLLYWOOD. LAND OF DREAMS. ALWAYS TIME TO DREAM, SO KEEP ON DREAMING.
PRETTY WOMAN? ANYONE?
FREE THE REST OF YOUR FRIENDS IF YOU CHOOSE. THAT'S UP TO YOU.
I SUGGEST YOU ALL GO HOME. TO YOUR FAMILIES.
I'M NOT AN ANIMAL.

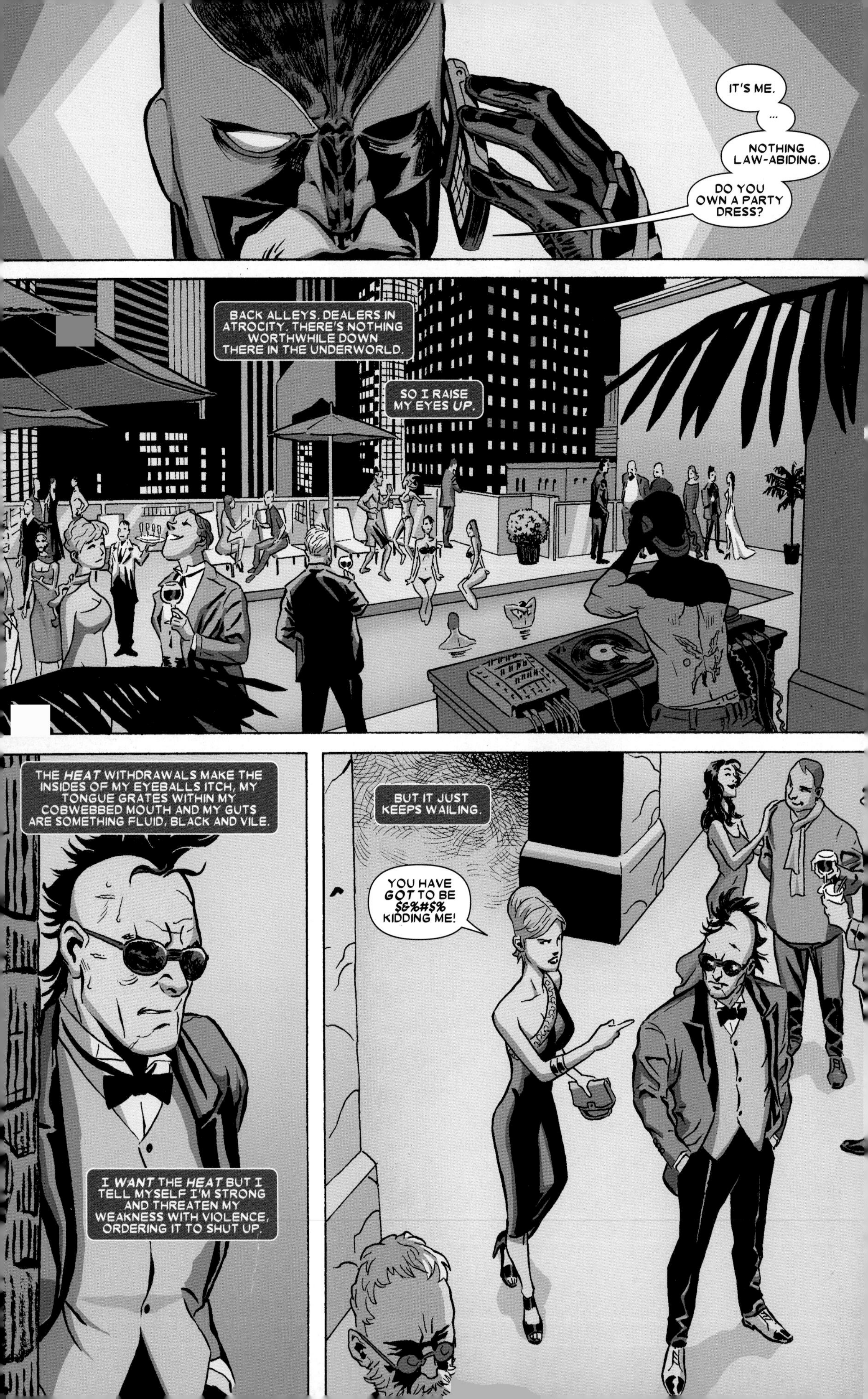
IT'S ME.
...
NOTHING LAW-ABIDING.
DO YOU OWN A PARTY DRESS?
BACK ALLEYS. DEALERS IN ATROCITY. THERE'S NOTHING WORTHWHILE DOWN THERE IN THE UNDERWORLD.
SO I RAISE MY EYES UP.
THE HEAT WITHDRAWALS MAKE THE INSIDES OF MY EYEBALLS ITCH, MY TONGUE GRATES WITHIN MY COBWEBBED MOUTH AND MY GUTS ARE SOMETHING FLUID, BLACK AND VILE.
I WANT THE HEAT BUT I TELL MYSELF I'M STRONG AND THREATEN MY WEAKNESS WITH VIOLENCE, ORDERING IT TO SHUT UP.
BUT IT JUST KEEPS WAILING.
YOU HAVE GOT TO BE $&%#$% KIDDING ME!

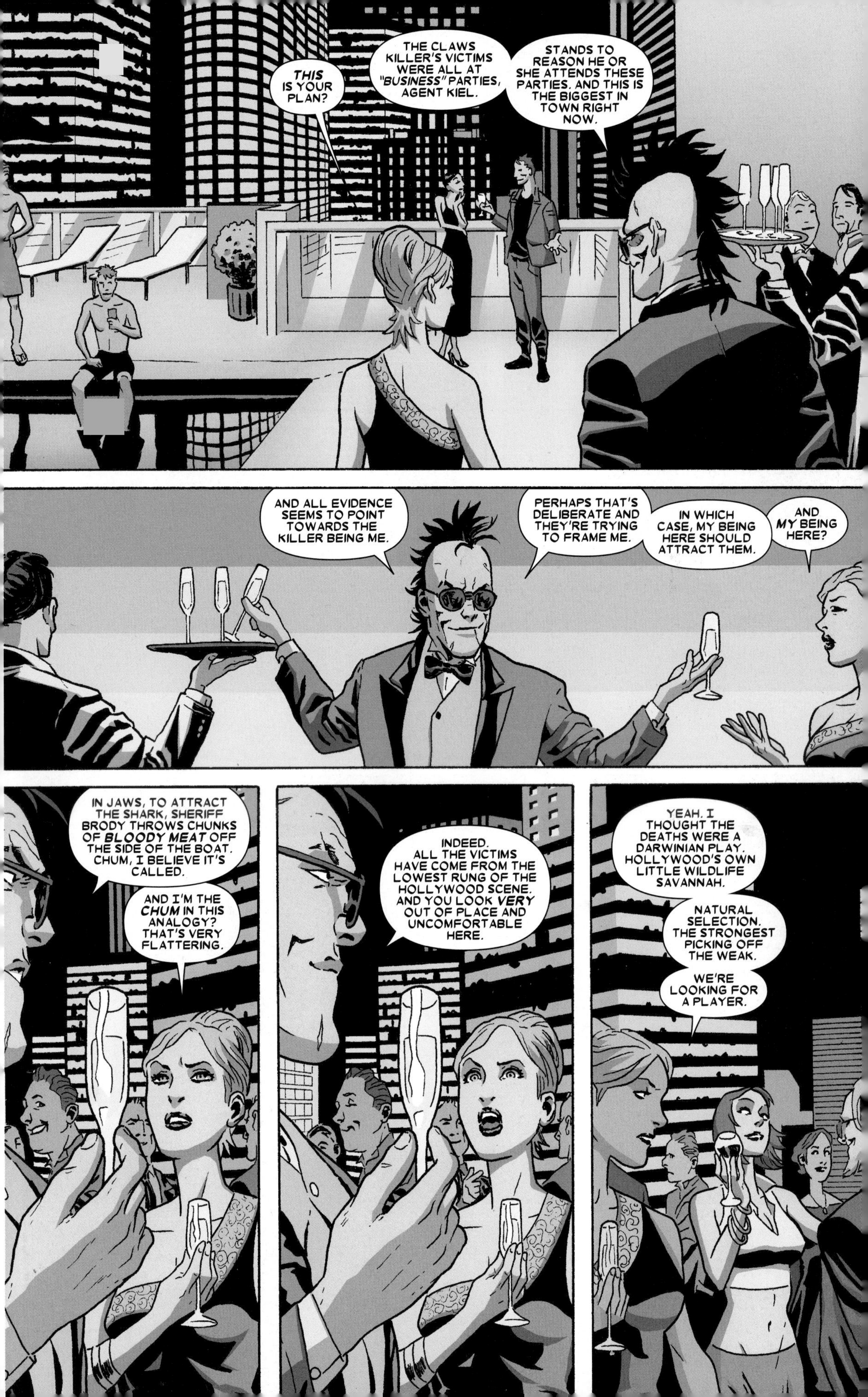
THIS IS YOUR PLAN?
THE CLAWS KILLER'S VICTIMS WERE ALL AT "BUSINESS" PARTIES, AGENT KIEL.
STANDS TO REASON HE OR SHE ATTENDS THESE PARTIES, AND THIS IS THE BIGGEST IN TOWN RIGHT NOW.
AND ALL EVIDENCE SEEMS TO POINT TOWARDS THE KILLER BEING ME.
PERHAPS THAT'S DELIBERATE AND THEY'RE TRYING TO FRAME ME.
IN WHICH CASE, MY BEING HERE SHOULD ATTRACT THEM.
AND MY BEING HERE?
IN JAWS, TO ATTRACT THE SHARK, SHERIFF BRODY THROWS CHUNKS OF BLOODY MEAT OFF THE SIDE OF THE BOAT. CHUM, I BELIEVE IT'S CALLED.
AND I'M THE CHUM IN THIS ANALOGY? THAT'S VERY FLATTERING.
INDEED. ALL THE VICTIMS HAVE COME FROM THE LOWEST RUNG OF THE HOLLYWOOD SCENE. AND YOU LOOK VERY OUT OF PLACE AND UNCOMFORTABLE HERE.
YEAH. I THOUGHT THE DEATHS WERE A DARWINIAN PLAY. HOLLYWOOD'S OWN LITTLE WILDLIFE SAVANNAH.
NATURAL SELECTION. THE STRONGEST PICKING OFF THE WEAK.
WE'RE LOOKING FOR A PLAYER.

UNDOUBTEDLY.

AND YOU'RE HERE TO GET NOTICED BY THEM.

SO GET NOTICED.

SHE LOOKS VERY GOOD.

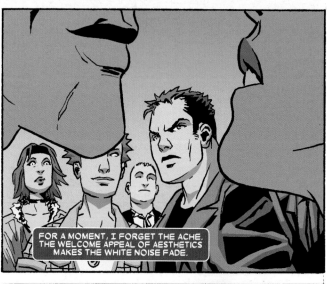

FOR A MOMENT, I FORGET THE ACHE. THE WELCOME APPEAL OF AESTHETICS MAKES THE WHITE NOISE FADE.

BUT WHEN THE HEAT CHANGES HANDS NEARBY I *SMELL* IT.

AND THEN I CAN THINK OF NOTHING ELSE.

AND MY SOLIPSISM OVERRIDES FEAR, AS EVER.

I TELL DONNA I NEED THE BATHROOM.

THIS ISN'T A LIE.

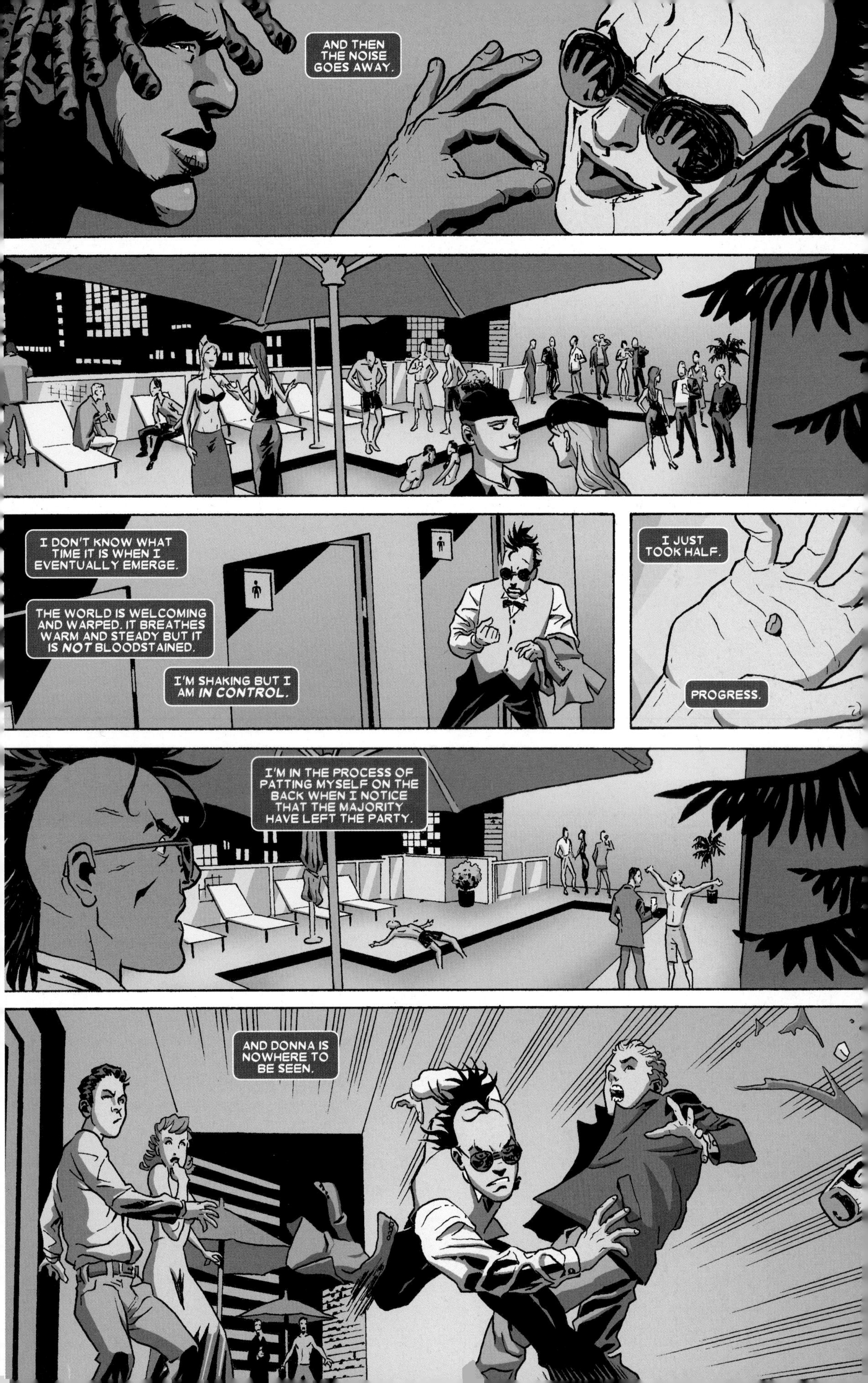
AND THEN THE NOISE GOES AWAY.
I DON'T KNOW WHAT TIME IT IS WHEN I EVENTUALLY EMERGE.
THE WORLD IS WELCOMING AND WARPED. IT BREATHES WARM AND STEADY BUT IT IS NOT BLOODSTAINED.
I'M SHAKING BUT I AM IN CONTROL.
I JUST TOOK HALF.
PROGRESS.
I'M IN THE PROCESS OF PATTING MYSELF ON THE BACK WHEN I NOTICE THAT THE MAJORITY HAVE LEFT THE PARTY.
AND DONNA IS NOWHERE TO BE SEEN.

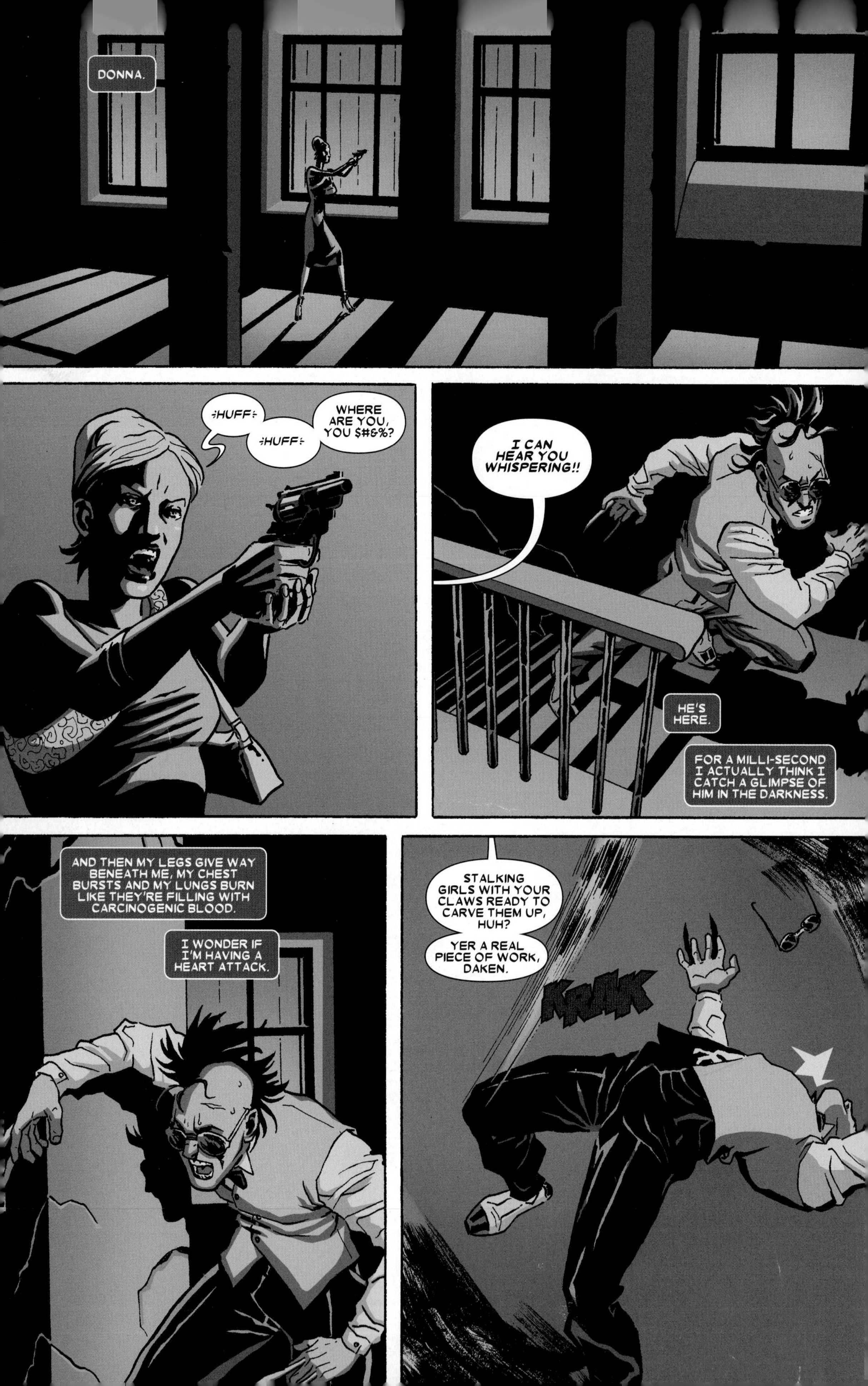
DONNA.
≠HUFF≠
≠HUFF≠
WHERE ARE YOU, YOU $#&%?
I CAN HEAR YOU WHISPERING!!
HE'S HERE.
FOR A MILLI-SECOND I ACTUALLY THINK I CATCH A GLIMPSE OF HIM IN THE DARKNESS.
AND THEN MY LEGS GIVE WAY BENEATH ME, MY CHEST BURSTS AND MY LUNGS BURN LIKE THEY'RE FILLING WITH CARCINOGENIC BLOOD.
I WONDER IF I'M HAVING A HEART ATTACK.
STALKING GIRLS WITH YOUR CLAWS READY TO CARVE THEM UP, HUH?
YER A REAL PIECE OF WORK, DAKEN.
KRAK

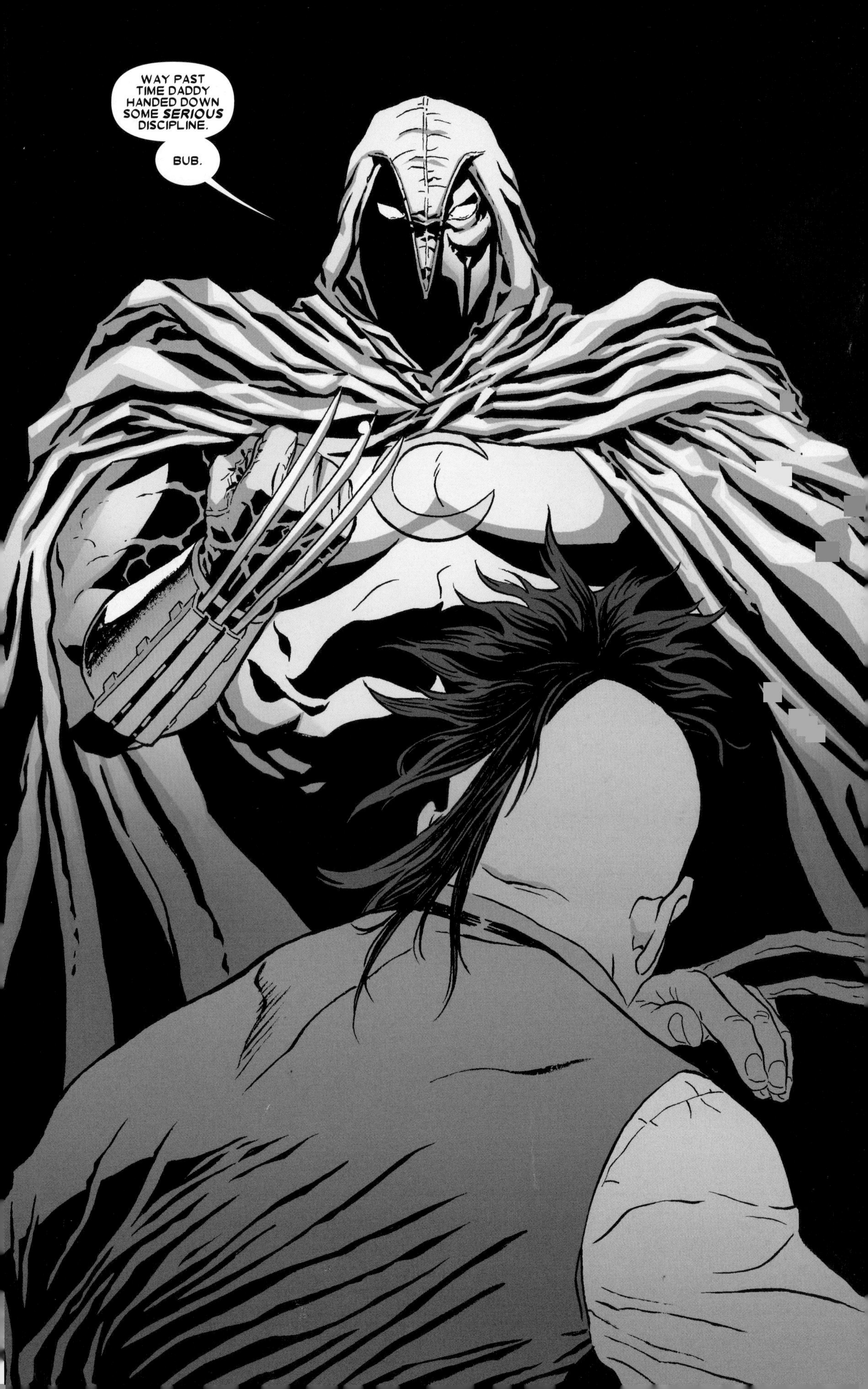
WAY PAST TIME DADDY HANDED DOWN SOME **SERIOUS** DISCIPLINE.
BUB.

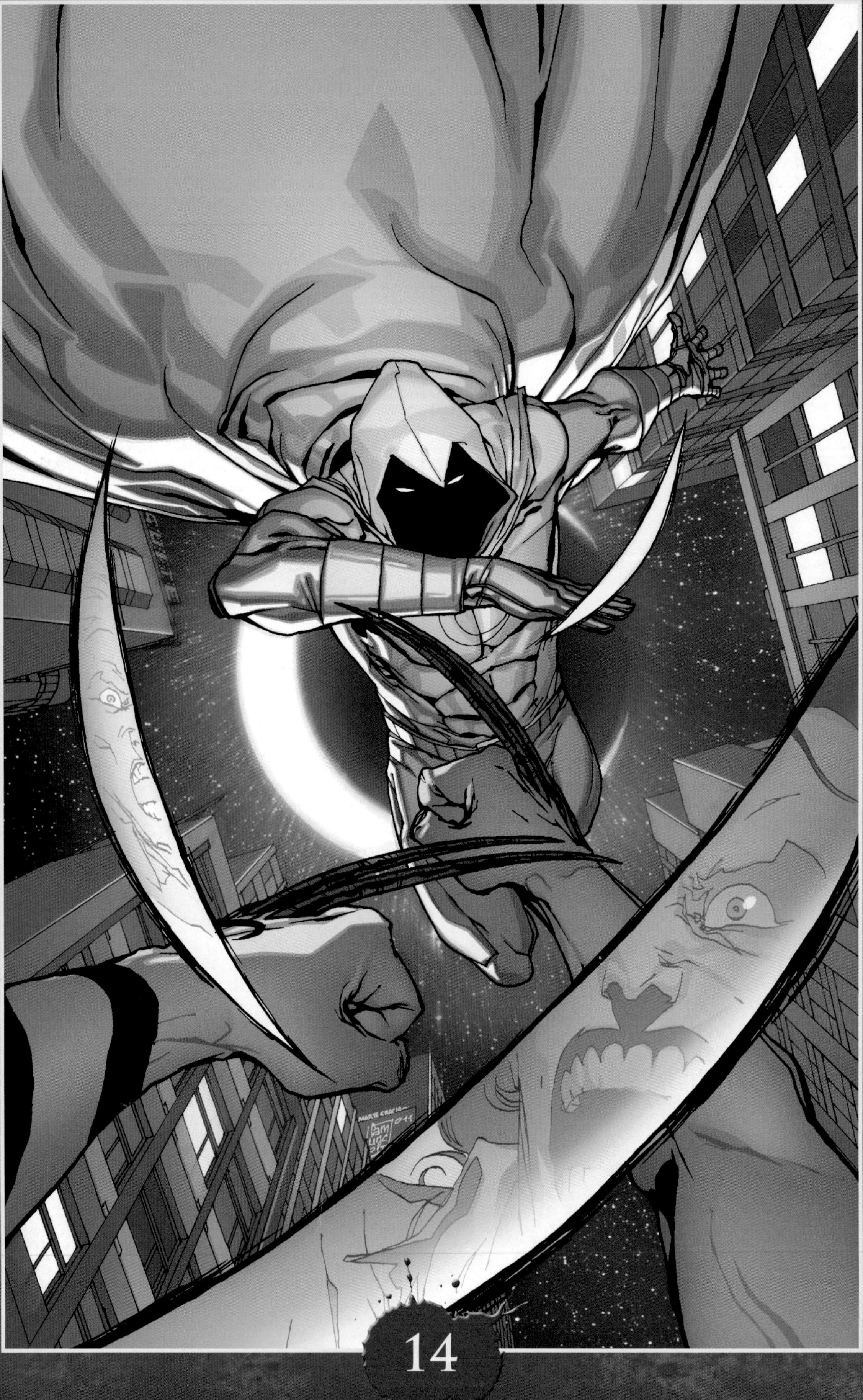

14

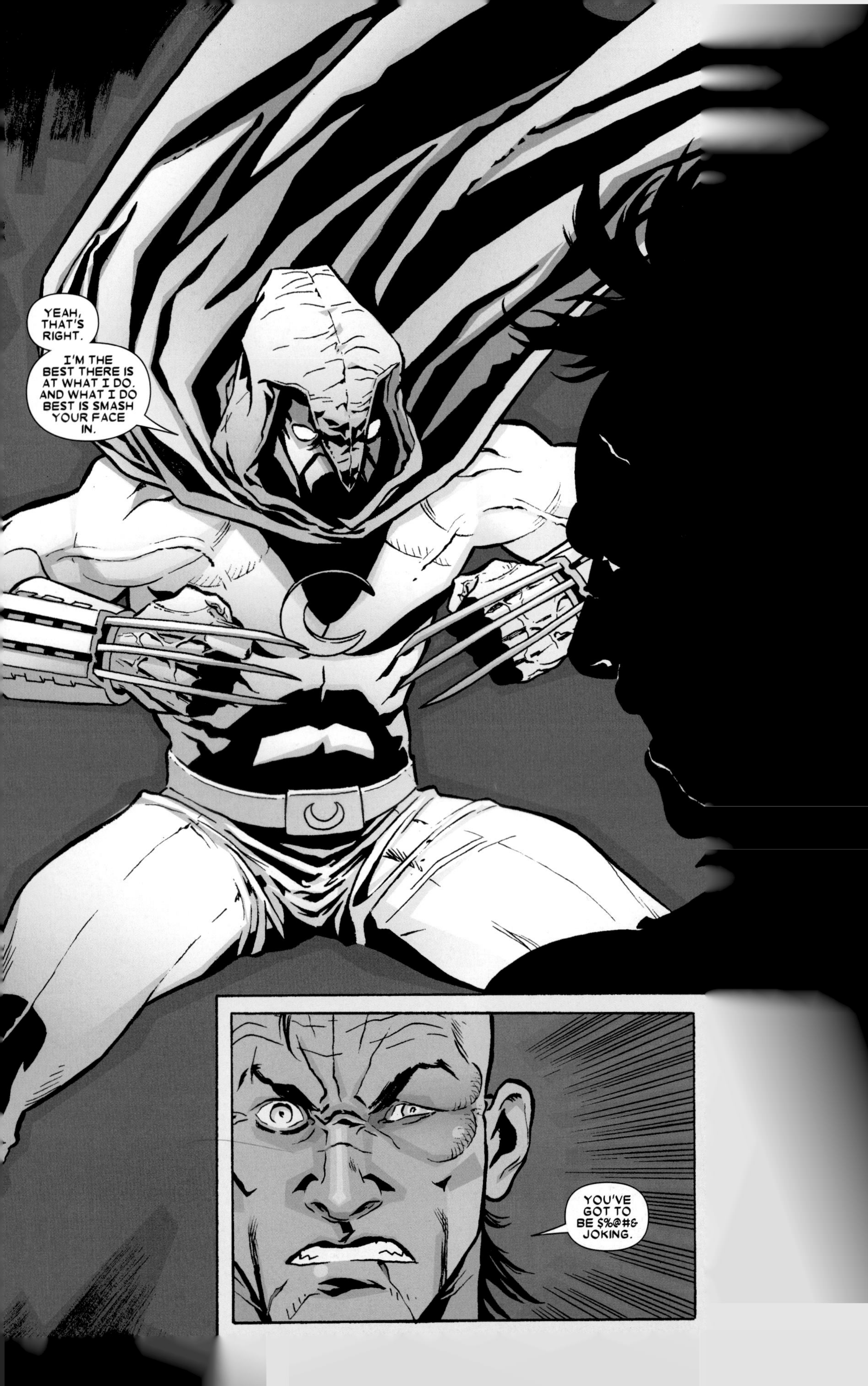
YEAH, THAT'S RIGHT.
I'M THE BEST THERE IS AT WHAT I DO. AND WHAT I DO BEST IS SMASH YOUR FACE IN.
YOU'VE GOT TO BE $%@#& JOKING.

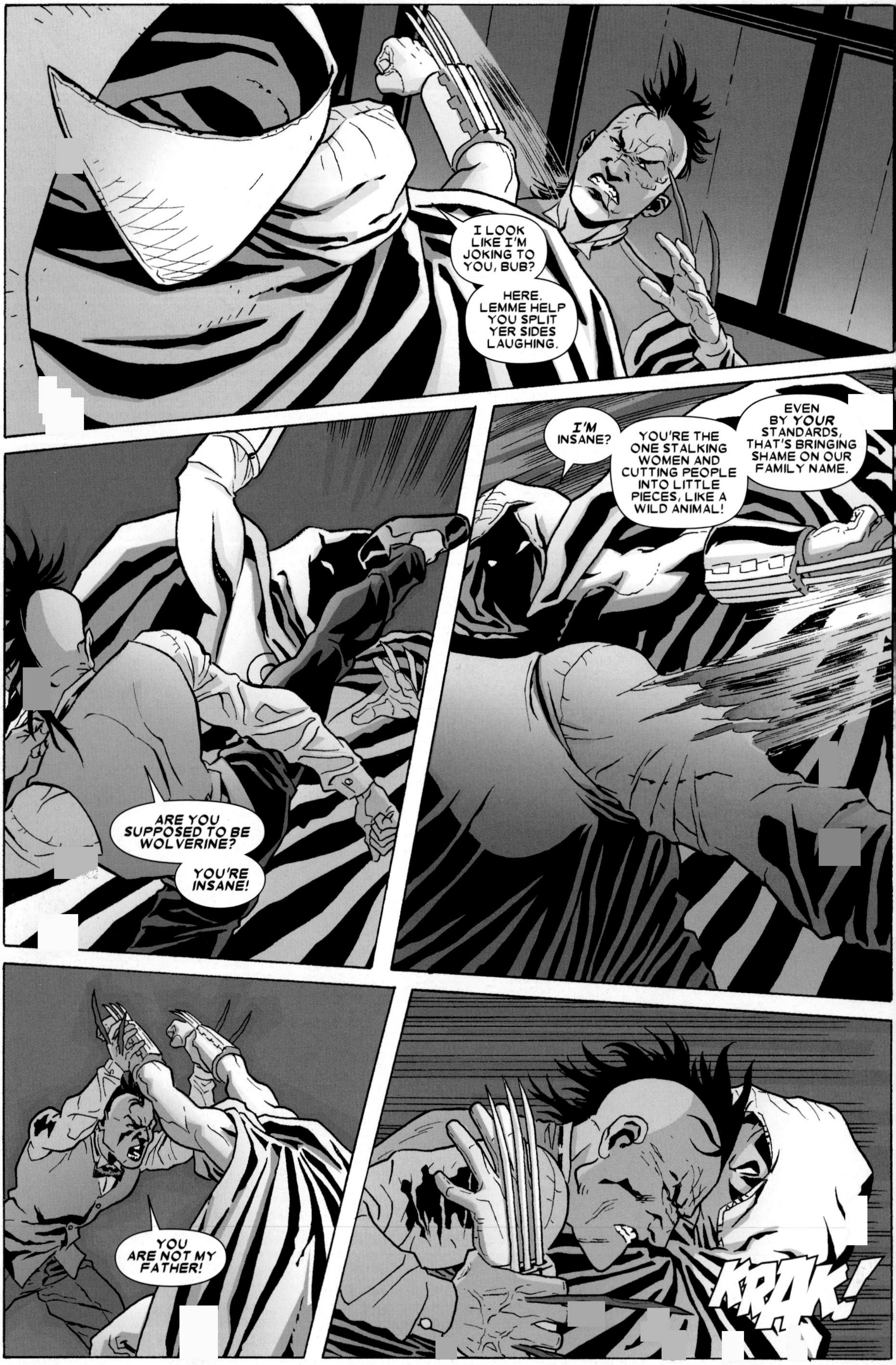
I LOOK LIKE I'M JOKING TO YOU, BUB?
HERE. LEMME HELP YOU SPLIT YER SIDES LAUGHING.
ARE YOU SUPPOSED TO BE WOLVERINE?
YOU'RE INSANE!
I'M INSANE?
YOU'RE THE ONE STALKING WOMEN AND CUTTING PEOPLE INTO LITTLE PIECES, LIKE A WILD ANIMAL!
EVEN BY YOUR STANDARDS, THAT'S BRINGING SHAME ON OUR FAMILY NAME.
YOU ARE NOT MY FATHER!
KRAK!

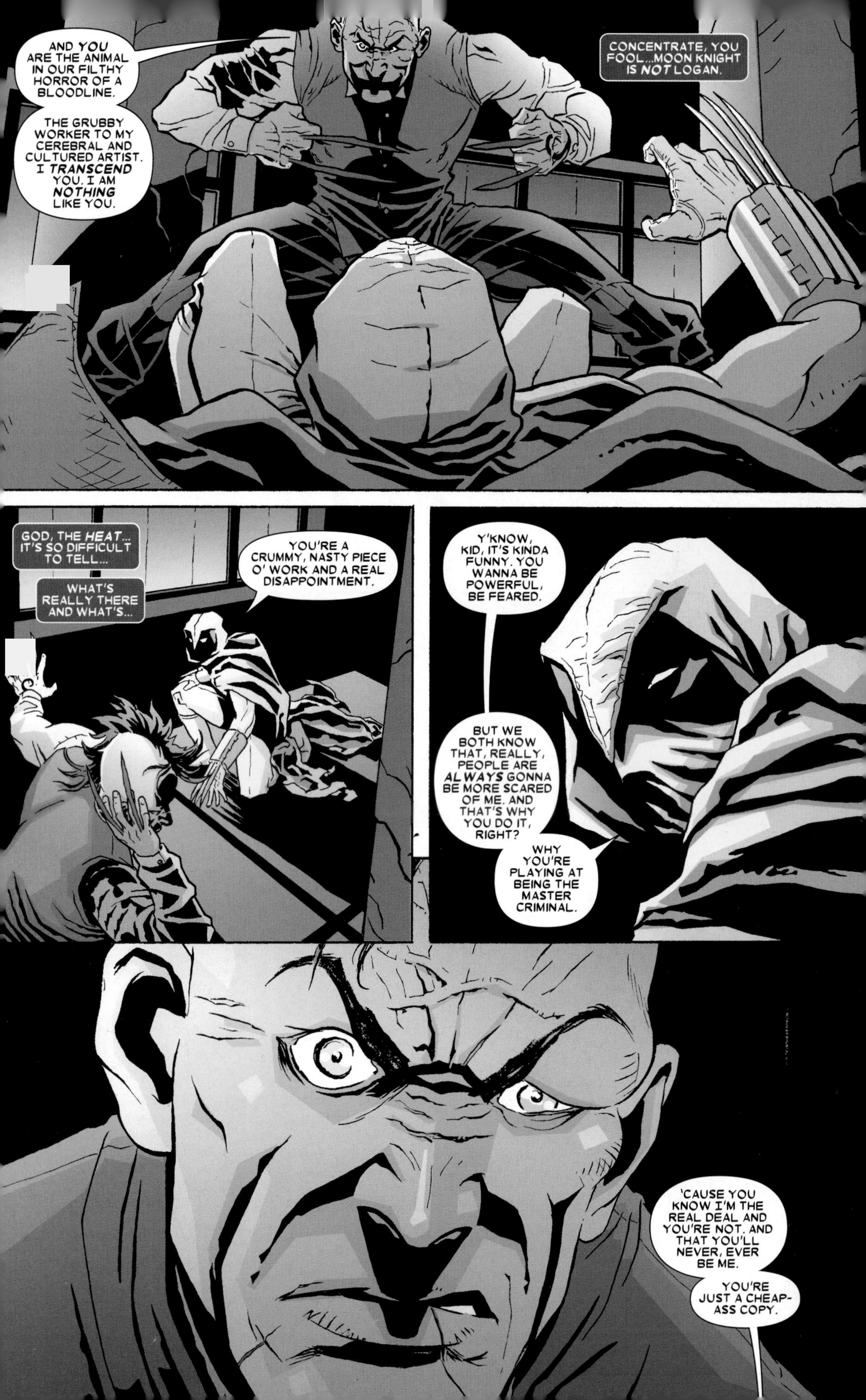
AND YOU ARE THE ANIMAL IN OUR FILTHY HORROR OF A BLOODLINE.
THE GRUBBY WORKER TO MY CEREBRAL AND CULTURED ARTIST. I TRANSCEND YOU. I AM NOTHING LIKE YOU.
CONCENTRATE, YOU FOOL...MOON KNIGHT IS NOT LOGAN.
GOD, THE HEAT... IT'S SO DIFFICULT TO TELL...
WHAT'S REALLY THERE AND WHAT'S...
YOU'RE A CRUMMY, NASTY PIECE O' WORK AND A REAL DISAPPOINTMENT.
Y'KNOW, KID, IT'S KINDA FUNNY. YOU WANNA BE POWERFUL, BE FEARED.
BUT WE BOTH KNOW THAT, REALLY, PEOPLE ARE ALWAYS GONNA BE MORE SCARED OF ME. AND THAT'S WHY YOU DO IT, RIGHT?
WHY YOU'RE PLAYING AT BEING THE MASTER CRIMINAL.
'CAUSE YOU KNOW I'M THE REAL DEAL AND YOU'RE NOT. AND THAT YOU'LL NEVER, EVER BE ME.
YOU'RE JUST A CHEAP-ASS COPY.

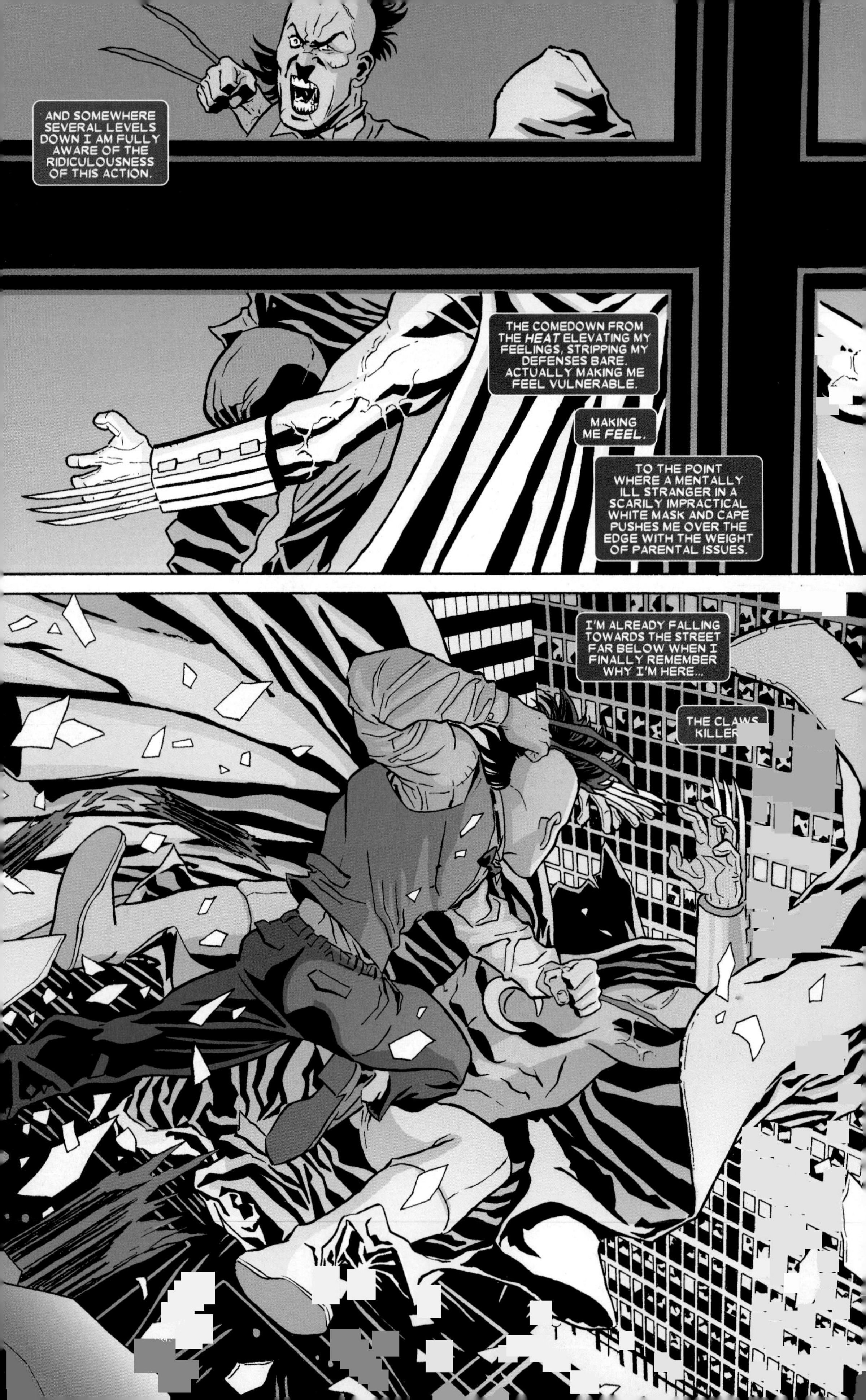
AND SOMEWHERE SEVERAL LEVELS DOWN I AM FULLY AWARE OF THE RIDICULOUSNESS OF THIS ACTION.
THE COMEDOWN FROM THE HEAT ELEVATING MY FEELINGS, STRIPPING MY DEFENSES BARE. ACTUALLY MAKING ME FEEL VULNERABLE.
MAKING ME FEEL.
TO THE POINT WHERE A MENTALLY ILL STRANGER IN A SCARILY IMPRACTICAL WHITE MASK AND CAPE PUSHES ME OVER THE EDGE WITH THE WEIGHT OF PARENTAL ISSUES.
I'M ALREADY FALLING TOWARDS THE STREET FAR BELOW WHEN I FINALLY REMEMBER WHY I'M HERE...
THE CLAWS KILLER

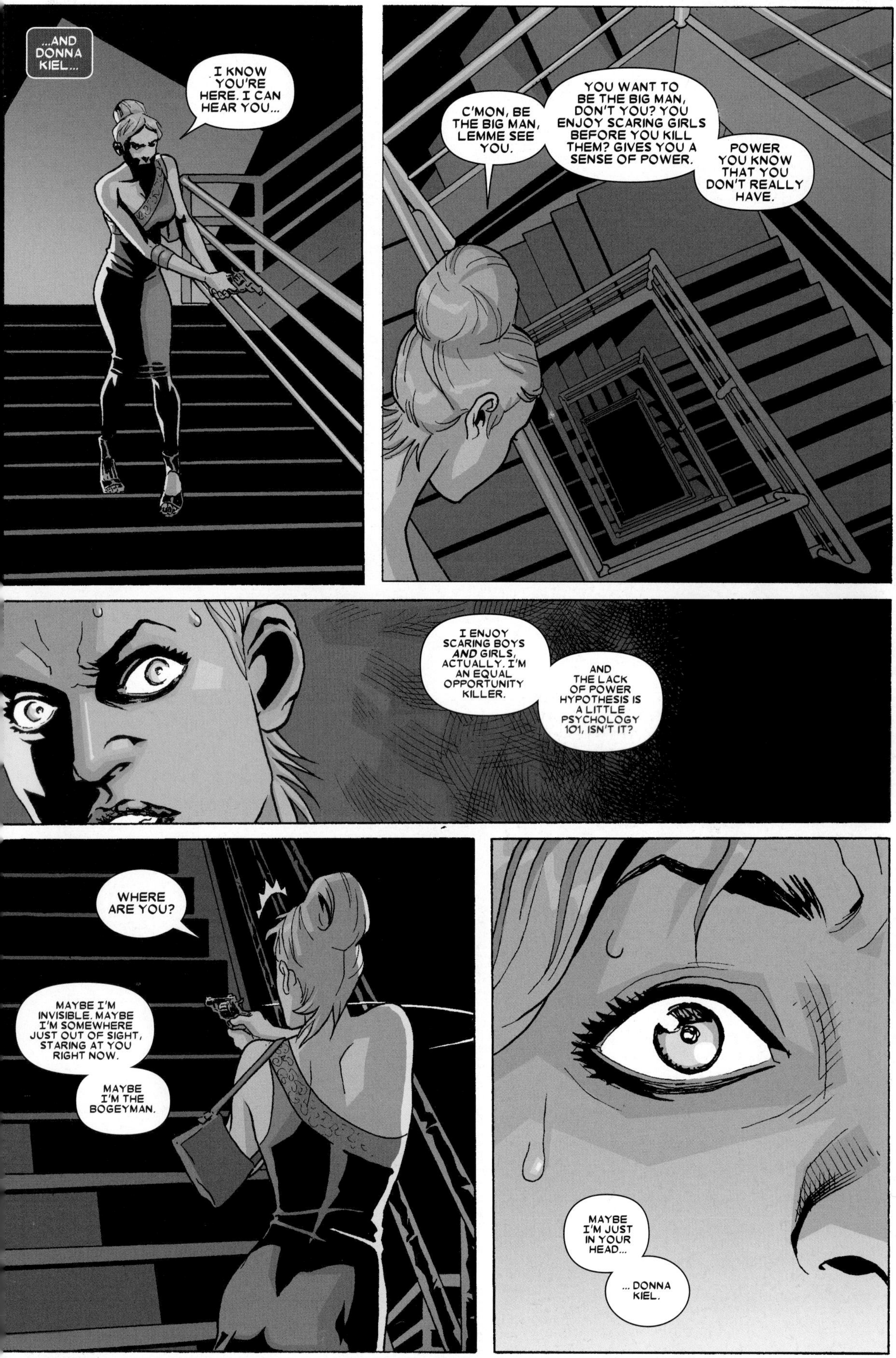
...AND DONNA KIEL...
I KNOW YOU'RE HERE. I CAN HEAR YOU...
C'MON, BE THE BIG MAN, LEMME SEE YOU.
YOU WANT TO BE THE BIG MAN, DON'T YOU? YOU ENJOY SCARING GIRLS BEFORE YOU KILL THEM? GIVES YOU A SENSE OF POWER.
POWER YOU KNOW THAT YOU DON'T REALLY HAVE.
I ENJOY SCARING BOYS *AND* GIRLS, ACTUALLY. I'M AN EQUAL OPPORTUNITY KILLER.
AND THE LACK OF POWER HYPOTHESIS IS A LITTLE PSYCHOLOGY 101, ISN'T IT?
WHERE ARE YOU?
MAYBE I'M INVISIBLE. MAYBE I'M SOMEWHERE JUST OUT OF SIGHT, STARING AT YOU RIGHT NOW.
MAYBE I'M THE BOGEYMAN.
MAYBE I'M JUST IN YOUR HEAD...
... DONNA KIEL.

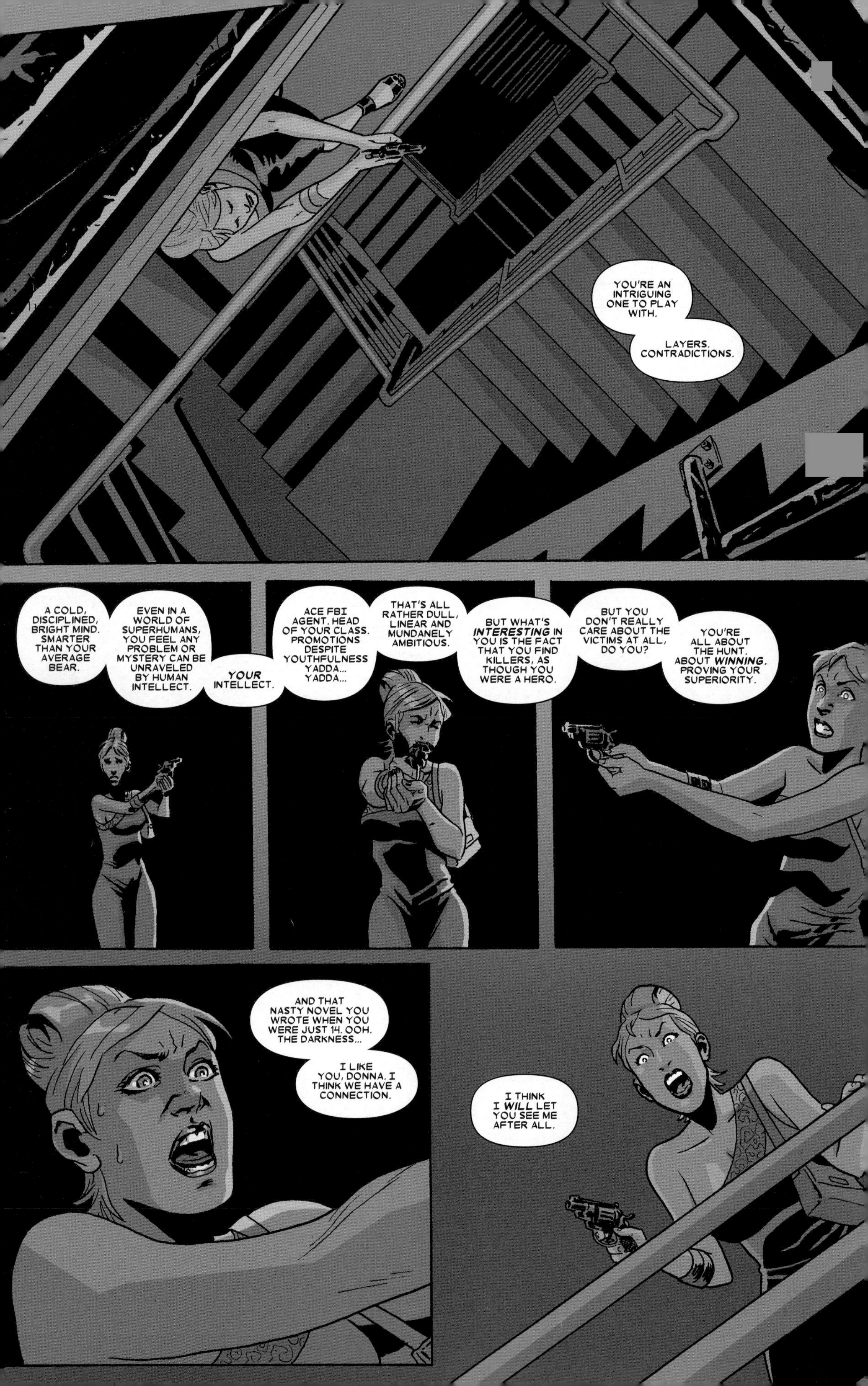
YOU'RE AN INTRIGUING ONE TO PLAY WITH.
LAYERS. CONTRADICTIONS.
A COLD, DISCIPLINED, BRIGHT MIND. SMARTER THAN YOUR AVERAGE BEAR.
EVEN IN A WORLD OF SUPERHUMANS, YOU FEEL ANY PROBLEM OR MYSTERY CAN BE UNRAVELED BY HUMAN INTELLECT.
YOUR INTELLECT.
ACE FBI AGENT. HEAD OF YOUR CLASS. PROMOTIONS DESPITE YOUTHFULNESS YADDA... YADDA...
THAT'S ALL RATHER DULL, LINEAR AND MUNDANELY AMBITIOUS.
BUT WHAT'S *INTERESTING* IN YOU IS THE FACT THAT YOU FIND KILLERS, AS THOUGH YOU WERE A HERO.
BUT YOU DON'T REALLY CARE ABOUT THE VICTIMS AT ALL, DO YOU?
YOU'RE ALL ABOUT THE HUNT. ABOUT *WINNING.* PROVING YOUR SUPERIORITY.
AND THAT NASTY NOVEL YOU WROTE WHEN YOU WERE JUST 14. OOH. THE DARKNESS...
I LIKE YOU, DONNA. I THINK WE HAVE A CONNECTION.
I THINK I *WILL* LET YOU SEE ME AFTER ALL.

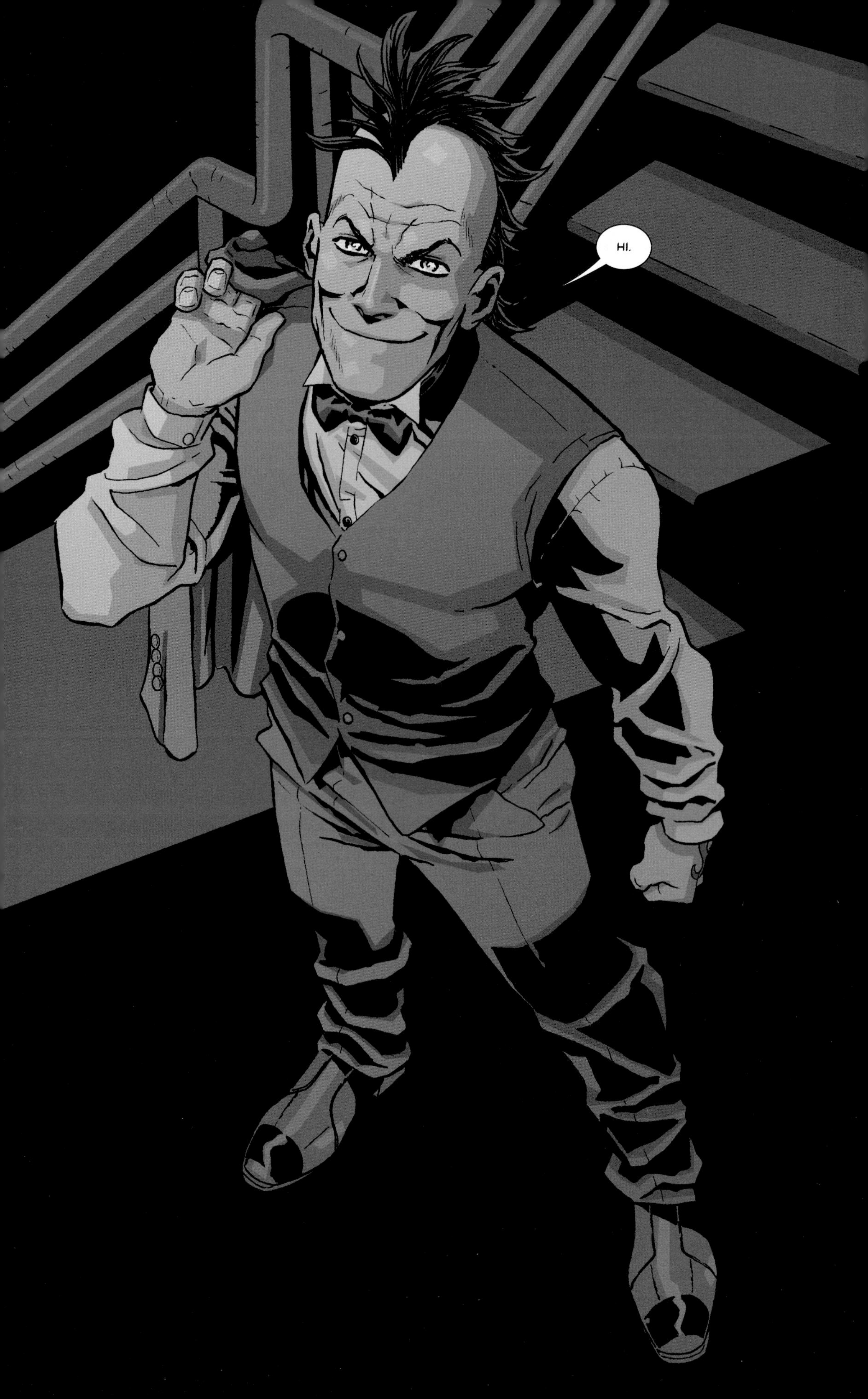
HI.

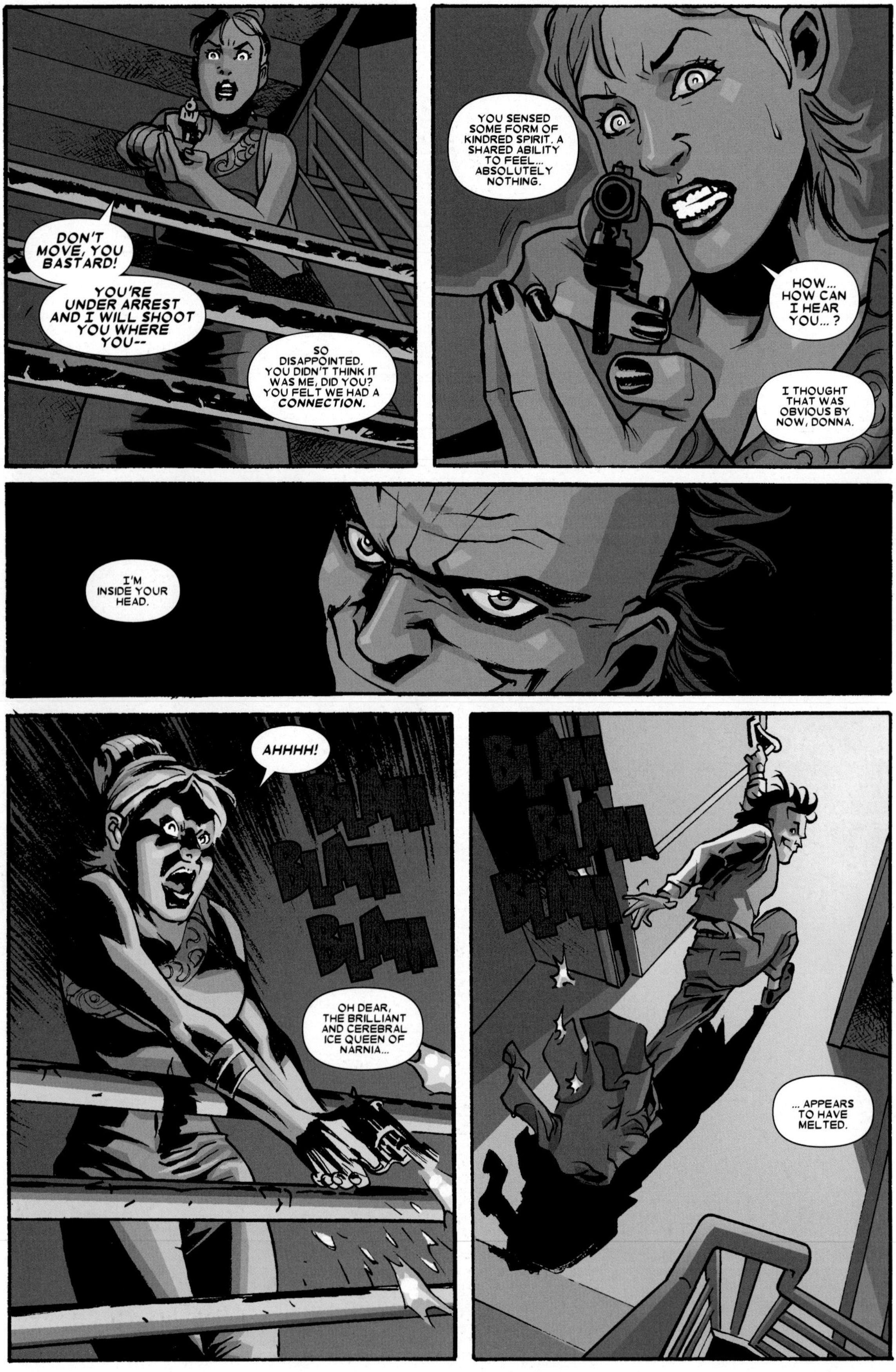

DON'T MOVE, YOU BASTARD!
YOU'RE UNDER ARREST AND I WILL SHOOT YOU WHERE YOU--
SO DISAPPOINTED. YOU DIDN'T THINK IT WAS ME, DID YOU? YOU FELT WE HAD A CONNECTION.
YOU SENSED SOME FORM OF KINDRED SPIRIT. A SHARED ABILITY TO FEEL... ABSOLUTELY NOTHING.
HOW... HOW CAN I HEAR YOU...?
I THOUGHT THAT WAS OBVIOUS BY NOW, DONNA.
I'M INSIDE YOUR HEAD.
AHHHH!
BLAM BLAM BLAM
OH DEAR, THE BRILLIANT AND CEREBRAL ICE QUEEN OF NARNIA...
BLAM BLAM BLAM
...APPEARS TO HAVE MELTED.

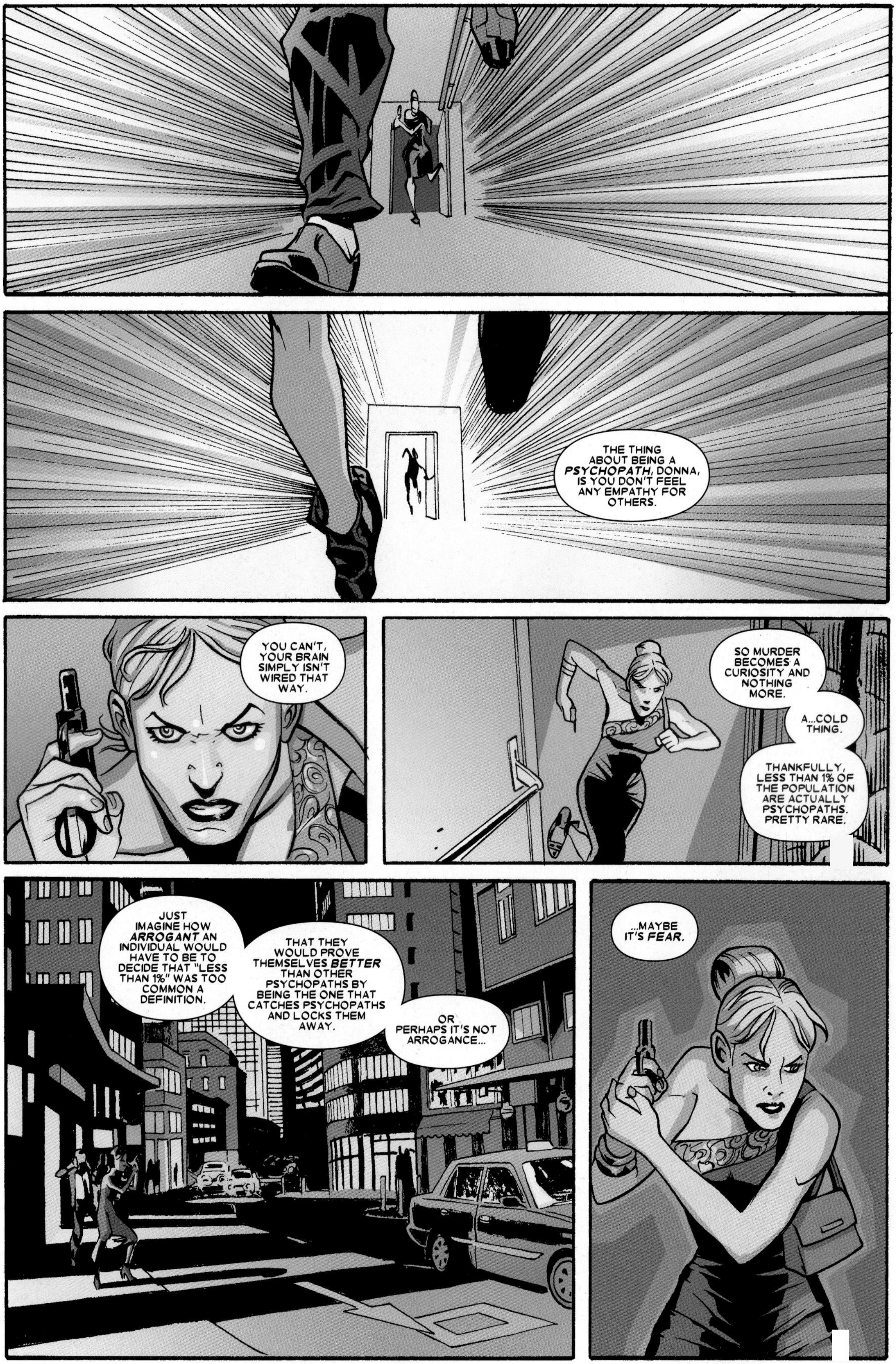
THE THING ABOUT BEING A *PSYCHOPATH,* DONNA, IS YOU DON'T FEEL ANY EMPATHY FOR OTHERS.
YOU CAN'T, YOUR BRAIN SIMPLY ISN'T WIRED THAT WAY.
SO MURDER BECOMES A CURIOSITY AND NOTHING MORE.
A...COLD THING.
THANKFULLY, LESS THAN 1% OF THE POPULATION ARE ACTUALLY PSYCHOPATHS. PRETTY RARE.
JUST IMAGINE HOW *ARROGANT* AN INDIVIDUAL WOULD HAVE TO BE TO DECIDE THAT "LESS THAN 1%" WAS TOO COMMON A DEFINITION.
THAT THEY WOULD PROVE THEMSELVES *BETTER* THAN OTHER PSYCHOPATHS BY BEING THE ONE THAT CATCHES PSYCHOPATHS AND LOCKS THEM AWAY.
OR PERHAPS IT'S NOT ARROGANCE...
...MAYBE IT'S *FEAR.*

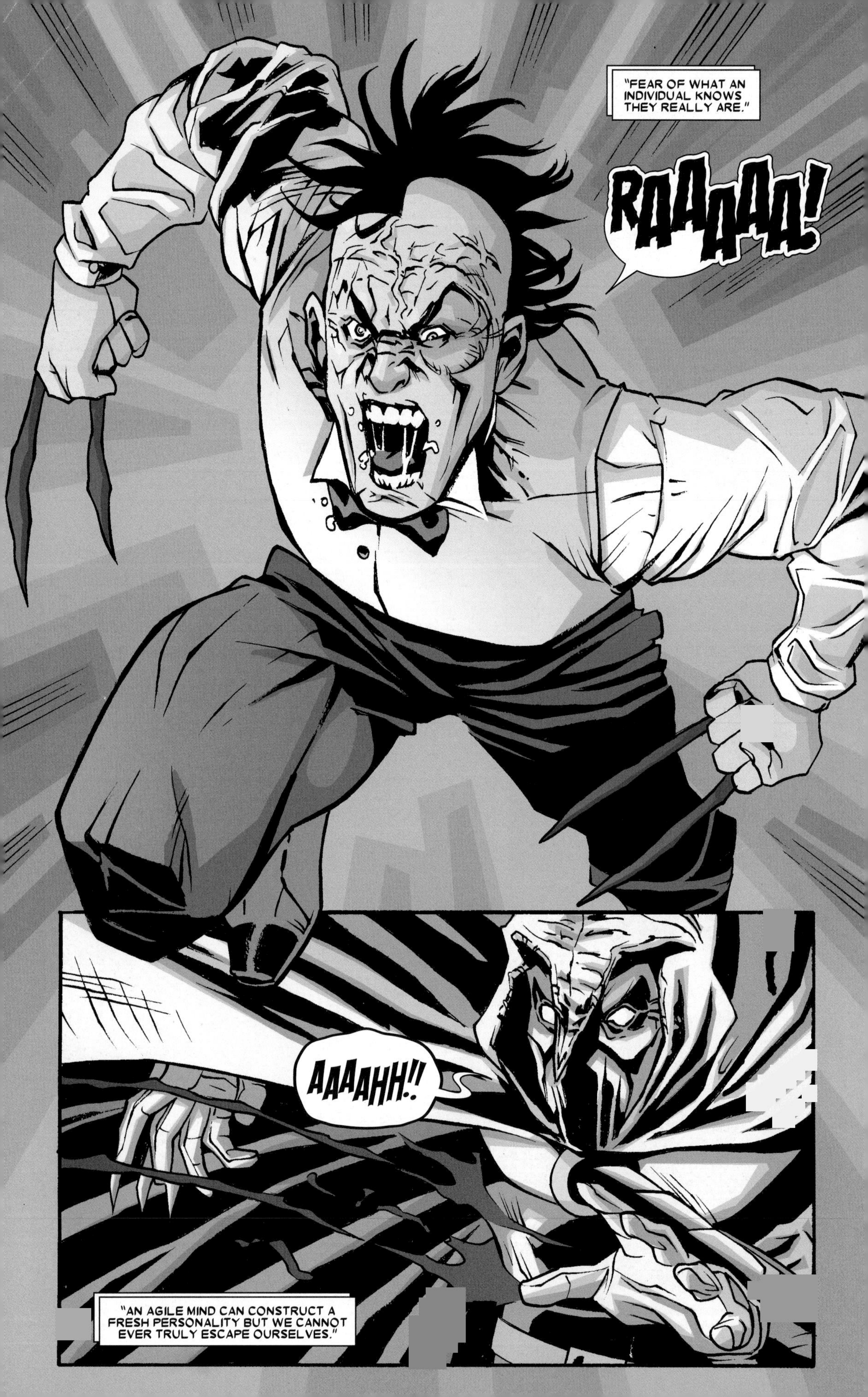
"FEAR OF WHAT AN INDIVIDUAL KNOWS THEY REALLY ARE."
RAAAAA!
AAAAHH!!
"AN AGILE MIND CAN CONSTRUCT A FRESH PERSONALITY BUT WE CANNOT EVER TRULY ESCAPE OURSELVES."

THIS IS **NOT** WHO I AM.

ANIMAL... INSANITY...

...I TURN MY BACK ON YOU.

NICE...*UNH*... WORK WITH THE CLAWS THERE.

IF YOU HADN'T KILLED MORE PEOPLE THAN CANCER AND CAR CRASHES COMBINED YOU'D BE MAKING YER DADDY PROUD RIGHT NOW.

I TAUGHT YOU GOOD.

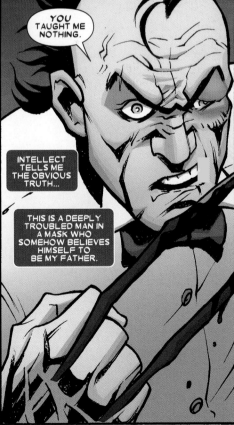

YOU TAUGHT ME NOTHING.

INTELLECT TELLS ME THE OBVIOUS TRUTH...

THIS IS A DEEPLY TROUBLED MAN IN A MASK WHO SOMEHOW BELIEVES HIMSELF TO BE MY FATHER.

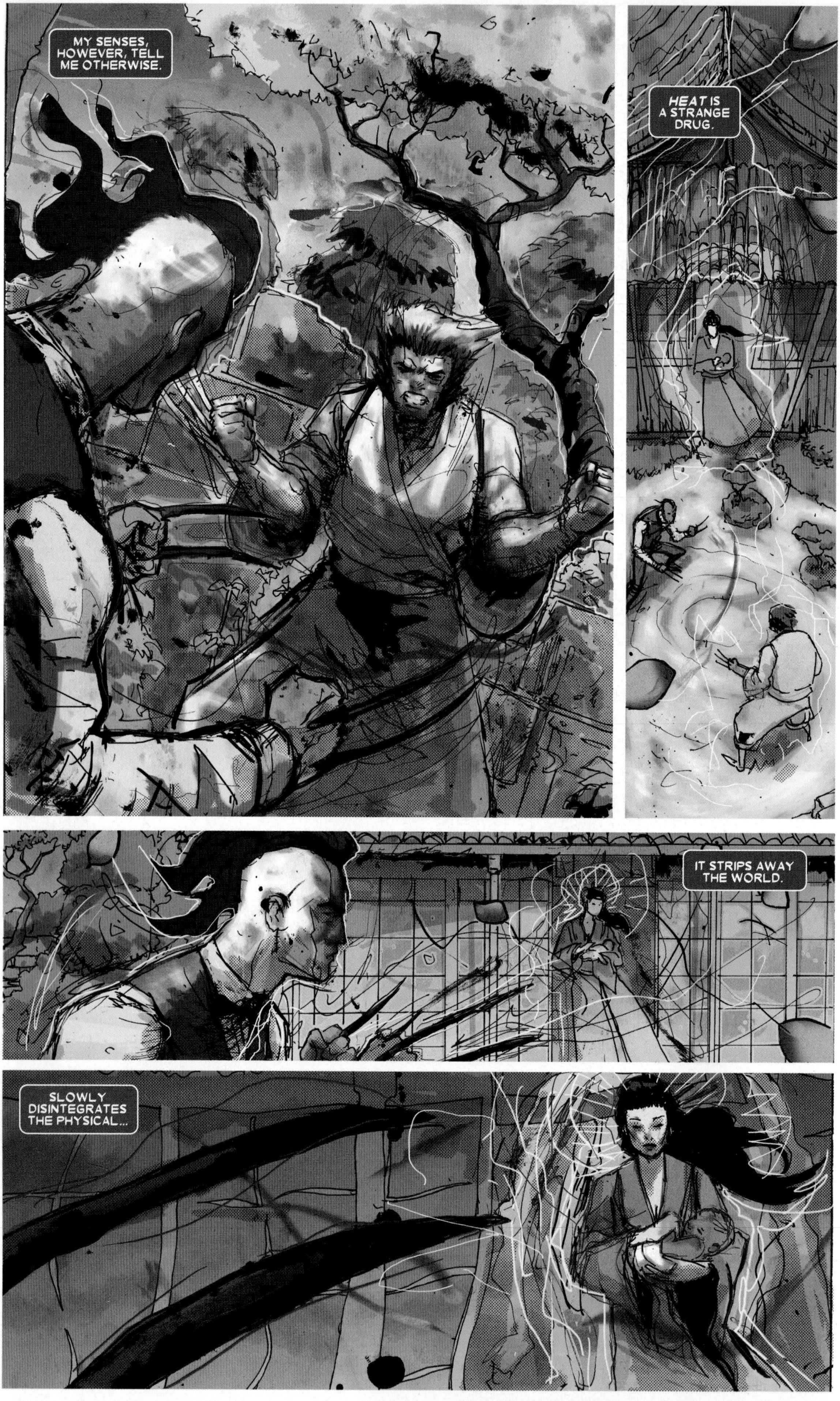
MY SENSES, HOWEVER, TELL ME OTHERWISE.
HEAT IS A STRANGE DRUG.
IT STRIPS AWAY THE WORLD.
SLOWLY DISINTEGRATES THE PHYSICAL...

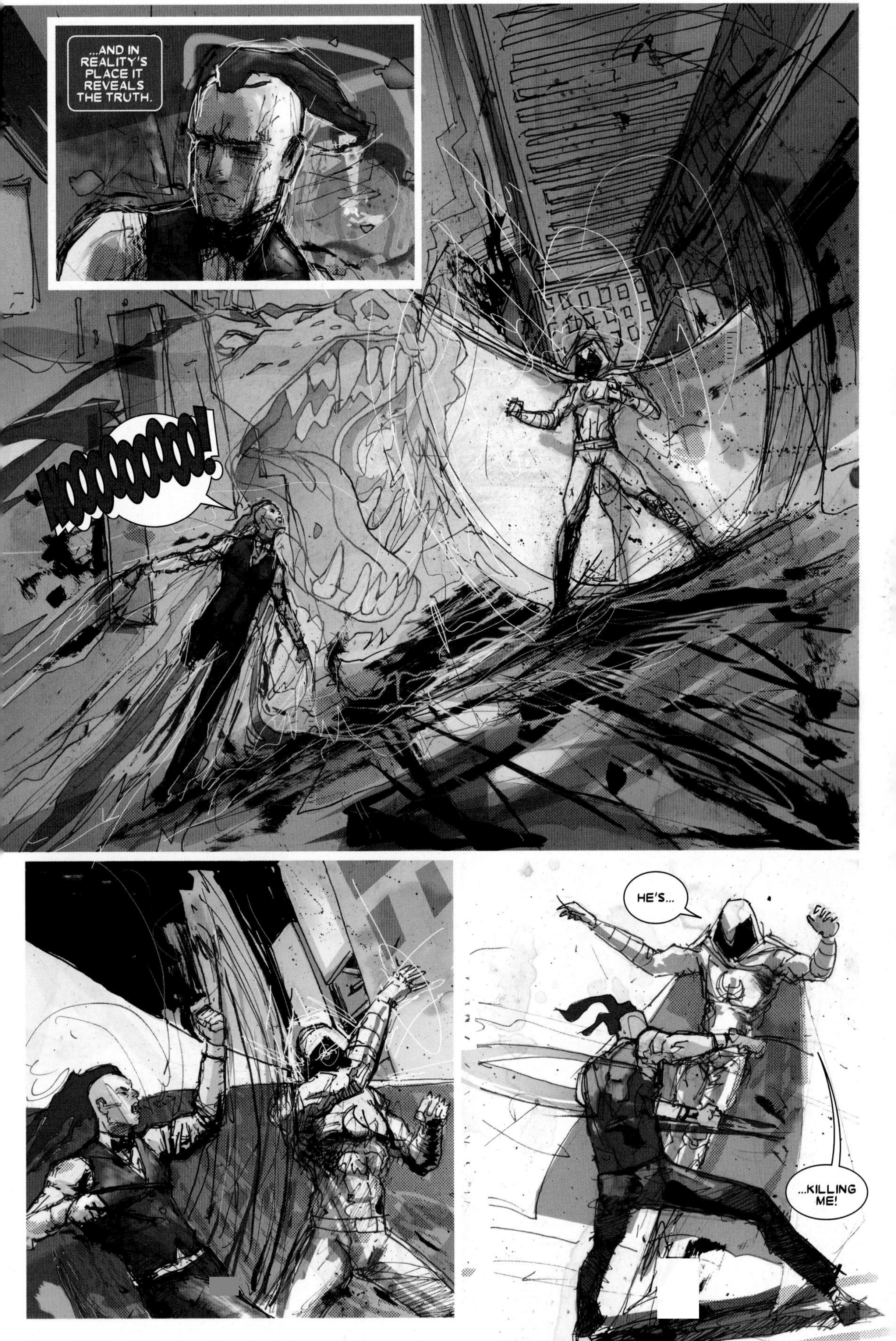
...AND IN REALITY'S PLACE IT REVEALS THE TRUTH.
NOOOOOOOOO!
HE'S...
...KILLING ME!

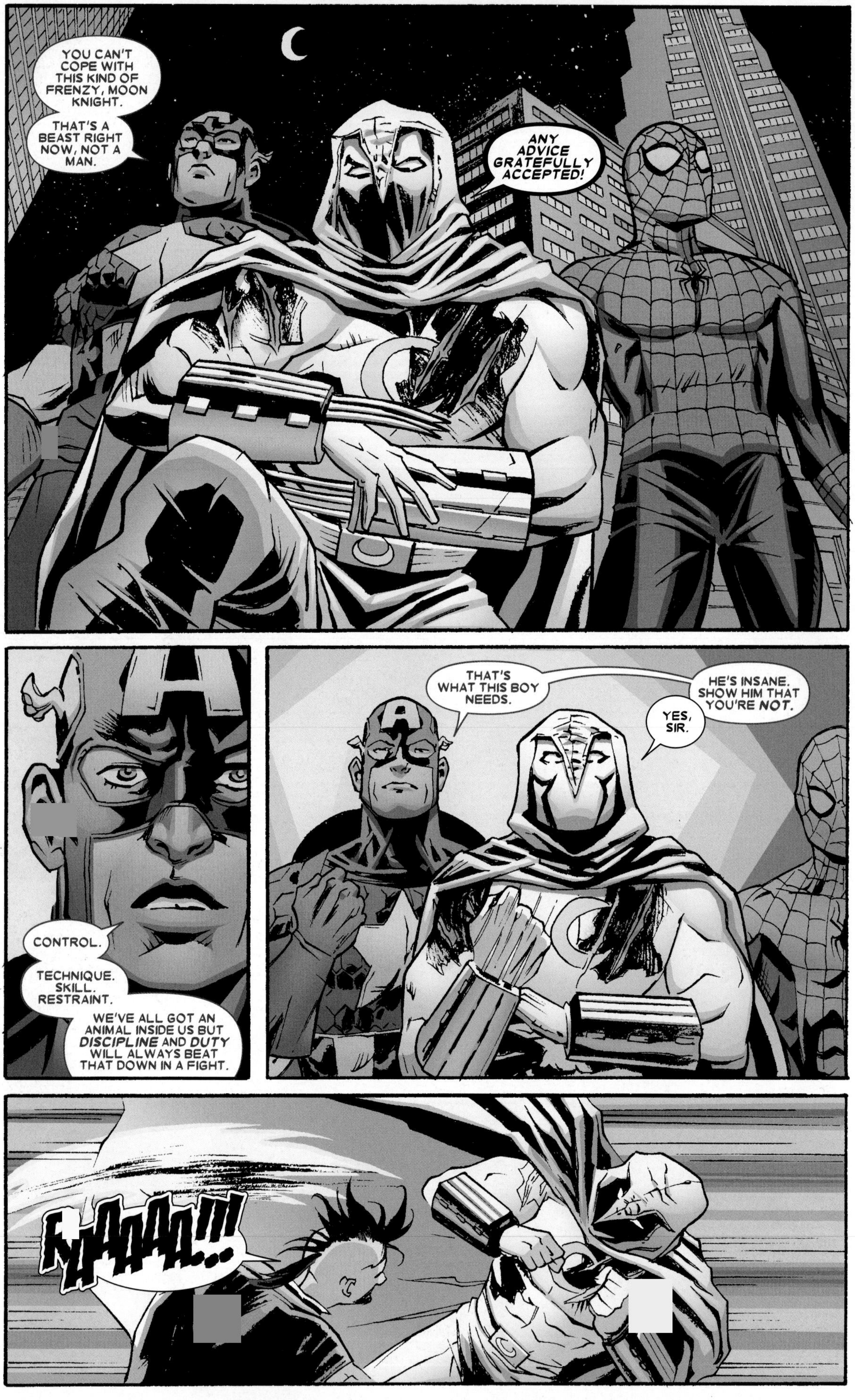
YOU CAN'T COPE WITH THIS KIND OF FRENZY, MOON KNIGHT.
THAT'S A BEAST RIGHT NOW, NOT A MAN.
ANY ADVICE GRATEFULLY ACCEPTED!
CONTROL.
TECHNIQUE. SKILL. RESTRAINT.
WE'VE ALL GOT AN ANIMAL INSIDE US BUT *DISCIPLINE* AND *DUTY* WILL ALWAYS BEAT THAT DOWN IN A FIGHT.
THAT'S WHAT THIS BOY NEEDS.
HE'S INSANE. SHOW HIM THAT YOU'RE *NOT*.
YES, SIR.

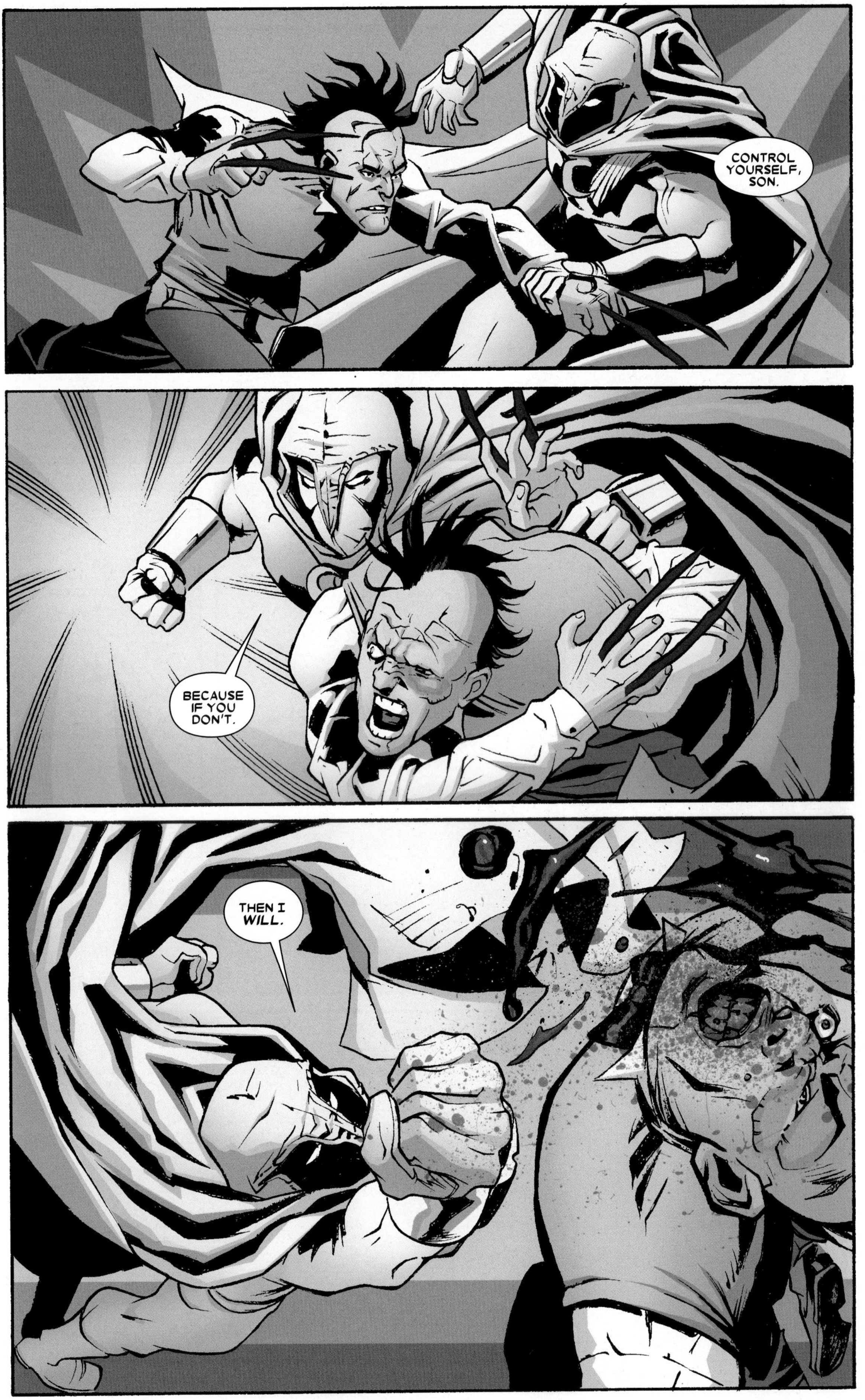
CONTROL YOURSELF, SON.
BECAUSE IF YOU DON'T.
THEN I *WILL.*

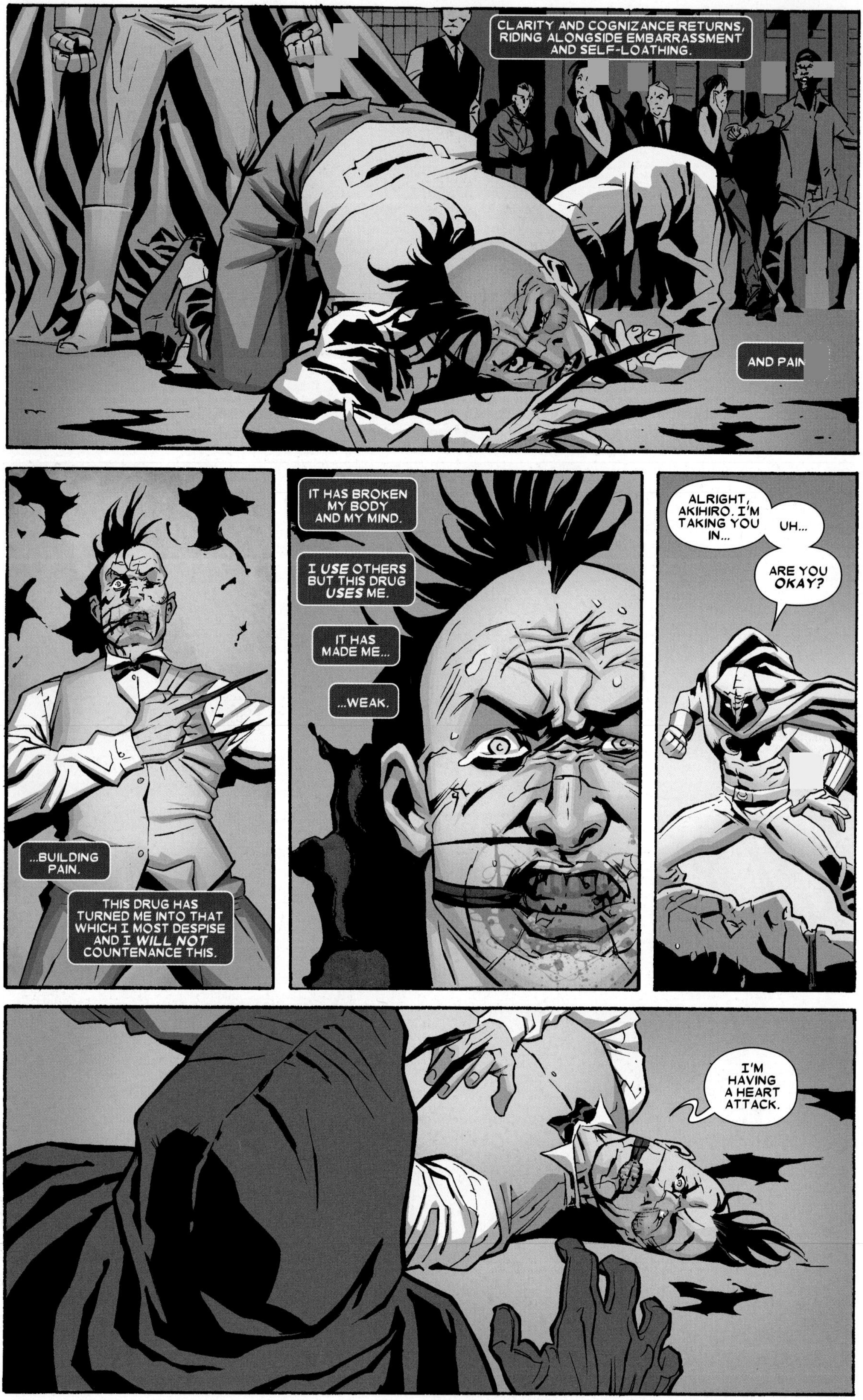
CLARITY AND COGNIZANCE RETURNS, RIDING ALONGSIDE EMBARRASSMENT AND SELF-LOATHING.
AND PAIN
...BUILDING PAIN.
THIS DRUG HAS TURNED ME INTO THAT WHICH I MOST DESPISE AND I WILL NOT COUNTENANCE THIS.
IT HAS BROKEN MY BODY AND MY MIND.
I USE OTHERS BUT THIS DRUG USES ME.
IT HAS MADE ME...
...WEAK.
ALRIGHT, AKIHIRO. I'M TAKING YOU IN...
UH...
ARE YOU OKAY?
I'M HAVING A HEART ATTACK.

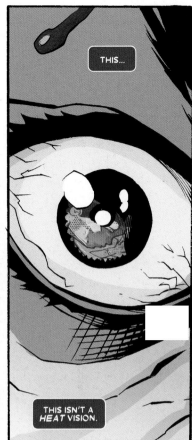

YOU'RE NOT FAKING?

UNH!!!

OKAY, HOLD ON! I'LL CALL 911!

JUST... HOLD ON.

THIS...

THIS ISN'T A *HEAT* VISION.

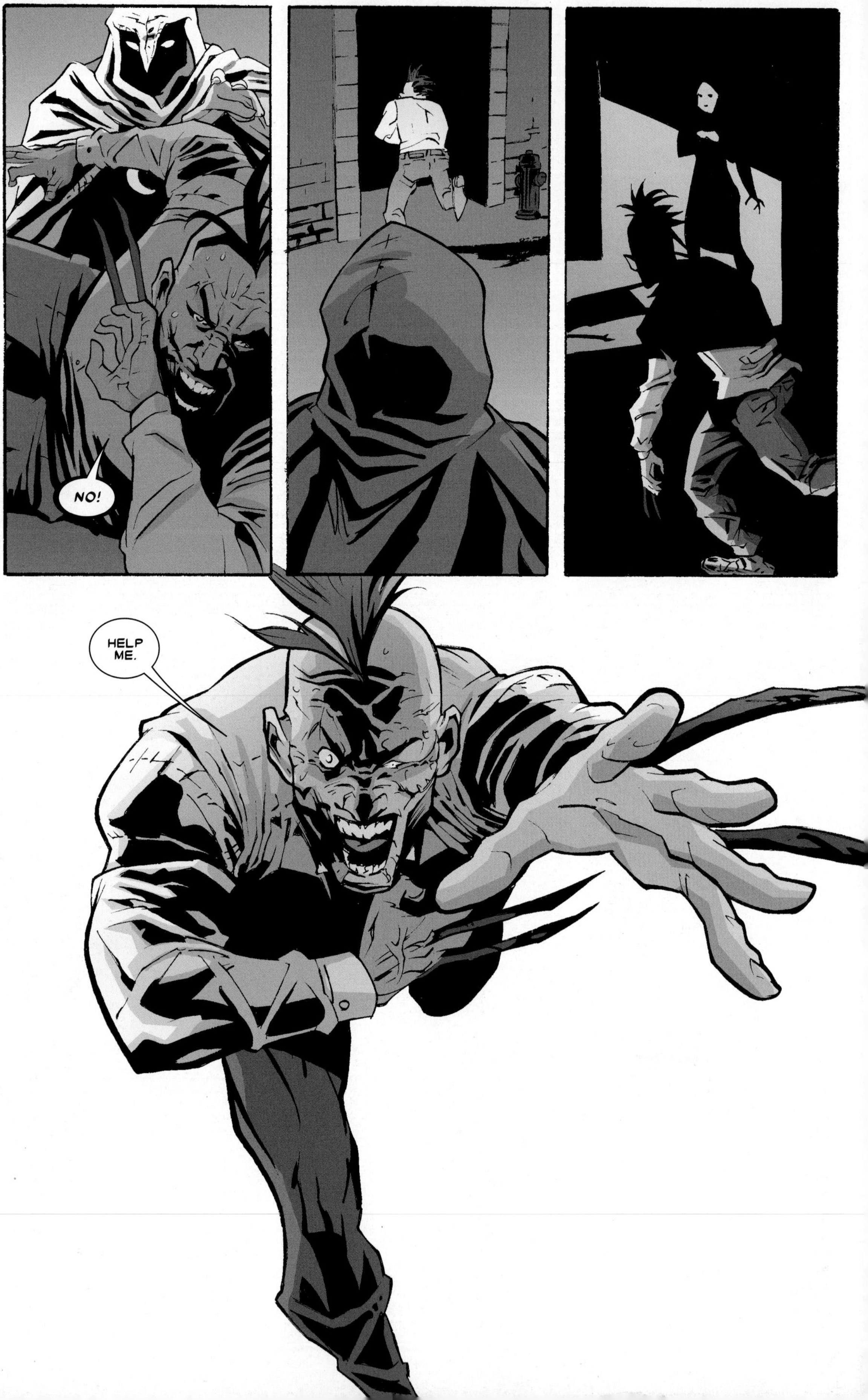
NO!
HELP ME.

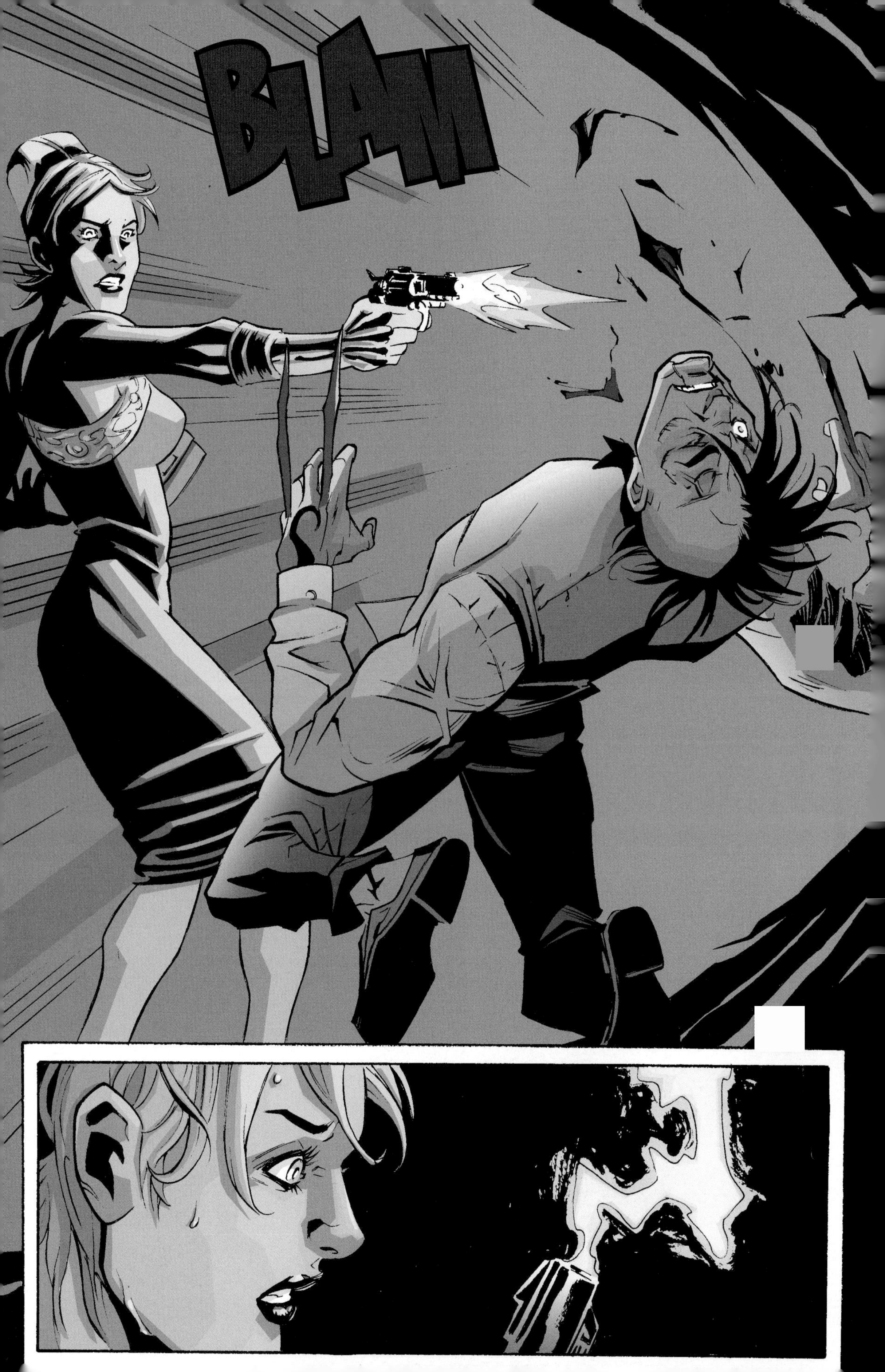
BLAM

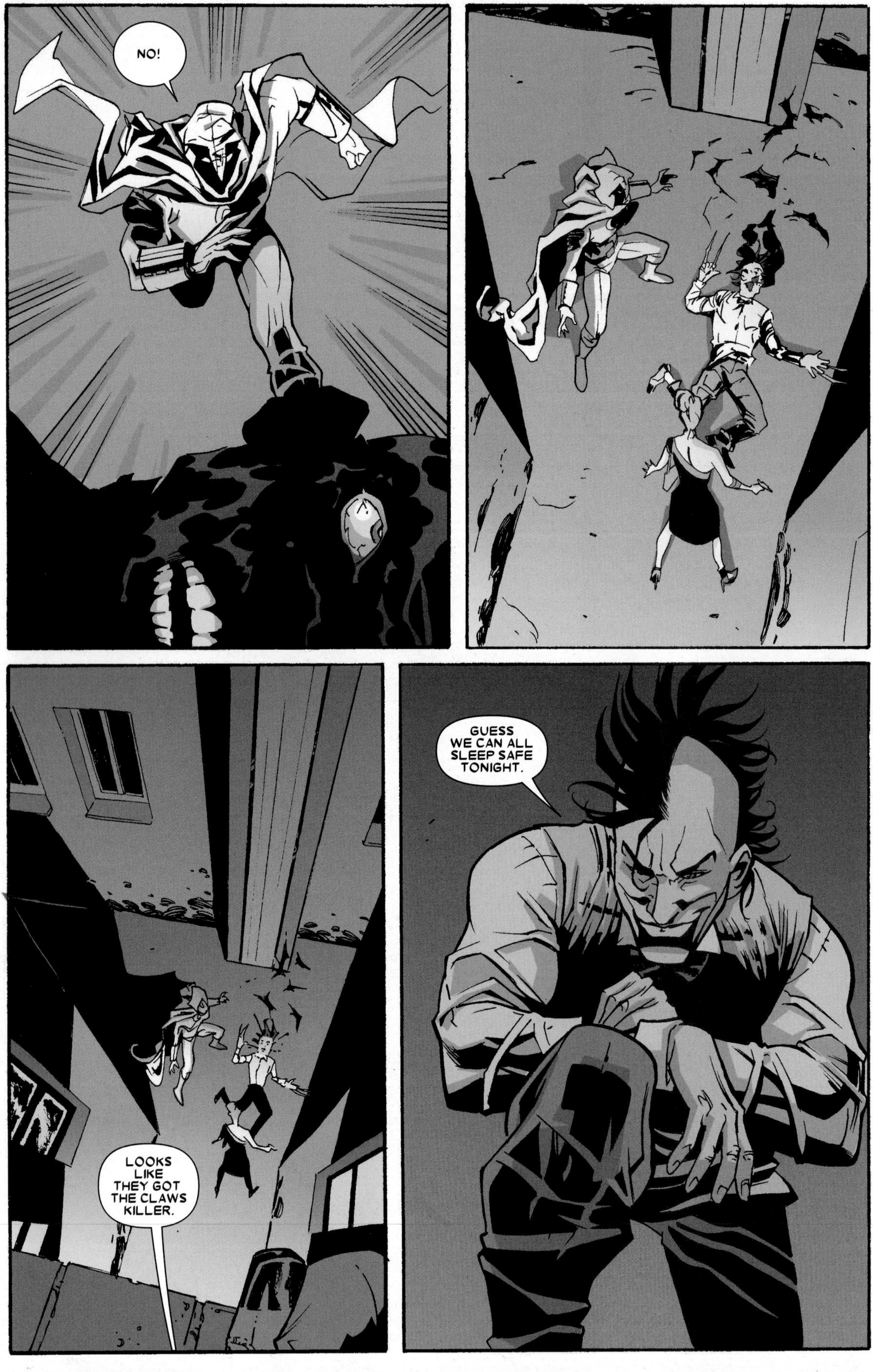
NO!
LOOKS LIKE THEY GOT THE CLAWS KILLER.
GUESS WE CAN ALL SLEEP SAFE TONIGHT.

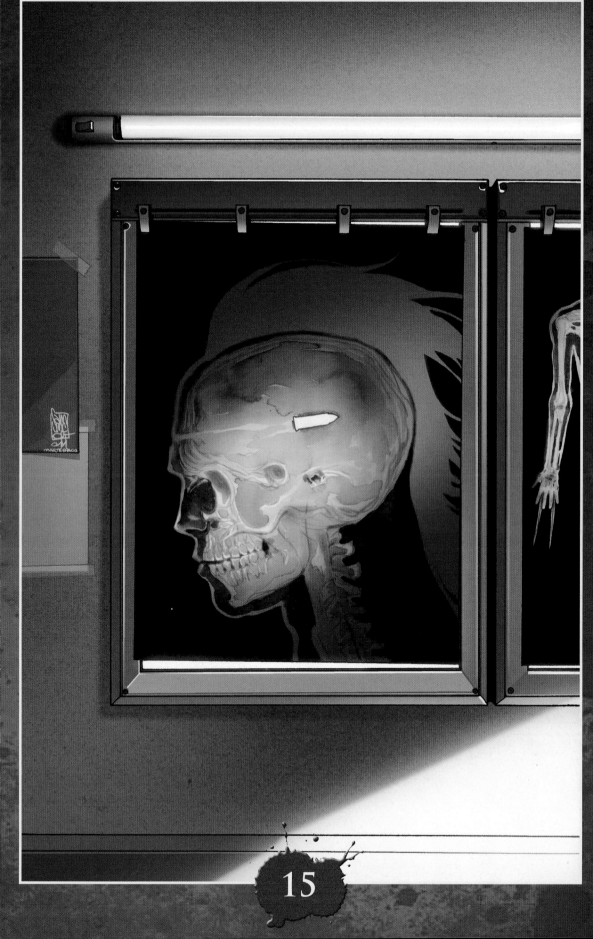

15

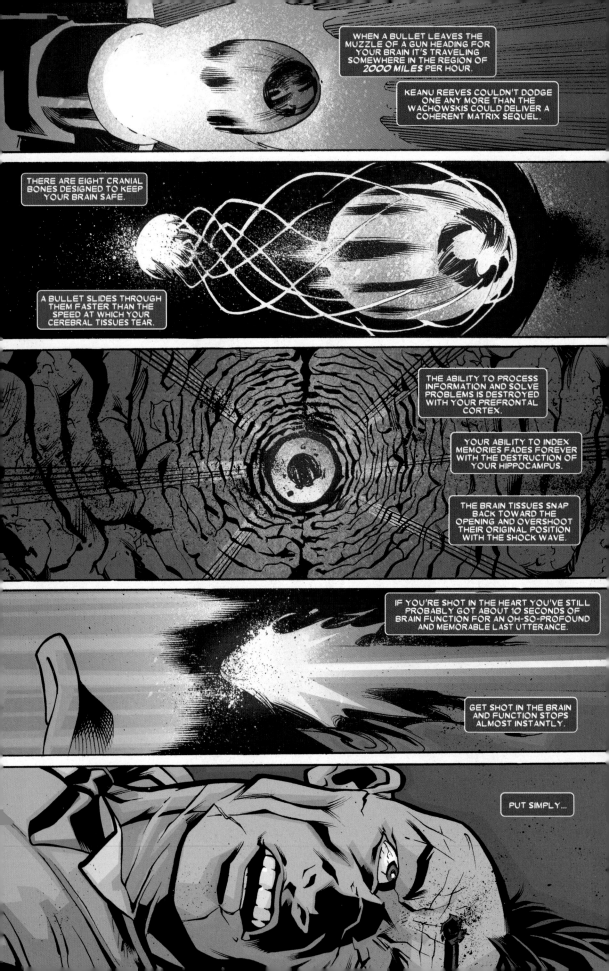

WHEN A BULLET LEAVES THE MUZZLE OF A GUN HEADING FOR YOUR BRAIN IT'S TRAVELING SOMEWHERE IN THE REGION OF *2000 MILES* PER HOUR.

KEANU REEVES COULDN'T DODGE ONE ANY MORE THAN THE WACHOWSKIS COULD DELIVER A COHERENT MATRIX SEQUEL.

THERE ARE EIGHT CRANIAL BONES DESIGNED TO KEEP YOUR BRAIN SAFE.

A BULLET SLIDES THROUGH THEM FASTER THAN THE SPEED AT WHICH YOUR CEREBRAL TISSUES TEAR.

THE ABILITY TO PROCESS INFORMATION AND SOLVE PROBLEMS IS DESTROYED WITH YOUR PREFRONTAL CORTEX.

YOUR ABILITY TO INDEX MEMORIES FADES FOREVER WITH THE DESTRUCTION OF YOUR HIPPOCAMPUS.

THE BRAIN TISSUES SNAP BACK TOWARD THE OPENING AND OVERSHOOT THEIR ORIGINAL POSITION WITH THE SHOCK WAVE.

IF YOU'RE SHOT IN THE HEART YOU'VE STILL PROBABLY GOT ABOUT 10 SECONDS OF BRAIN FUNCTION FOR AN OH-SO-PROFOUND AND MEMORABLE LAST UTTERANCE.

GET SHOT IN THE BRAIN AND FUNCTION STOPS ALMOST INSTANTLY.

PUT SIMPLY...

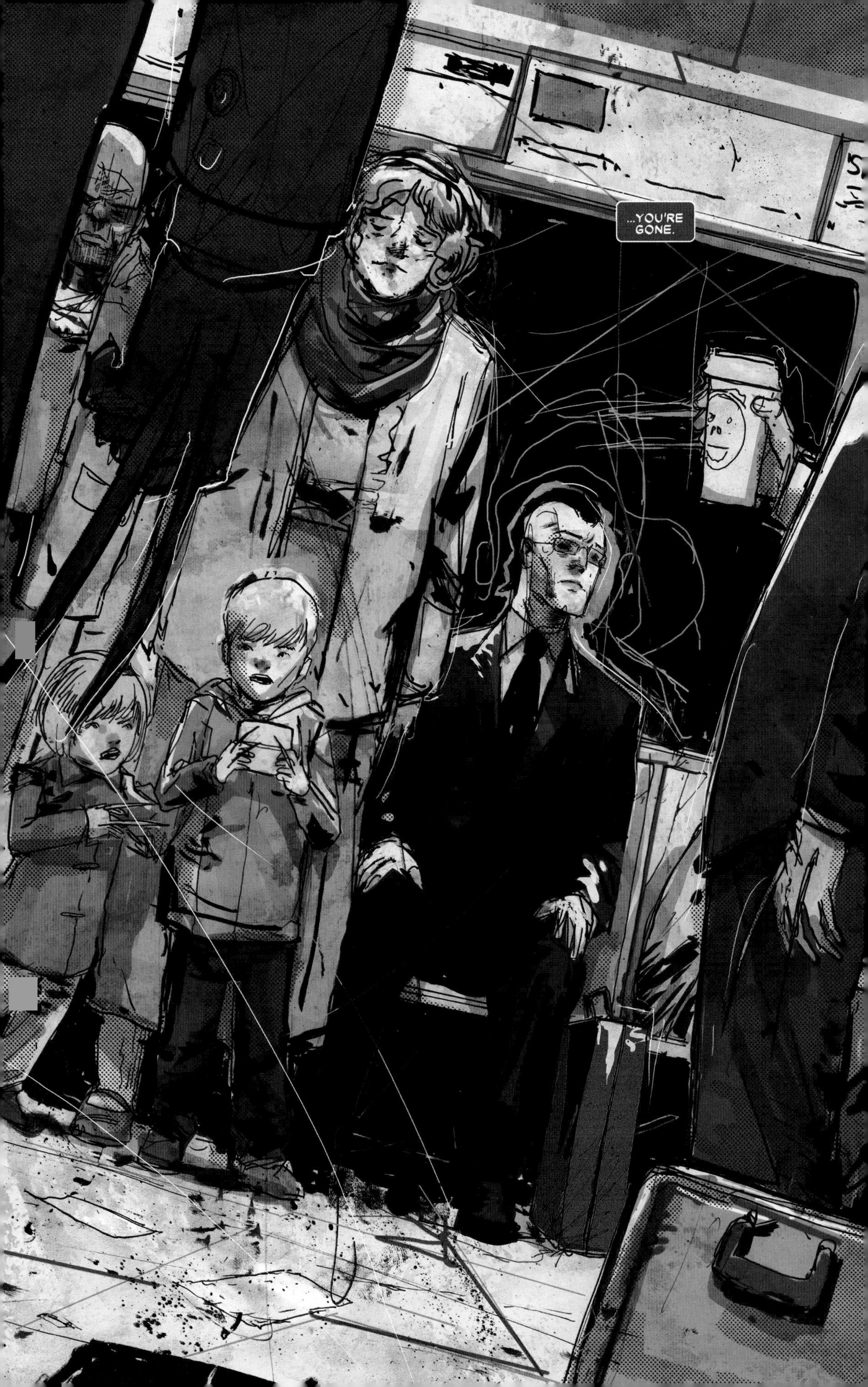
...YOU'RE GONE.

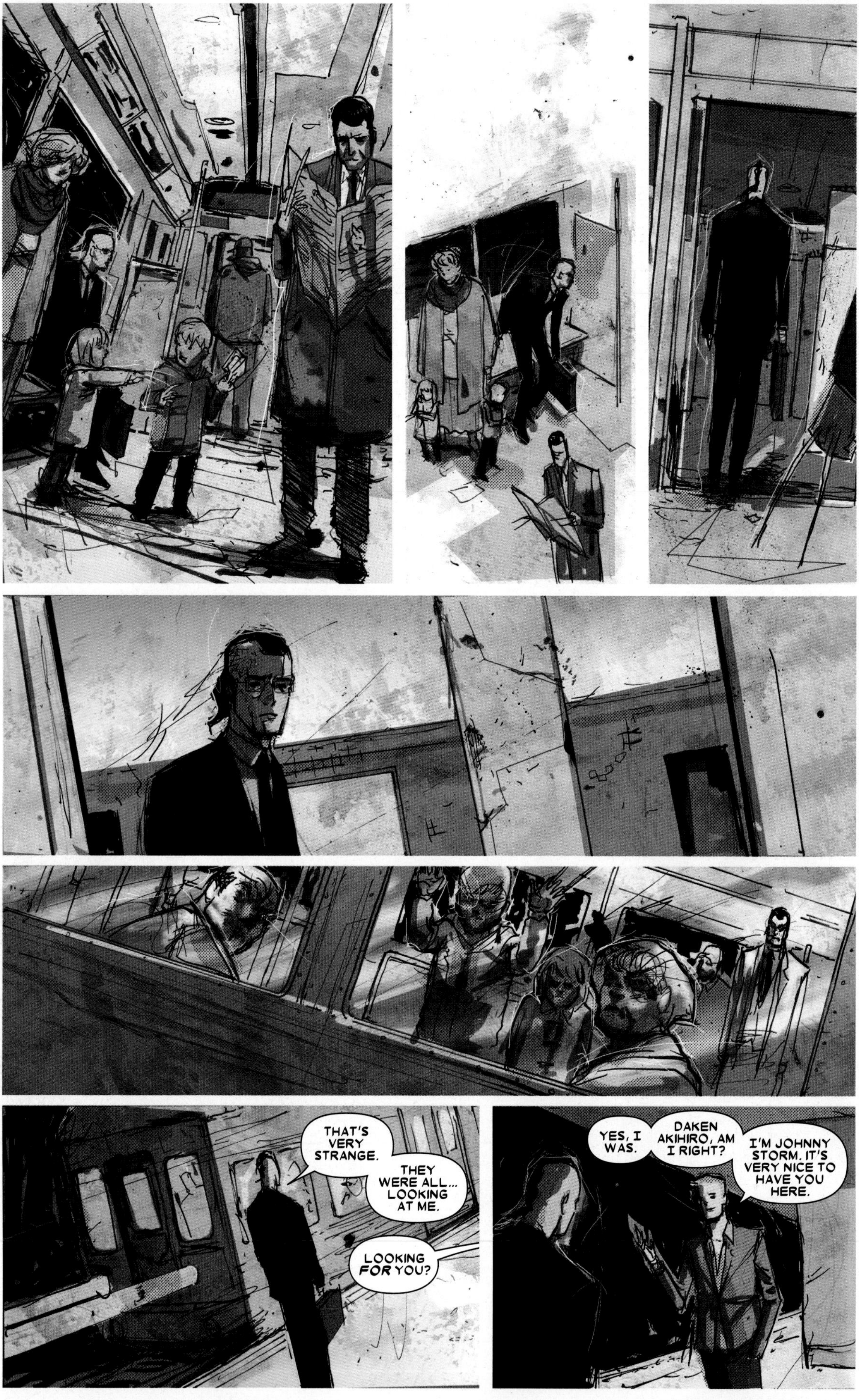
THAT'S VERY STRANGE.
THEY WERE ALL... LOOKING AT ME.
LOOKING FOR YOU?
YES, I WAS.
DAKEN AKIHIRO, AM I RIGHT?
I'M JOHNNY STORM. IT'S VERY NICE TO HAVE YOU HERE.

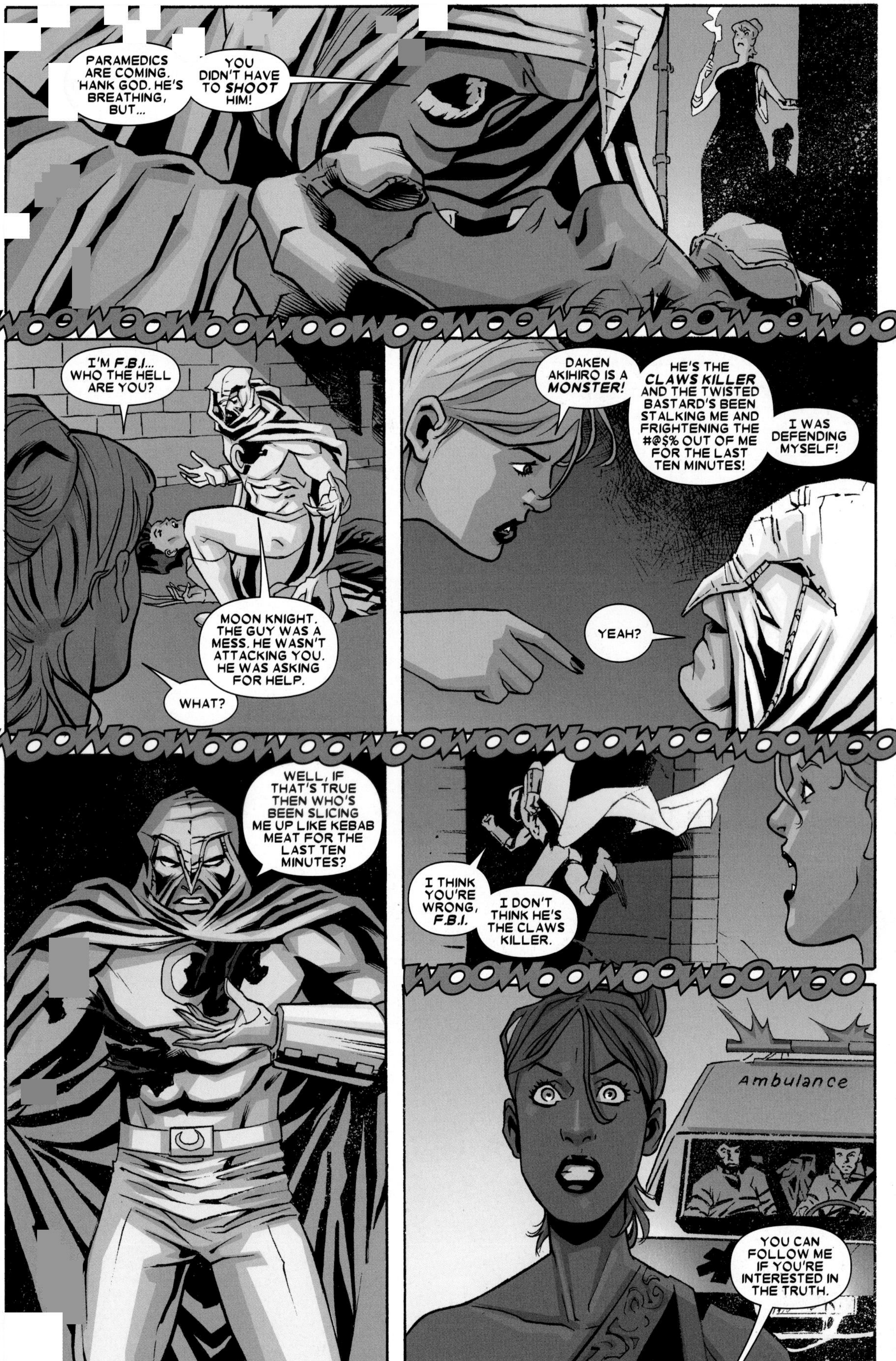
PARAMEDICS ARE COMING. HANK GOD. HE'S BREATHING, BUT...
YOU DIDN'T HAVE TO SHOOT HIM!
WOOWOOWOOWOOWOOWOOWOOWOOWOOWOO
I'M F.B.I... WHO THE HELL ARE YOU?
MOON KNIGHT. THE GUY WAS A MESS. HE WASN'T ATTACKING YOU. HE WAS ASKING FOR HELP.
WHAT?
DAKEN AKIHIRO IS A MONSTER!
HE'S THE CLAWS KILLER AND THE TWISTED BASTARD'S BEEN STALKING ME AND FRIGHTENING THE #@$% OUT OF ME FOR THE LAST TEN MINUTES!
I WAS DEFENDING MYSELF!
YEAH?
WOOWOOWOOWOOWOOWOOWOOWOOWOOWOO
WELL, IF THAT'S TRUE THEN WHO'S BEEN SLICING ME UP LIKE KEBAB MEAT FOR THE LAST TEN MINUTES?
I THINK YOU'RE WRONG, F.B.I.
I DON'T THINK HE'S THE CLAWS KILLER.
WOOWOOWOOWOOWOOWOO
Ambulance
YOU CAN FOLLOW ME IF YOU'RE INTERESTED IN THE TRUTH.

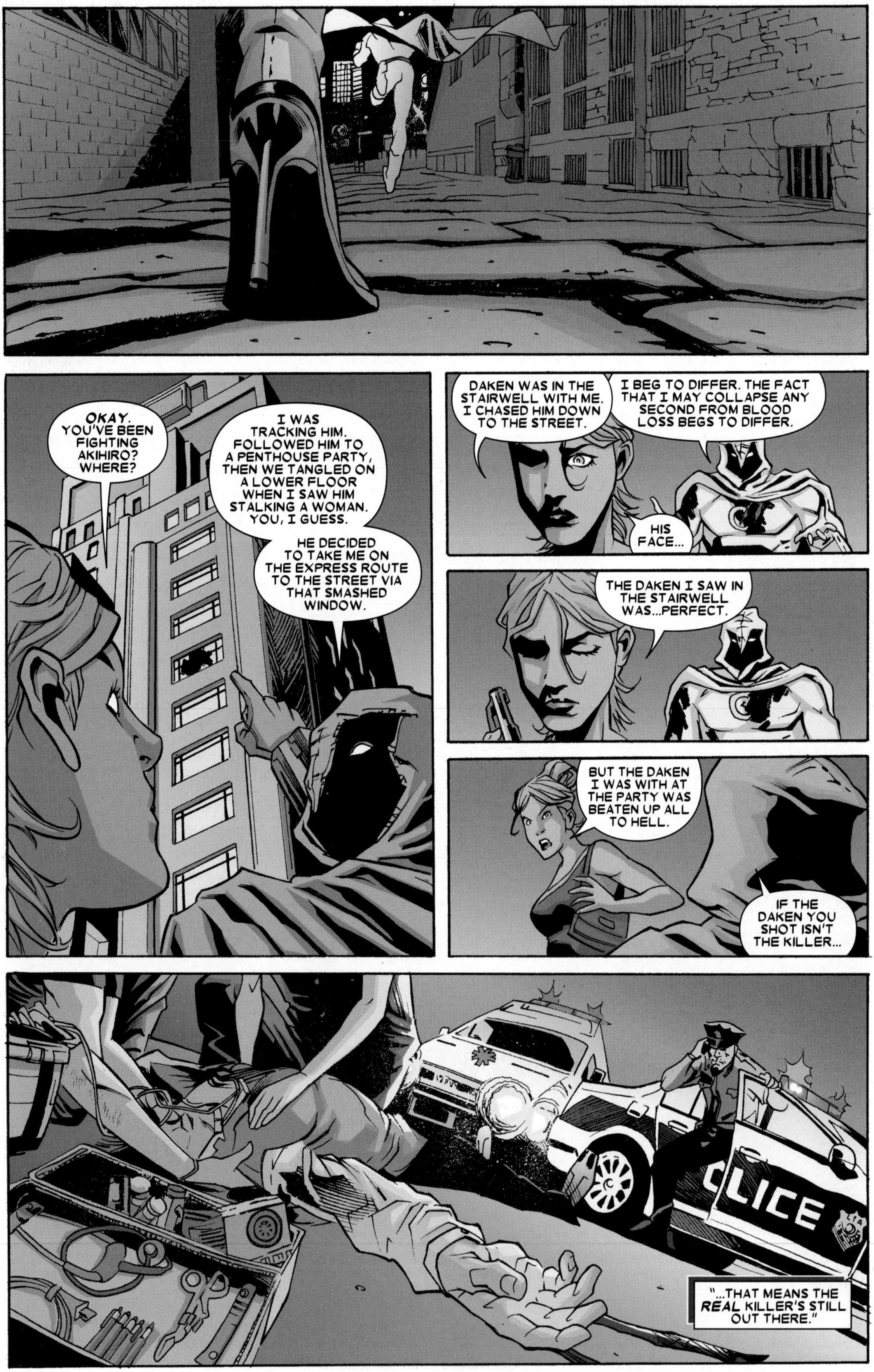
OKAY. YOU'VE BEEN FIGHTING AKIHIRO? WHERE?
I WAS TRACKING HIM. FOLLOWED HIM TO A PENTHOUSE PARTY, THEN WE TANGLED ON A LOWER FLOOR WHEN I SAW HIM STALKING A WOMAN. YOU, I GUESS.
HE DECIDED TO TAKE ME ON THE EXPRESS ROUTE TO THE STREET VIA THAT SMASHED WINDOW.
DAKEN WAS IN THE STAIRWELL WITH ME. I CHASED HIM DOWN TO THE STREET.
I BEG TO DIFFER. THE FACT THAT I MAY COLLAPSE ANY SECOND FROM BLOOD LOSS BEGS TO DIFFER.
HIS FACE...
THE DAKEN I SAW IN THE STAIRWELL WAS...PERFECT.
BUT THE DAKEN I WAS WITH AT THE PARTY WAS BEATEN UP ALL TO HELL.
IF THE DAKEN YOU SHOT ISN'T THE KILLER...
"...THAT MEANS THE REAL KILLER'S STILL OUT THERE."

HE'S WITH ME.

YOU WERE RIGHT. HERE'S DAKEN AND I FIGHTING.

FIGURED ANY BUILDING WITH A MILLIONAIRE'S PENTHOUSE WOULD HAVE SECURITY CAMERAS.

I DON'T KNOW WHAT'S MORE DISTURBING. THE THOUGHT THAT THE CLAWS KILLER MIGHT STILL BE ON THE LOOSE...

...OR HOW BADLY I WANT THAT TO BE TRUE.

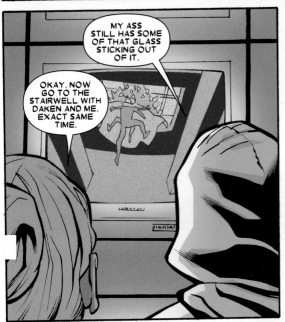

MY ASS STILL HAS SOME OF THAT GLASS STICKING OUT OF IT.

OKAY. NOW GO TO THE STAIRWELL WITH DAKEN AND ME. EXACT SAME TIME.

THERE HE IS.

WHAT'S WITH THE BLUR EFFECT?

IT WAS DEFINITELY DAKEN. I SAW HIM. HE SPOKE TO ME.

SOMEONE'S THERE...BUT IT'S ALMOST LIKE THEY'VE GOT SOME KIND OF PERSONAL CLOAKING DEVICE.

HEY, LOOK ON THE BRIGHT SIDE...

AT LEAST YOU KNOW YOU'RE NOT TOTALLY CRAZY.

BUT...

...HOW COULD HE KNOW ALL THE THINGS HE SAID TO ME?

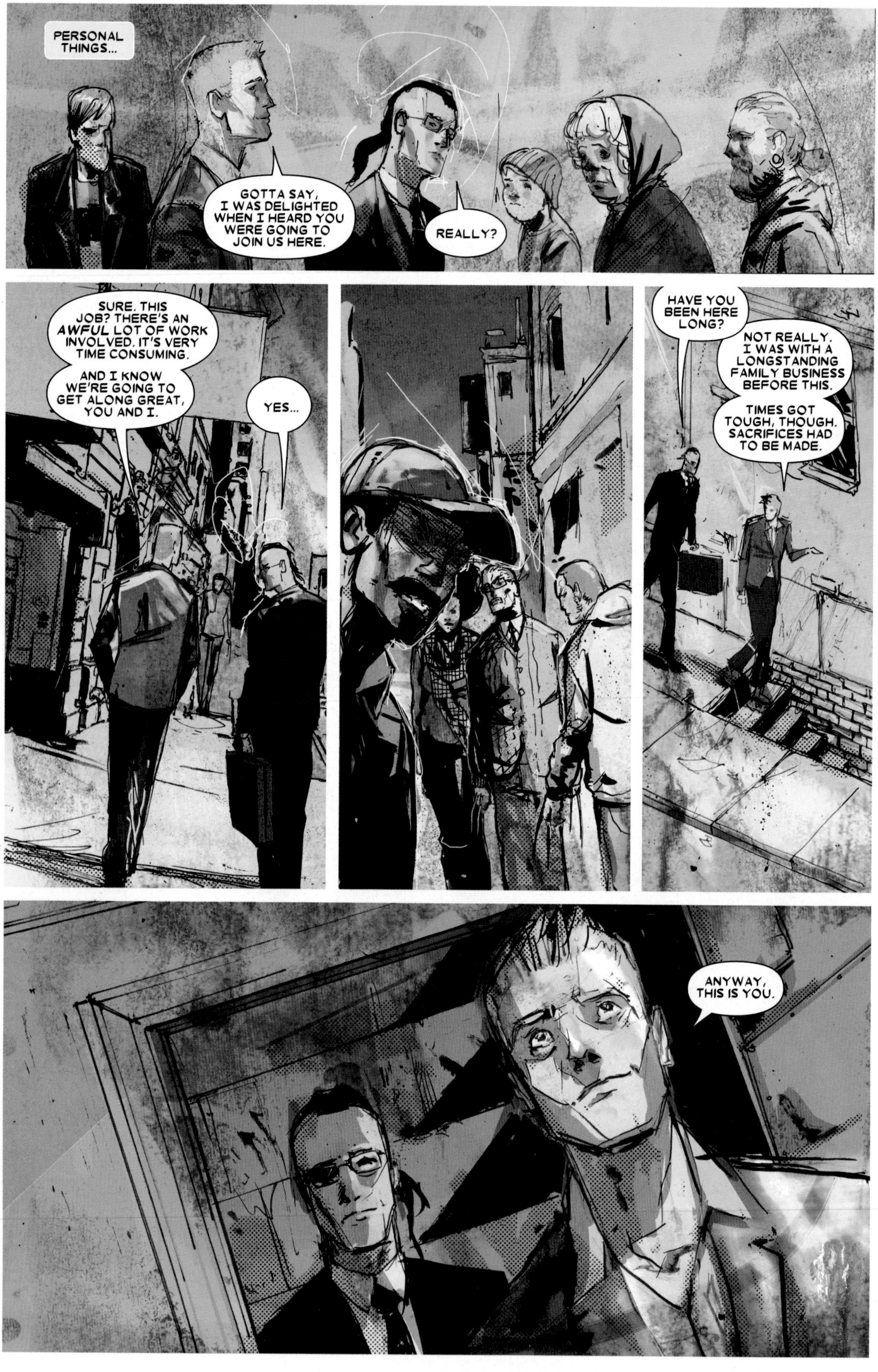
PERSONAL THINGS...
GOTTA SAY, I WAS DELIGHTED WHEN I HEARD YOU WERE GOING TO JOIN US HERE.
REALLY?
SURE. THIS JOB? THERE'S AN AWFUL LOT OF WORK INVOLVED. IT'S VERY TIME CONSUMING.
AND I KNOW WE'RE GOING TO GET ALONG GREAT, YOU AND I.
YES...
HAVE YOU BEEN HERE LONG?
NOT REALLY. I WAS WITH A LONGSTANDING FAMILY BUSINESS BEFORE THIS.
TIMES GOT TOUGH, THOUGH. SACRIFICES HAD TO BE MADE.
ANYWAY, THIS IS YOU.

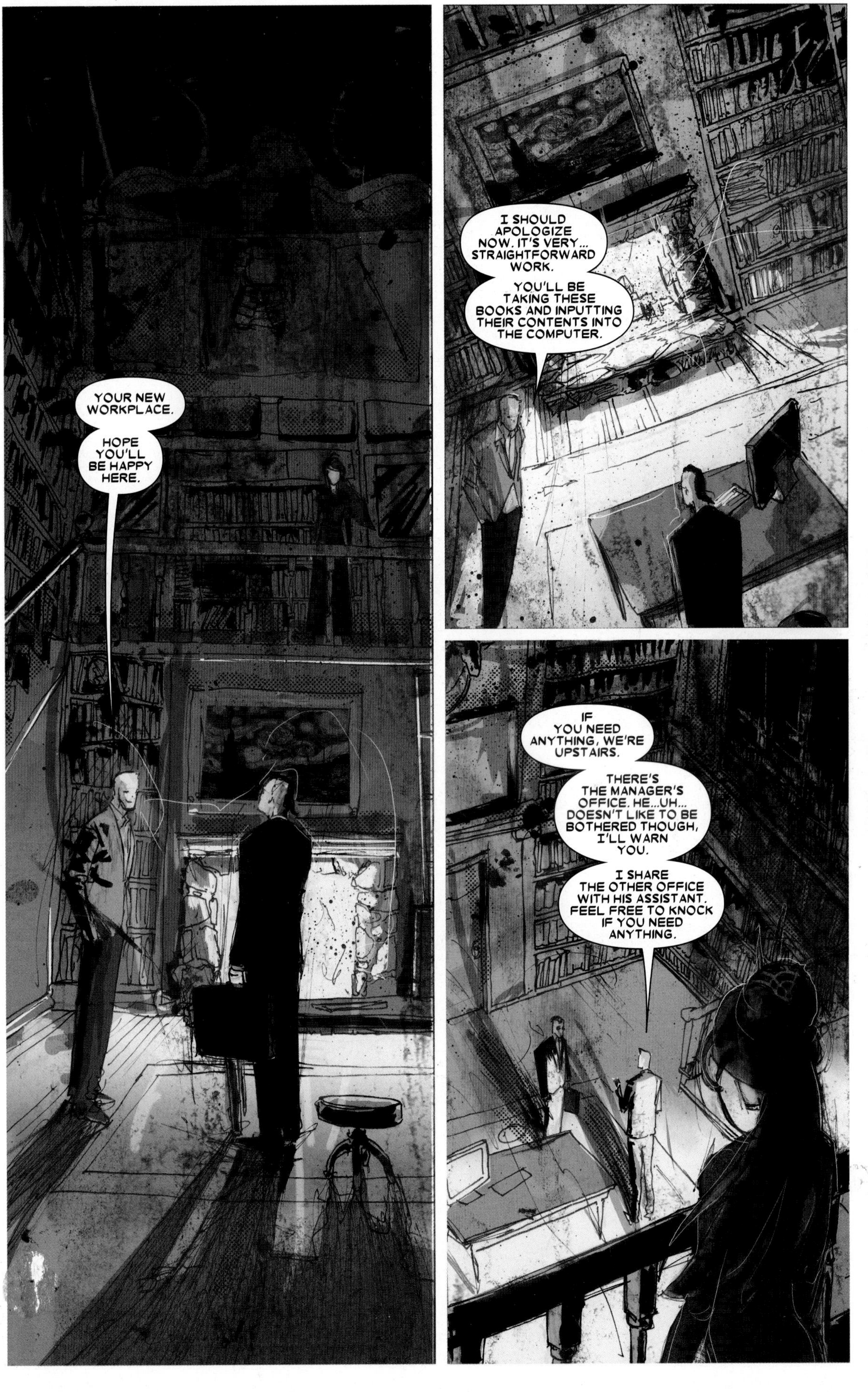
YOUR NEW WORKPLACE.
HOPE YOU'LL BE HAPPY HERE.
I SHOULD APOLOGIZE NOW. IT'S VERY... STRAIGHTFORWARD WORK.
YOU'LL BE TAKING THESE BOOKS AND INPUTTING THEIR CONTENTS INTO THE COMPUTER.
IF YOU NEED ANYTHING, WE'RE UPSTAIRS.
THERE'S THE MANAGER'S OFFICE. HE...UH... DOESN'T LIKE TO BE BOTHERED THOUGH, I'LL WARN YOU.
I SHARE THE OTHER OFFICE WITH HIS ASSISTANT. FEEL FREE TO KNOCK IF YOU NEED ANYTHING.

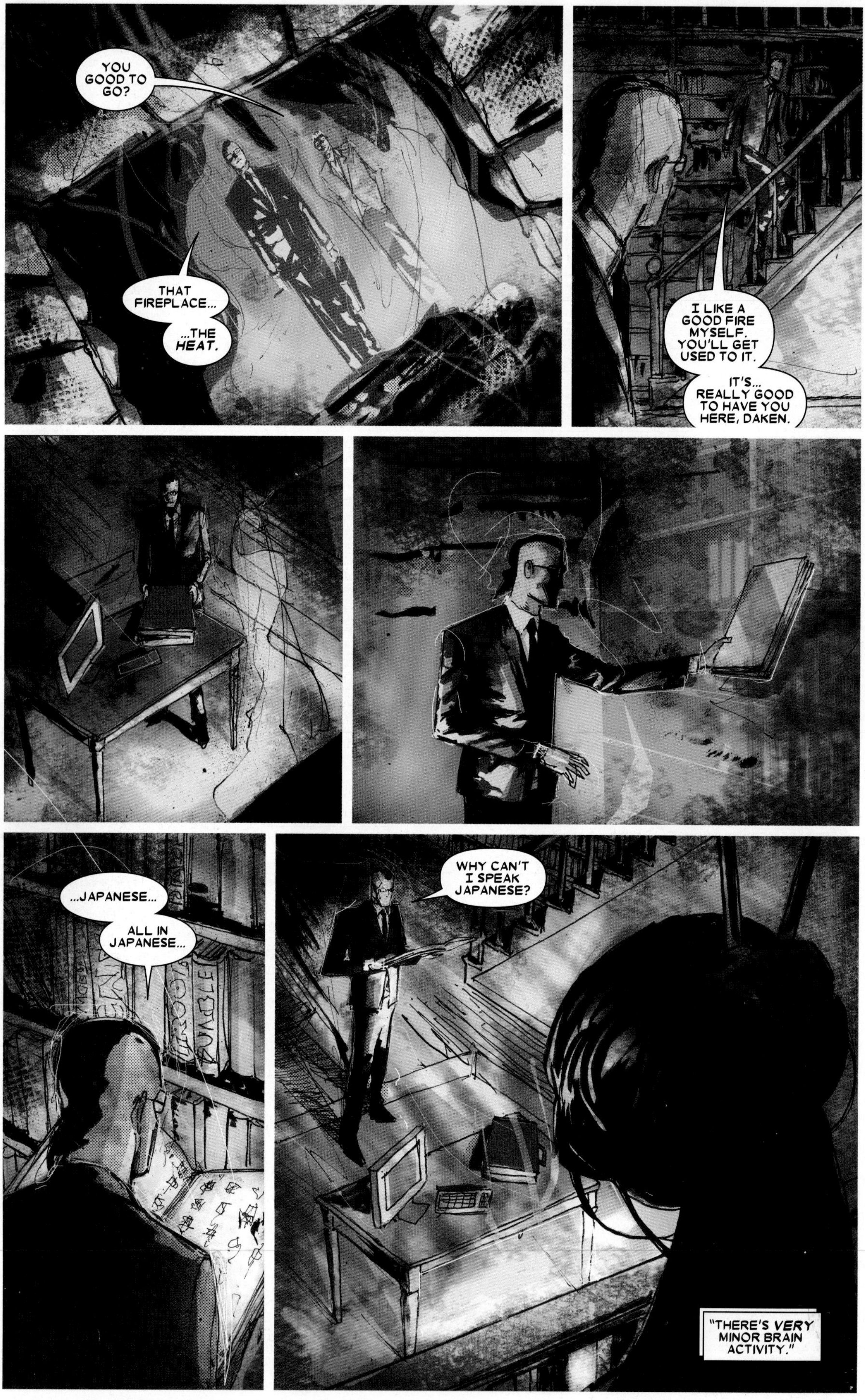
YOU GOOD TO GO?
THAT FIREPLACE...
...THE *HEAT.*
I LIKE A GOOD FIRE MYSELF. YOU'LL GET USED TO IT.
IT'S... REALLY GOOD TO HAVE YOU HERE, DAKEN.
...JAPANESE...
ALL IN JAPANESE...
WHY CAN'T I SPEAK JAPANESE?
"THERE'S *VERY* MINOR BRAIN ACTIVITY."

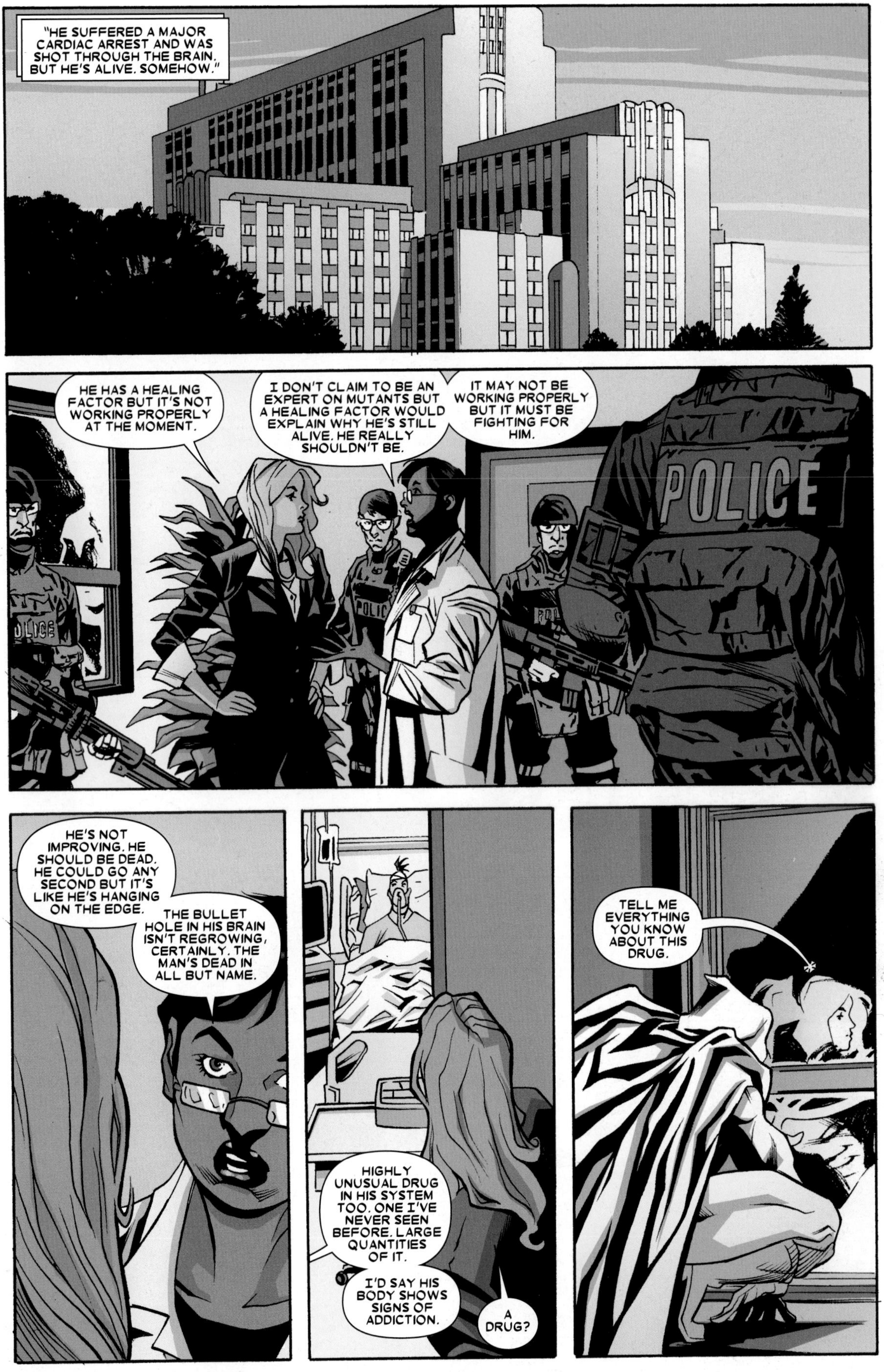
"HE SUFFERED A MAJOR CARDIAC ARREST AND WAS SHOT THROUGH THE BRAIN. BUT HE'S ALIVE. SOMEHOW."
HE HAS A HEALING FACTOR BUT IT'S NOT WORKING PROPERLY AT THE MOMENT.
I DON'T CLAIM TO BE AN EXPERT ON MUTANTS BUT A HEALING FACTOR WOULD EXPLAIN WHY HE'S STILL ALIVE. HE REALLY SHOULDN'T BE.
IT MAY NOT BE WORKING PROPERLY BUT IT MUST BE FIGHTING FOR HIM.
POLICE
HE'S NOT IMPROVING. HE SHOULD BE DEAD. HE COULD GO ANY SECOND BUT IT'S LIKE HE'S HANGING ON THE EDGE.
THE BULLET HOLE IN HIS BRAIN ISN'T REGROWING, CERTAINLY. THE MAN'S DEAD IN ALL BUT NAME.
HIGHLY UNUSUAL DRUG IN HIS SYSTEM TOO. ONE I'VE NEVER SEEN BEFORE. LARGE QUANTITIES OF IT.
I'D SAY HIS BODY SHOWS SIGNS OF ADDICTION.
A DRUG?
TELL ME EVERYTHING YOU KNOW ABOUT THIS DRUG.

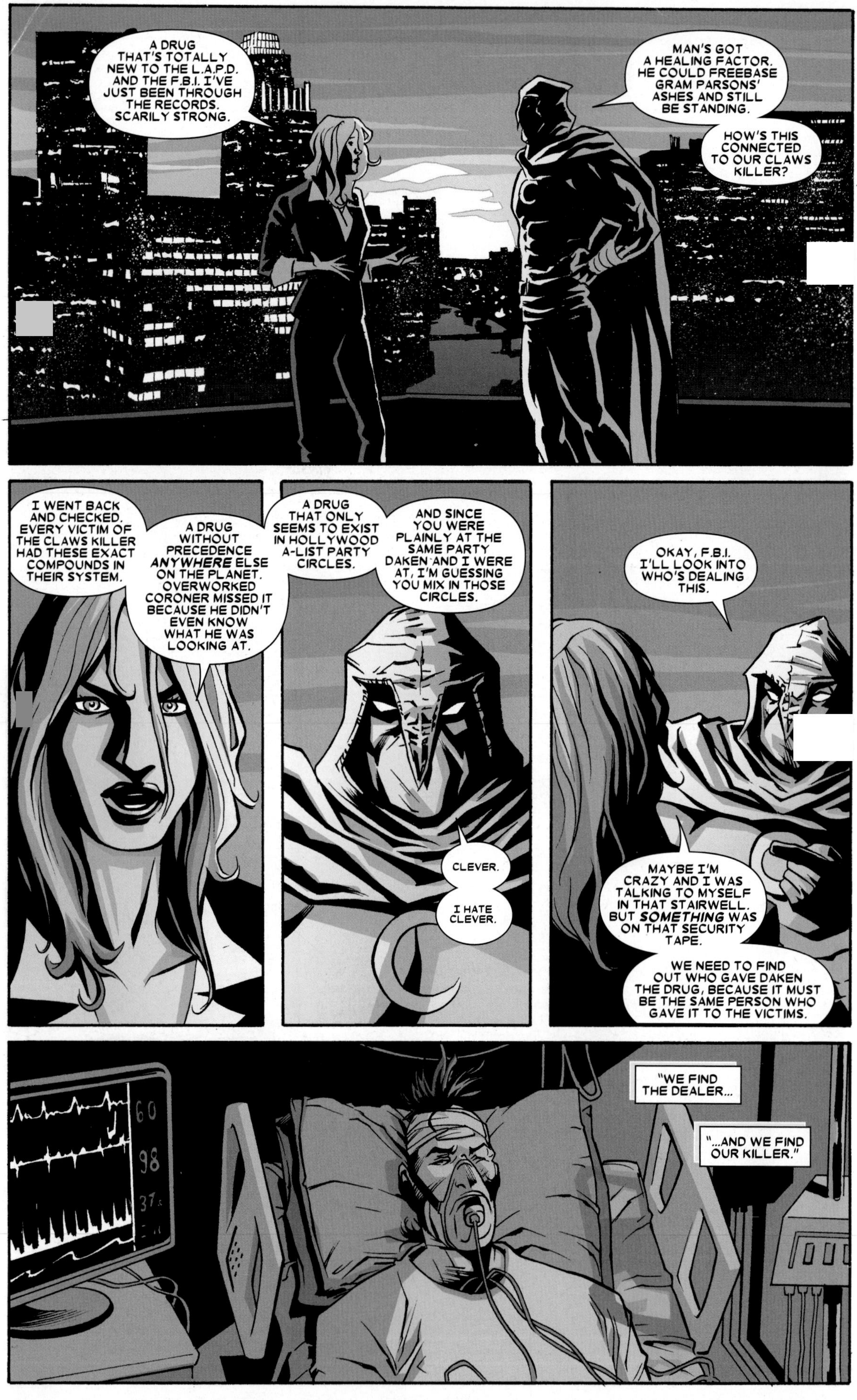

A DRUG THAT'S TOTALLY NEW TO THE L.A.P.D. AND THE F.B.I. I'VE JUST BEEN THROUGH THE RECORDS. SCARILY STRONG.
MAN'S GOT A HEALING FACTOR. HE COULD FREEBASE GRAM PARSONS' ASHES AND STILL BE STANDING.
HOW'S THIS CONNECTED TO OUR CLAWS KILLER?
I WENT BACK AND CHECKED. EVERY VICTIM OF THE CLAWS KILLER HAD THESE EXACT COMPOUNDS IN THEIR SYSTEM.
A DRUG WITHOUT PRECEDENCE *ANYWHERE* ELSE ON THE PLANET. OVERWORKED CORONER MISSED IT BECAUSE HE DIDN'T EVEN KNOW WHAT HE WAS LOOKING AT.
A DRUG THAT ONLY SEEMS TO EXIST IN HOLLYWOOD A-LIST PARTY CIRCLES.
AND SINCE YOU WERE PLAINLY AT THE SAME PARTY DAKEN AND I WERE AT, I'M GUESSING YOU MIX IN THOSE CIRCLES.
CLEVER.
I HATE CLEVER.
OKAY, F.B.I. I'LL LOOK INTO WHO'S DEALING THIS.
MAYBE I'M CRAZY AND I WAS TALKING TO MYSELF IN THAT STAIRWELL. BUT *SOMETHING* WAS ON THAT SECURITY TAPE.
WE NEED TO FIND OUT WHO GAVE DAKEN THE DRUG, BECAUSE IT MUST BE THE SAME PERSON WHO GAVE IT TO THE VICTIMS.
"WE FIND THE DEALER...
"...AND WE FIND OUR KILLER."

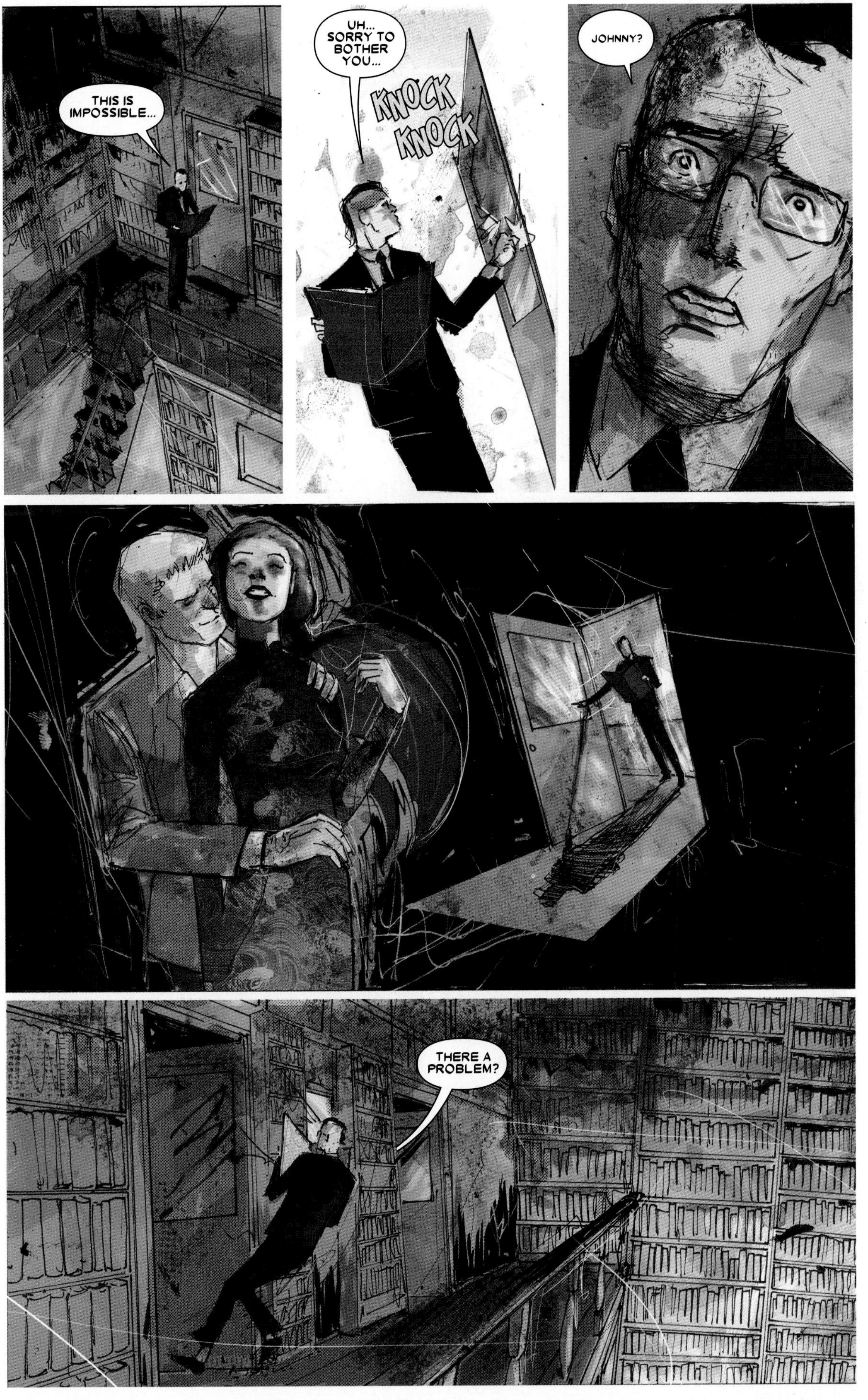
THIS IS IMPOSSIBLE...
UH... SORRY TO BOTHER YOU...
KNOCK KNOCK
JOHNNY?
THERE A PROBLEM?

YOU SPEAK JAPANESE FINE AND YOU CAN READ IT, TOO.

TAKE A BREATH AND LOOK AT IT AGAIN.

UH...I'M... UH...I'M SORRY TO TROUBLE YOU BUT...THERE'S BEEN SOME KIND OF MISTAKE...

I'M NEW HERE AND...WELL, ALL THESE BOOKS ARE IN JAPANESE AND I DON'T SPEAK...

I REALLY DON'T...

OH.

THEY'RE NAMES.

PEOPLE'S NAMES. FILLING THE BOOKS.

ALL THE BOOKS.

WHO ARE THESE PEOPLE?

THEY'RE THE NAMES OF ALL THE PEOPLE YOU'VE MURDERED, DAKEN.

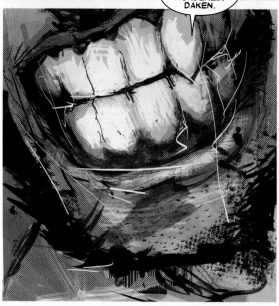

BOOM!

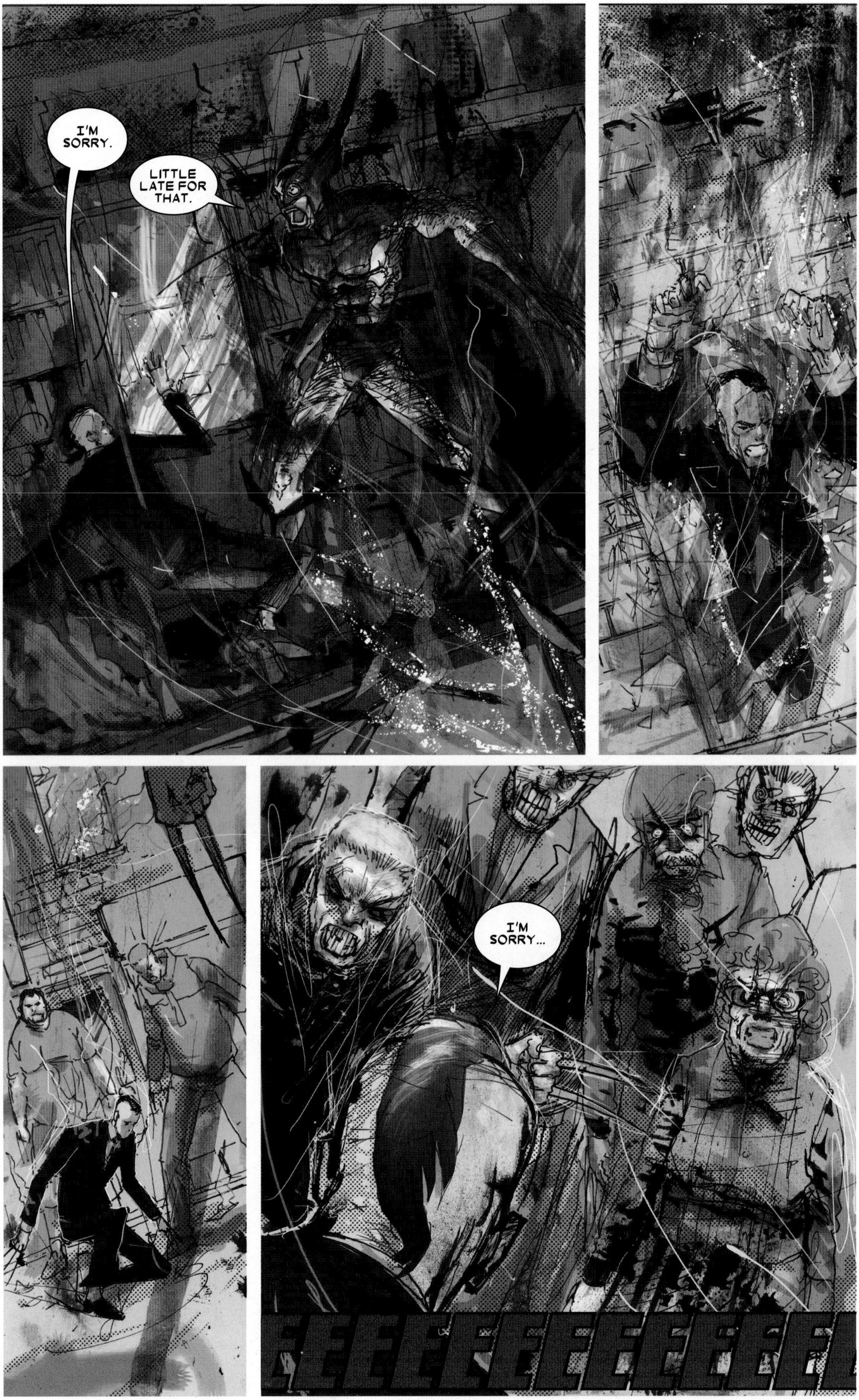
I'M SORRY.
LITTLE LATE FOR THAT.
I'M SORRY...
EEEEEEEEEEEE

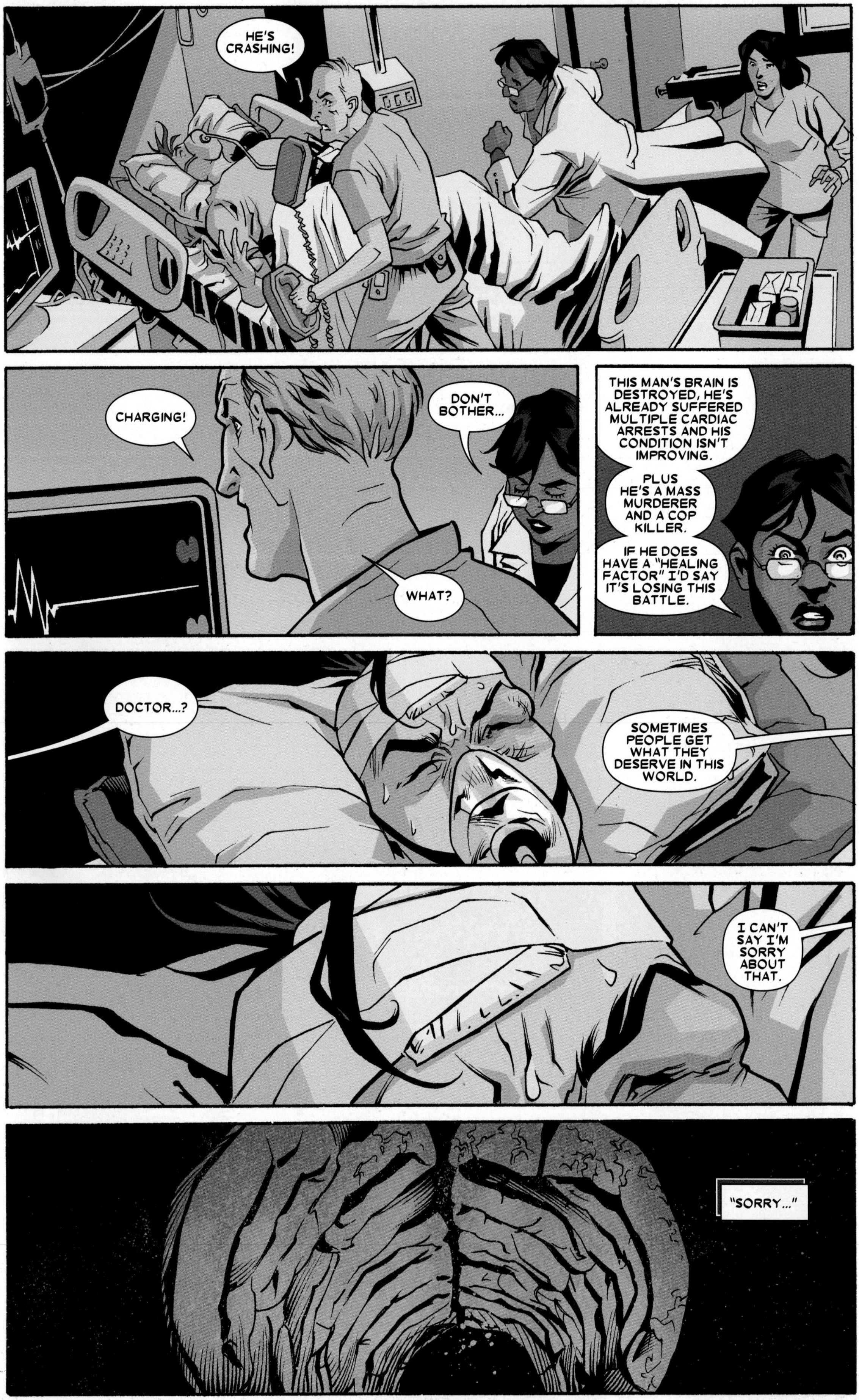
HE'S CRASHING!
CHARGING!
DON'T BOTHER...
WHAT?
THIS MAN'S BRAIN IS DESTROYED, HE'S ALREADY SUFFERED MULTIPLE CARDIAC ARRESTS AND HIS CONDITION ISN'T IMPROVING.
PLUS HE'S A MASS MURDERER AND A COP KILLER.
IF HE DOES HAVE A "HEALING FACTOR" I'D SAY IT'S LOSING THIS BATTLE.
DOCTOR...?
SOMETIMES PEOPLE GET WHAT THEY DESERVE IN THIS WORLD.
I CAN'T SAY I'M SORRY ABOUT THAT.
"SORRY..."

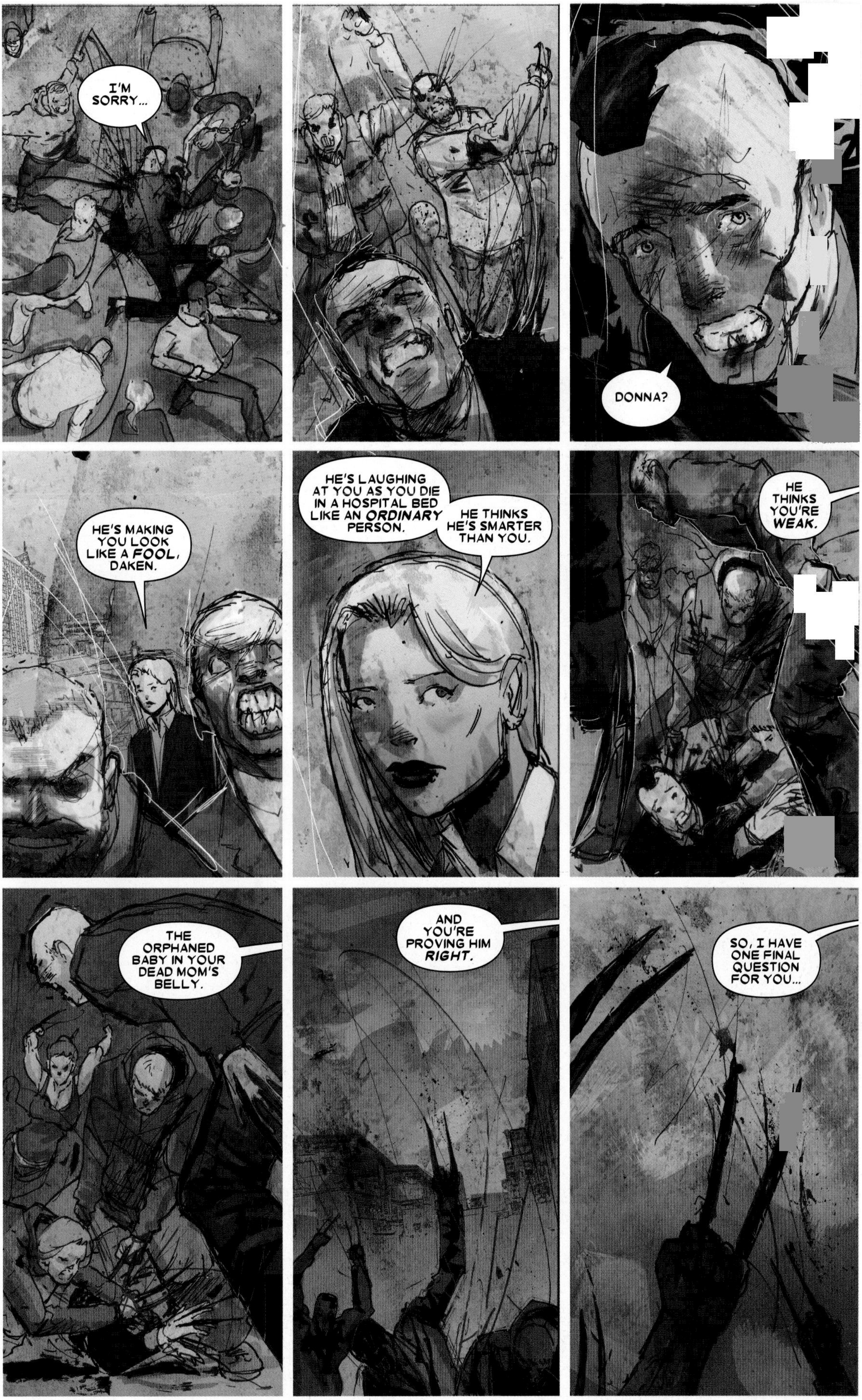
I'M SORRY...
DONNA?
HE'S MAKING YOU LOOK LIKE A FOOL, DAKEN.
HE'S LAUGHING AT YOU AS YOU DIE IN A HOSPITAL BED LIKE AN ORDINARY PERSON.
HE THINKS HE'S SMARTER THAN YOU.
HE THINKS YOU'RE WEAK.
THE ORPHANED BABY IN YOUR DEAD MOM'S BELLY.
AND YOU'RE PROVING HIM RIGHT.
SO, I HAVE ONE FINAL QUESTION FOR YOU...

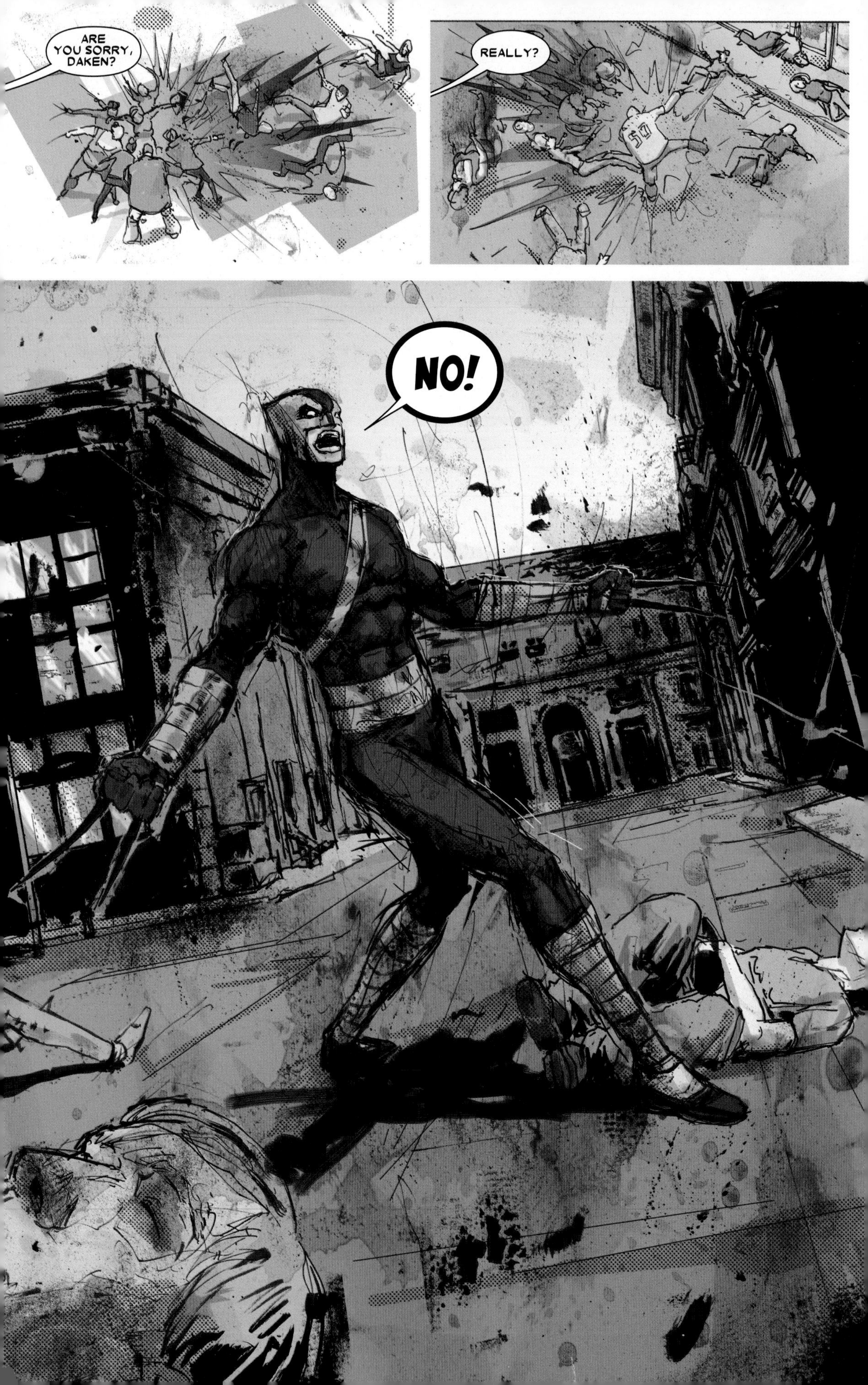
ARE YOU SORRY, DAKEN?
REALLY?
NO!

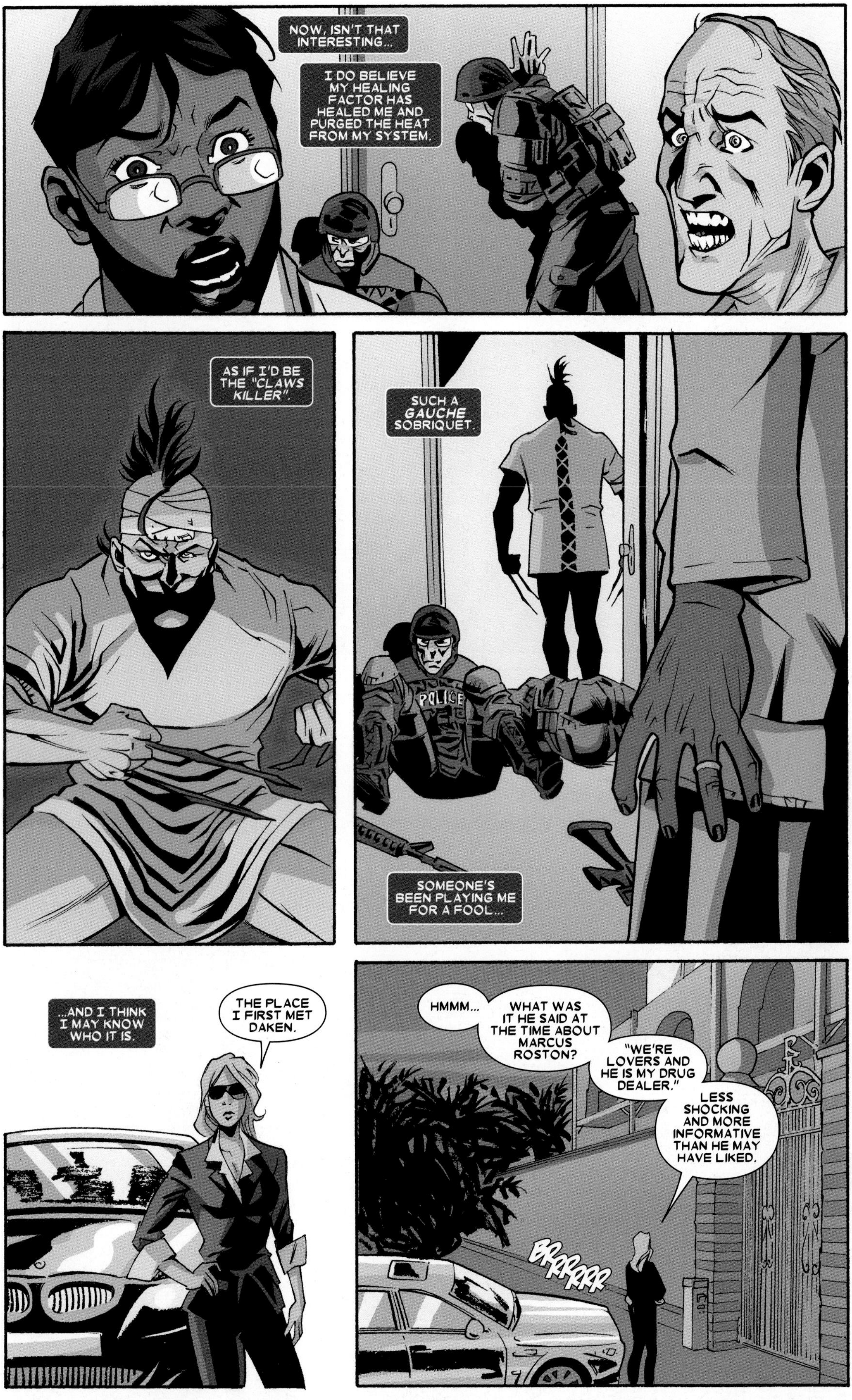
NOW, ISN'T THAT INTERESTING...
I DO BELIEVE MY HEALING FACTOR HAS HEALED ME AND PURGED THE HEAT FROM MY SYSTEM.
AS IF I'D BE THE "CLAWS KILLER".
SUCH A GAUCHE SOBRIQUET.
POLICE
SOMEONE'S BEEN PLAYING ME FOR A FOOL...
...AND I THINK I MAY KNOW WHO IT IS.
THE PLACE I FIRST MET DAKEN.
HMMM...
WHAT WAS IT HE SAID AT THE TIME ABOUT MARCUS ROSTON?
"WE'RE LOVERS AND HE IS MY DRUG DEALER."
LESS SHOCKING AND MORE INFORMATIVE THAN HE MAY HAVE LIKED.
BRRRRRR

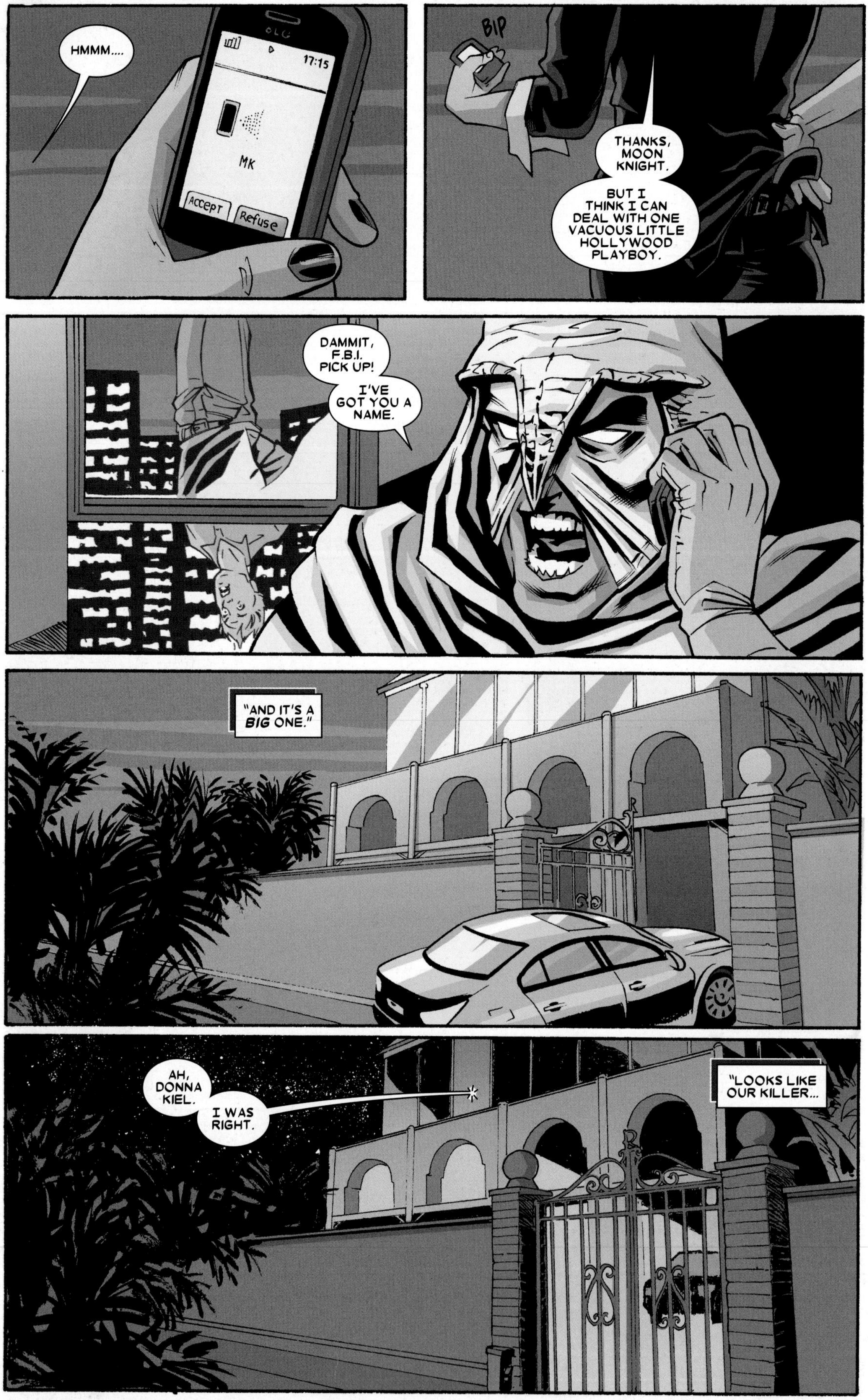
HMMM....
17:15
MK
Accept
Refuse
BIP
THANKS, MOON KNIGHT.
BUT I THINK I CAN DEAL WITH ONE VACUOUS LITTLE HOLLYWOOD PLAYBOY.
DAMMIT, F.B.I. PICK UP!
I'VE GOT YOU A NAME.
"AND IT'S A *BIG* ONE."
AH, DONNA KIEL.
I WAS RIGHT.
"LOOKS LIKE OUR KILLER...

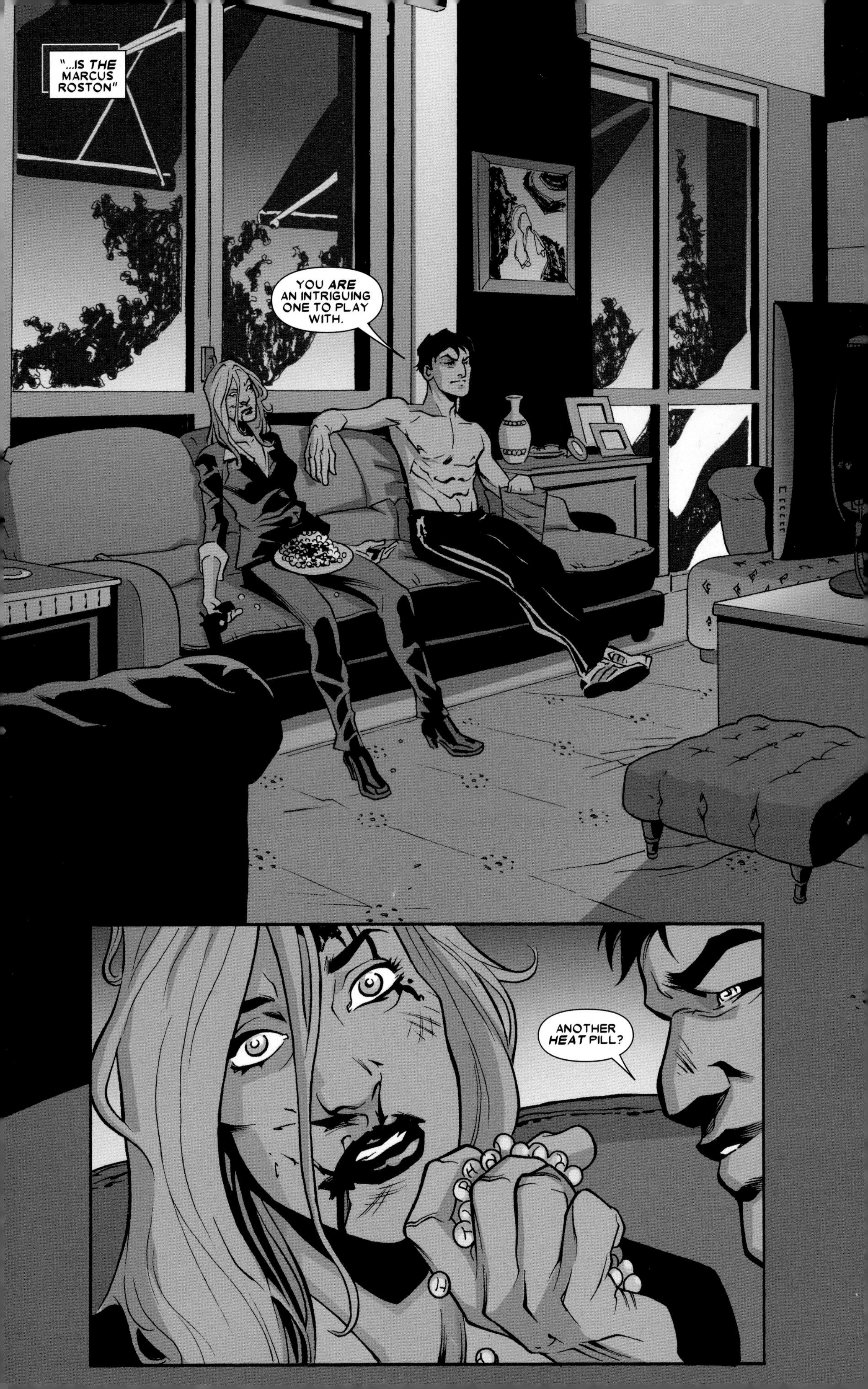
"...IS *THE* MARCUS ROSTON"
YOU *ARE* AN INTRIGUING ONE TO PLAY WITH.
ANOTHER *HEAT* PILL?

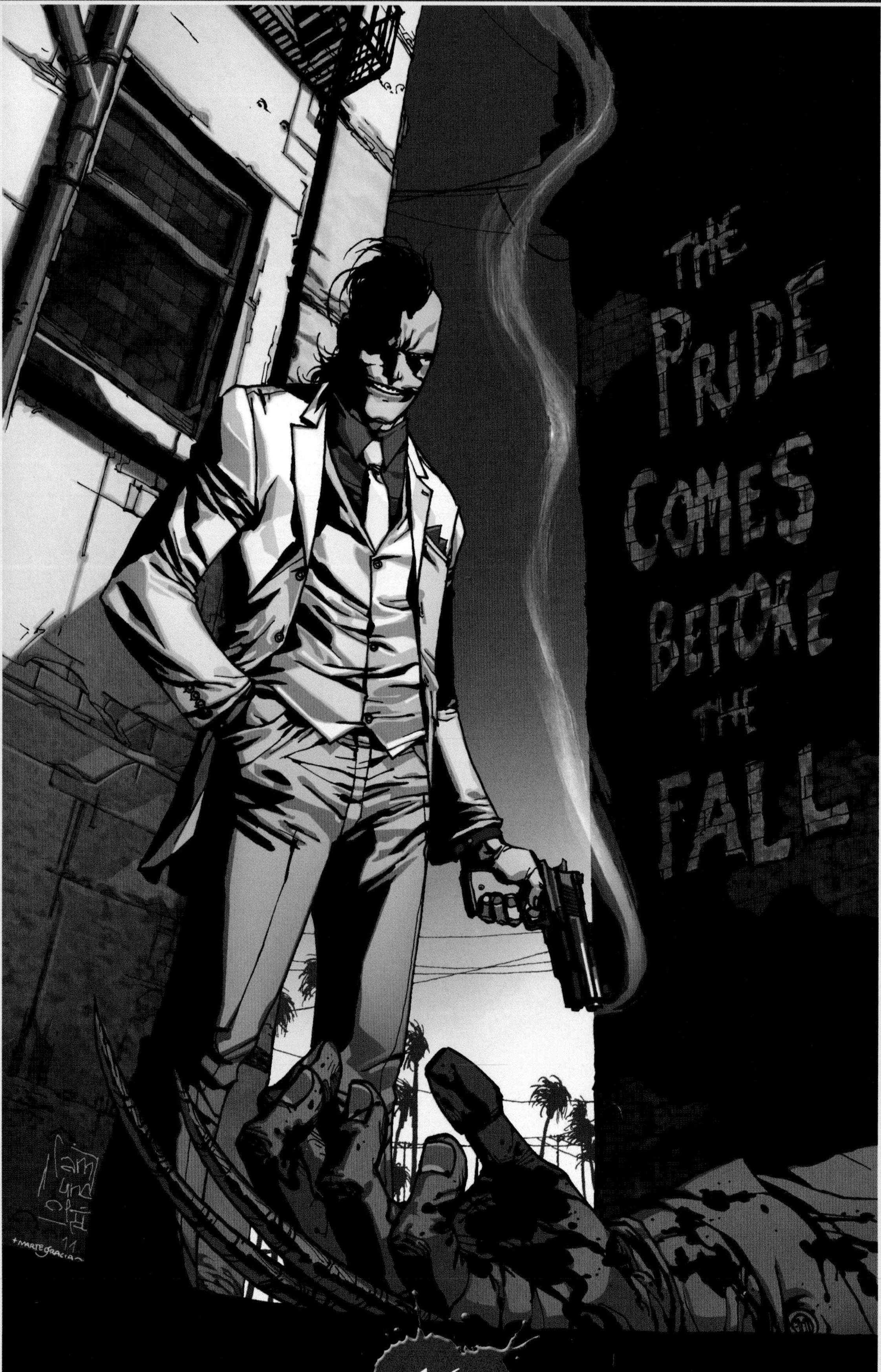
THE PRIDE COMES BEFORE THE FALL

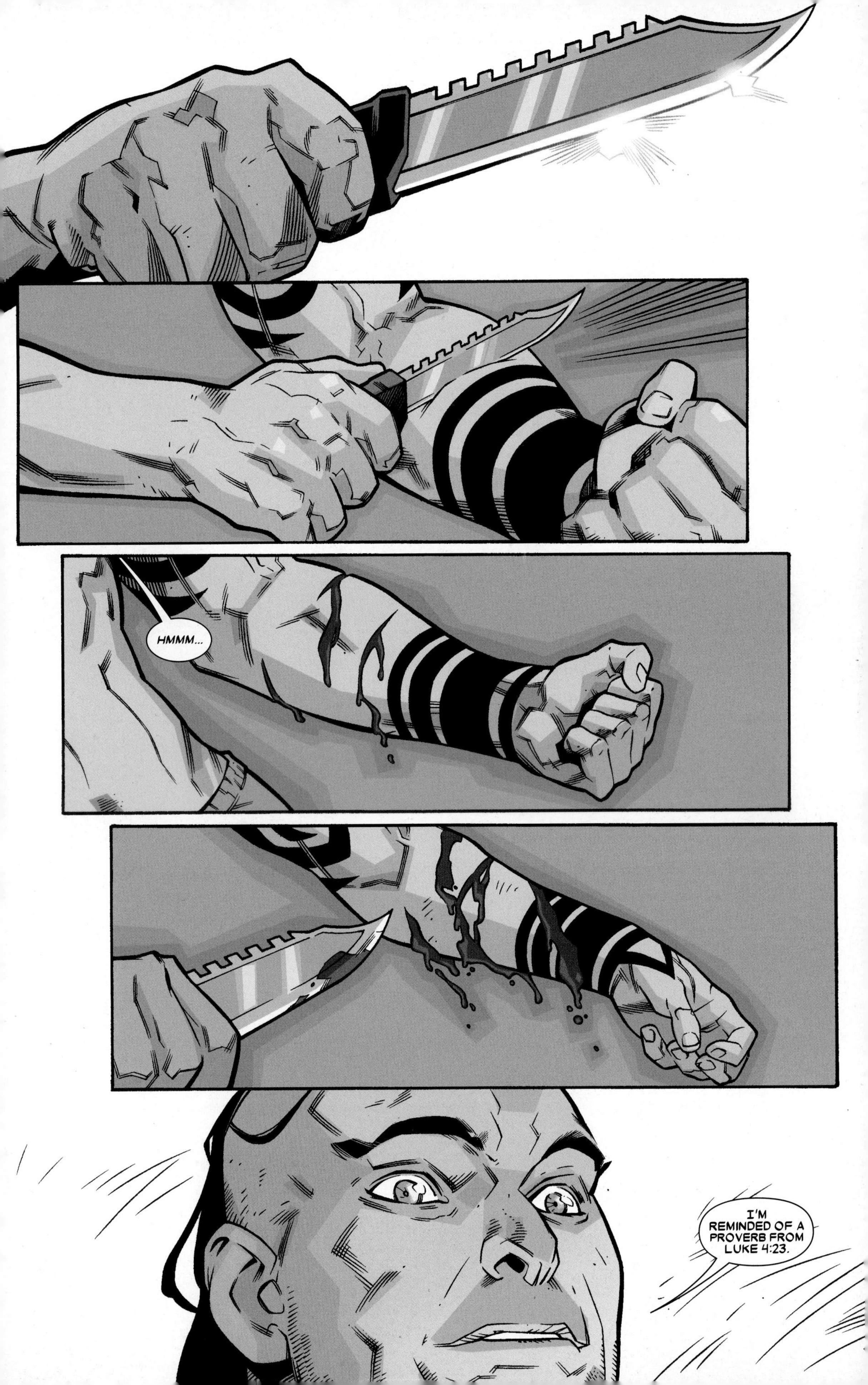
HMMM...
I'M REMINDED OF A PROVERB FROM LUKE 4:23.

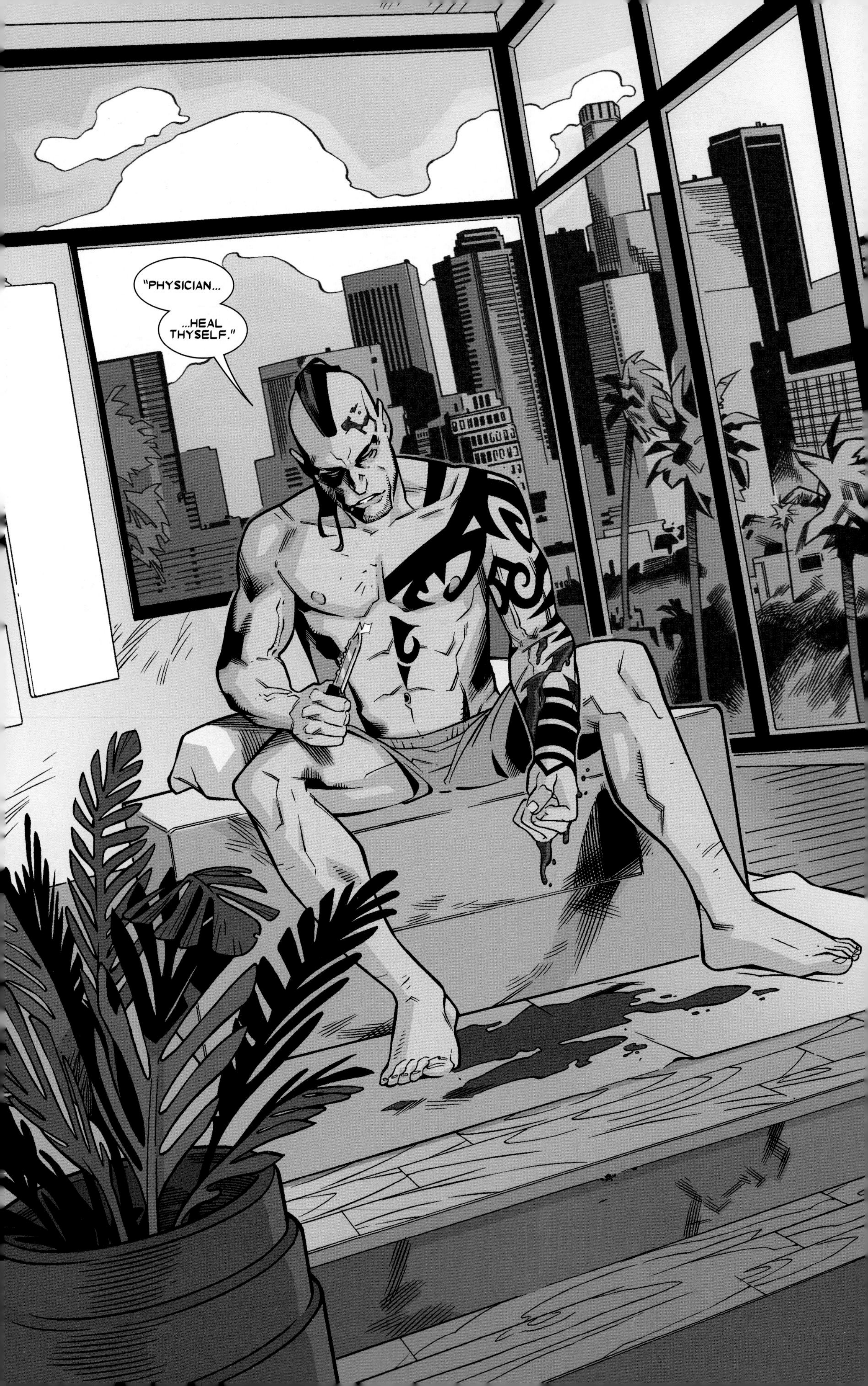
"PHYSICIAN...
...HEAL THYSELF."

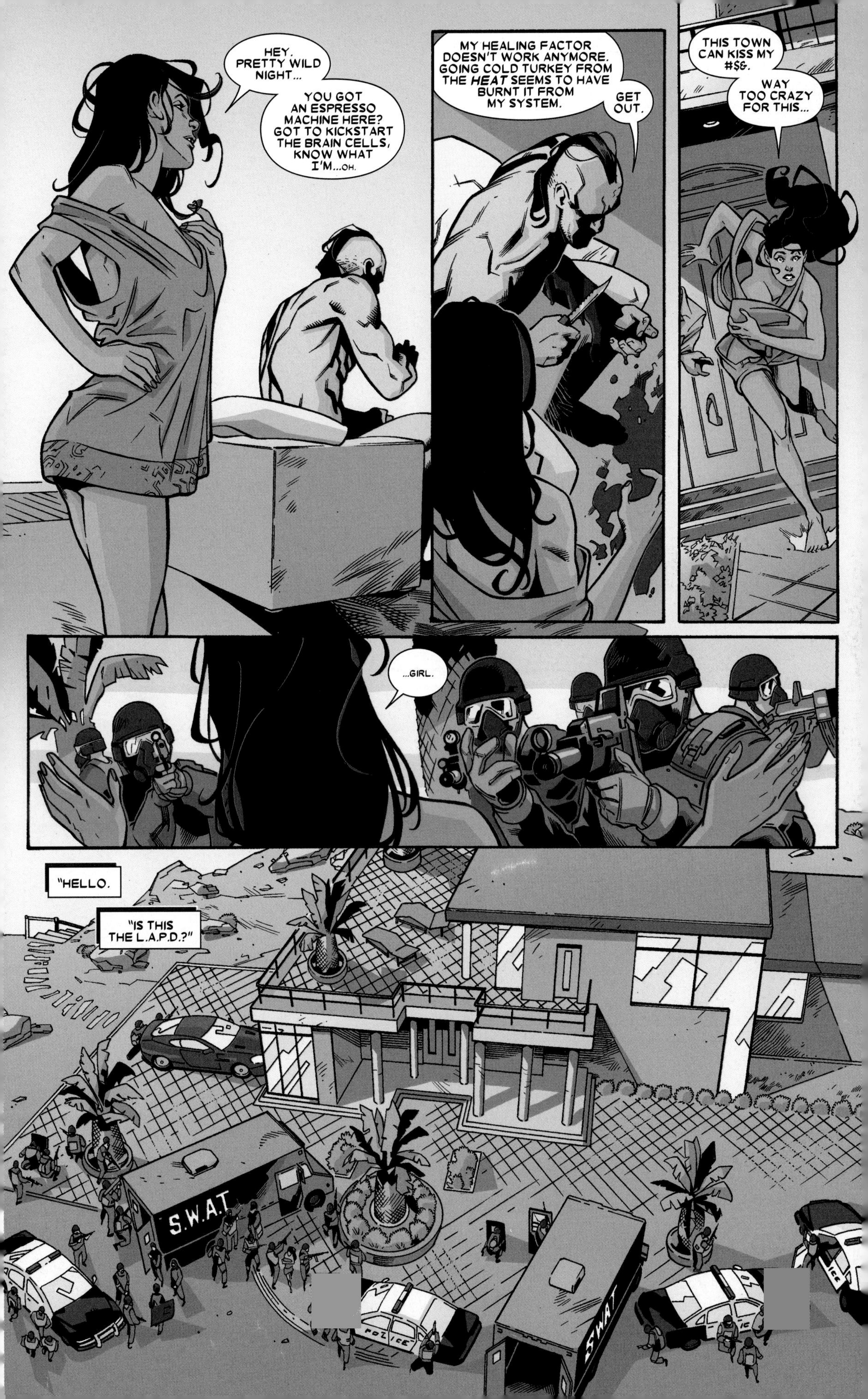
HEY. PRETTY WILD NIGHT...
YOU GOT AN ESPRESSO MACHINE HERE? GOT TO KICKSTART THE BRAIN CELLS, KNOW WHAT I'M...OH.
MY HEALING FACTOR DOESN'T WORK ANYMORE. GOING COLD TURKEY FROM THE HEAT SEEMS TO HAVE BURNT IT FROM MY SYSTEM.
GET OUT.
THIS TOWN CAN KISS MY #$&.
WAY TOO CRAZY FOR THIS...
...GIRL.
"HELLO.
"IS THIS THE L.A.P.D.?"
S.W.A.T.
POLICE
S.W.A.T.

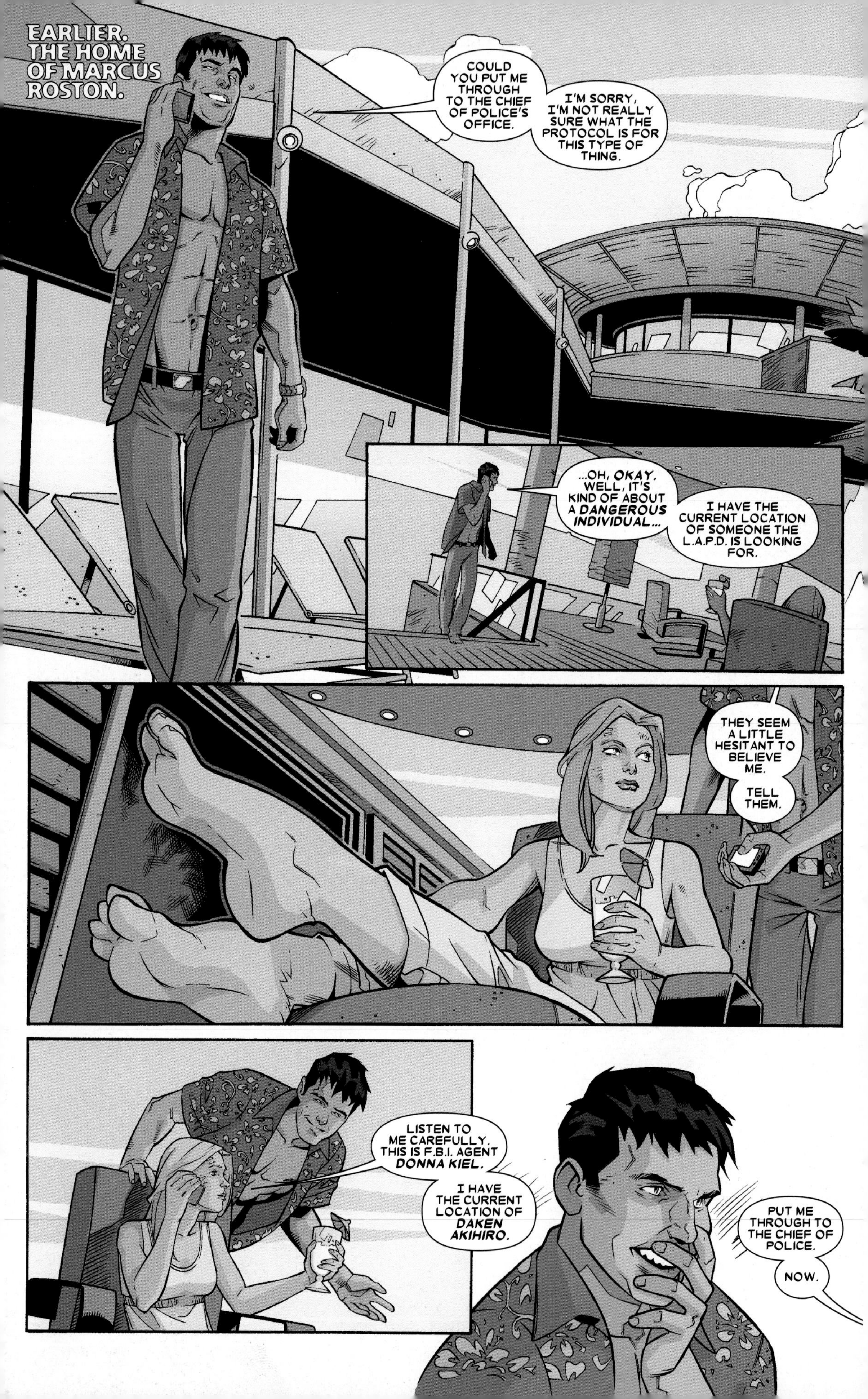
EARLIER. THE HOME OF MARCUS ROSTON.
COULD YOU PUT ME THROUGH TO THE CHIEF OF POLICE'S OFFICE.
I'M SORRY, I'M NOT REALLY SURE WHAT THE PROTOCOL IS FOR THIS TYPE OF THING.
...OH, OKAY. WELL, IT'S KIND OF ABOUT A DANGEROUS INDIVIDUAL...
I HAVE THE CURRENT LOCATION OF SOMEONE THE L.A.P.D. IS LOOKING FOR.
THEY SEEM A LITTLE HESITANT TO BELIEVE ME.
TELL THEM.
LISTEN TO ME CAREFULLY. THIS IS F.B.I. AGENT DONNA KIEL.
I HAVE THE CURRENT LOCATION OF DAKEN AKIHIRO.
PUT ME THROUGH TO THE CHIEF OF POLICE.
NOW.

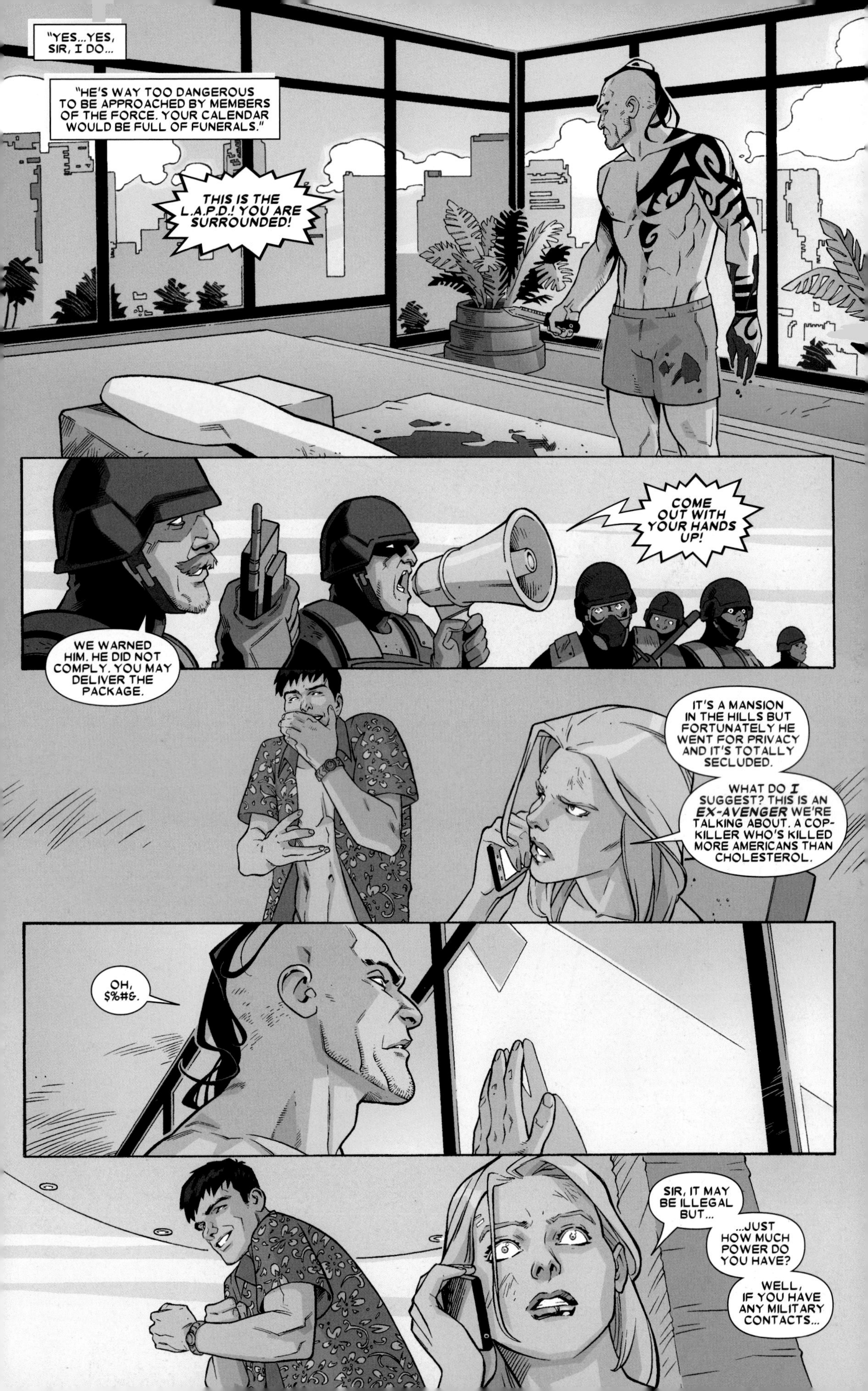

"YES...YES, SIR, I DO...
"HE'S WAY TOO DANGEROUS TO BE APPROACHED BY MEMBERS OF THE FORCE. YOUR CALENDAR WOULD BE FULL OF FUNERALS."
THIS IS THE L.A.P.D.! YOU ARE SURROUNDED!
COME OUT WITH YOUR HANDS UP!
WE WARNED HIM. HE DID NOT COMPLY. YOU MAY DELIVER THE PACKAGE.
IT'S A MANSION IN THE HILLS BUT FORTUNATELY HE WENT FOR PRIVACY AND IT'S TOTALLY SECLUDED.
WHAT DO *I* SUGGEST? THIS IS AN ***EX-AVENGER*** WE'RE TALKING ABOUT. A COP-KILLER WHO'S KILLED MORE AMERICANS THAN CHOLESTEROL.
OH, $%#&.
SIR, IT MAY BE ILLEGAL BUT...
...JUST HOW MUCH POWER DO YOU HAVE?
WELL, IF YOU HAVE ANY MILITARY CONTACTS...

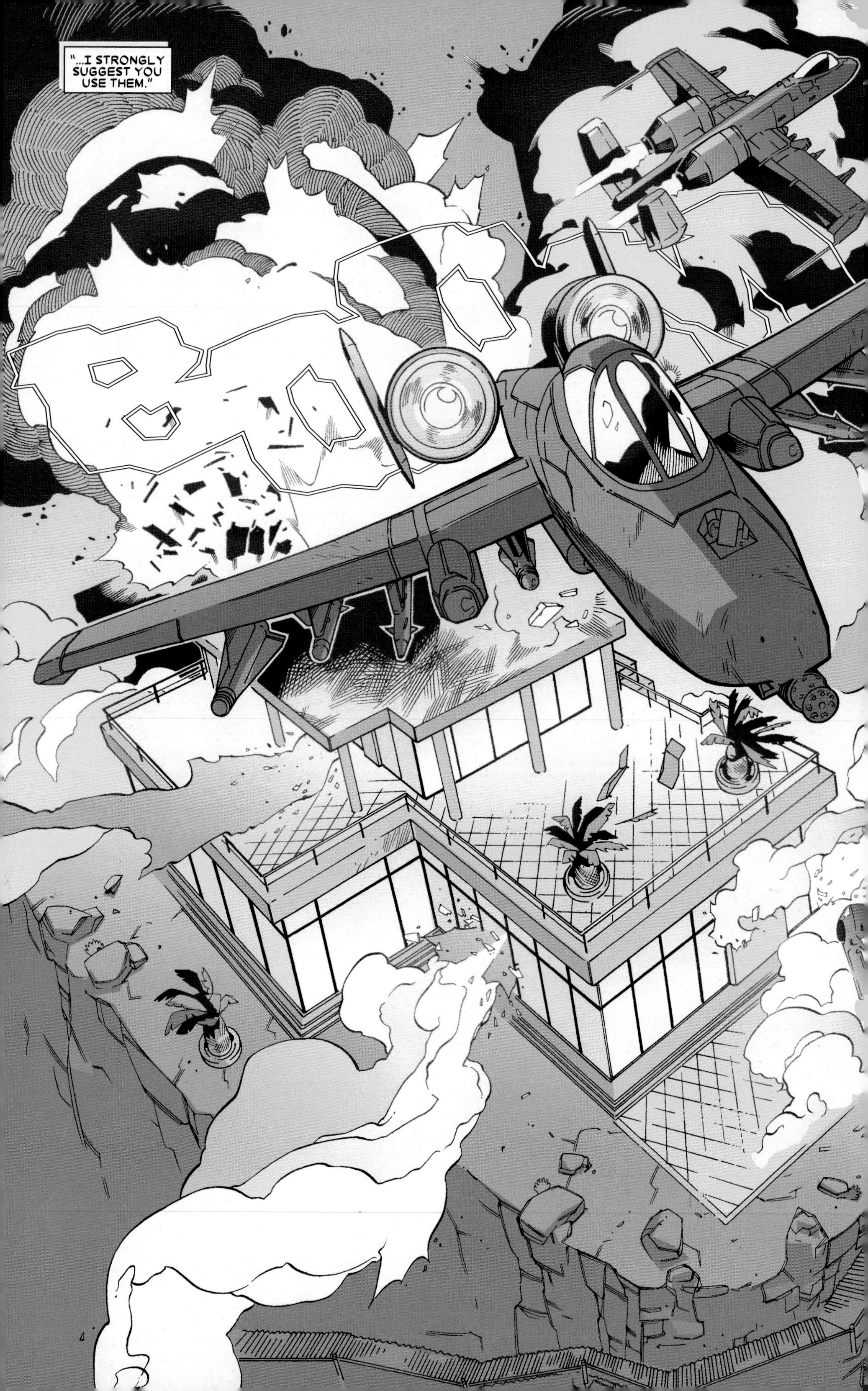
"...I STRONGLY SUGGEST YOU USE THEM."

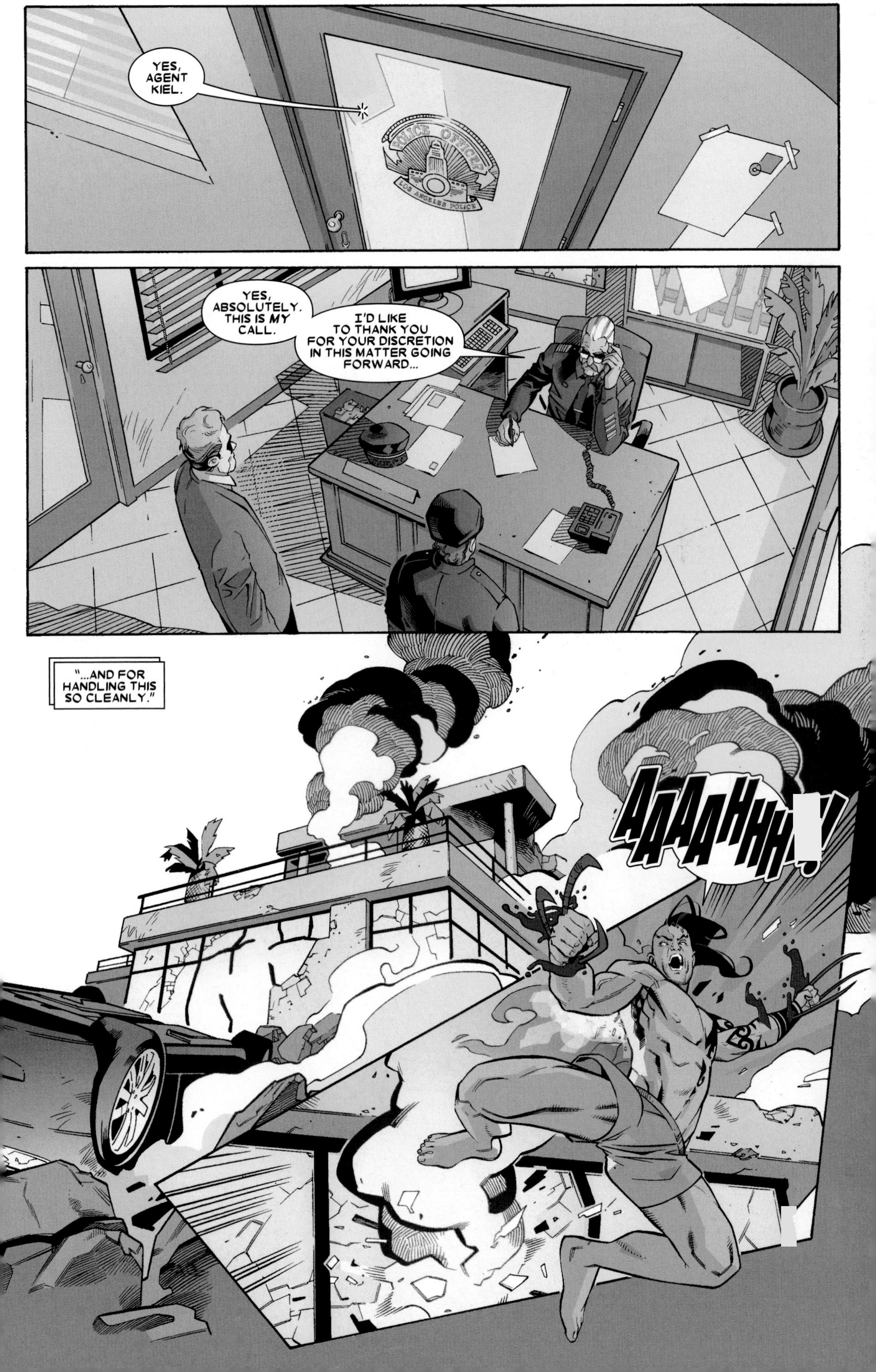
YES, AGENT KIEL.
POLICE OFFICER
LOS ANGELES POLICE
YES, ABSOLUTELY. THIS IS MY CALL.
I'D LIKE TO THANK YOU FOR YOUR DISCRETION IN THIS MATTER GOING FORWARD...
"...AND FOR HANDLING THIS SO CLEANLY."
AAAAHHH

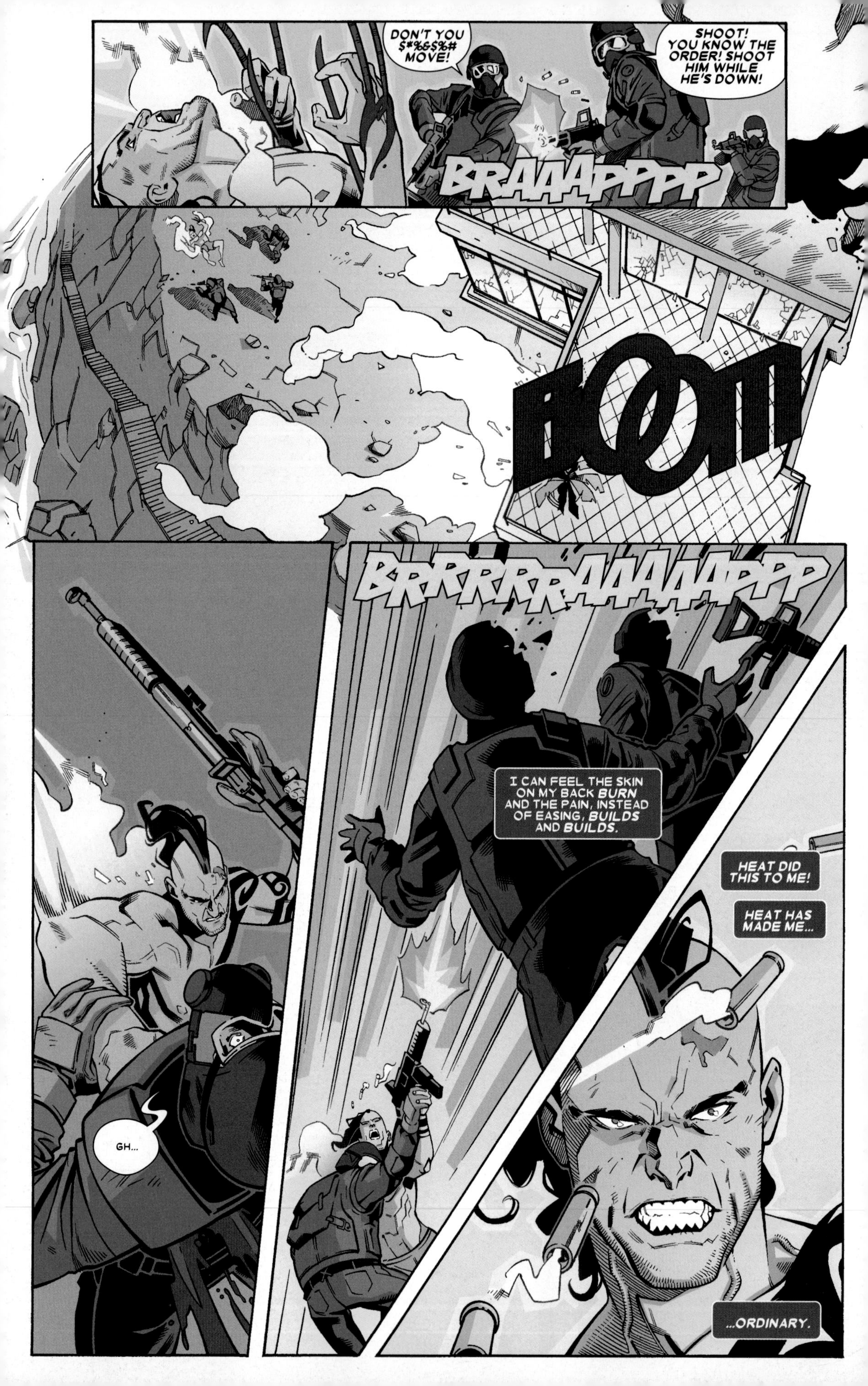
DON'T YOU $*%&$%# MOVE!
SHOOT! YOU KNOW THE ORDER! SHOOT HIM WHILE HE'S DOWN!
BRAAAPPPP
BOOM
BRRRRRAAAAAPPP
I CAN FEEL THE SKIN ON MY BACK BURN AND THE PAIN, INSTEAD OF EASING, BUILDS AND BUILDS.
HEAT DID THIS TO ME!
HEAT HAS MADE ME...
GH...
...ORDINARY.

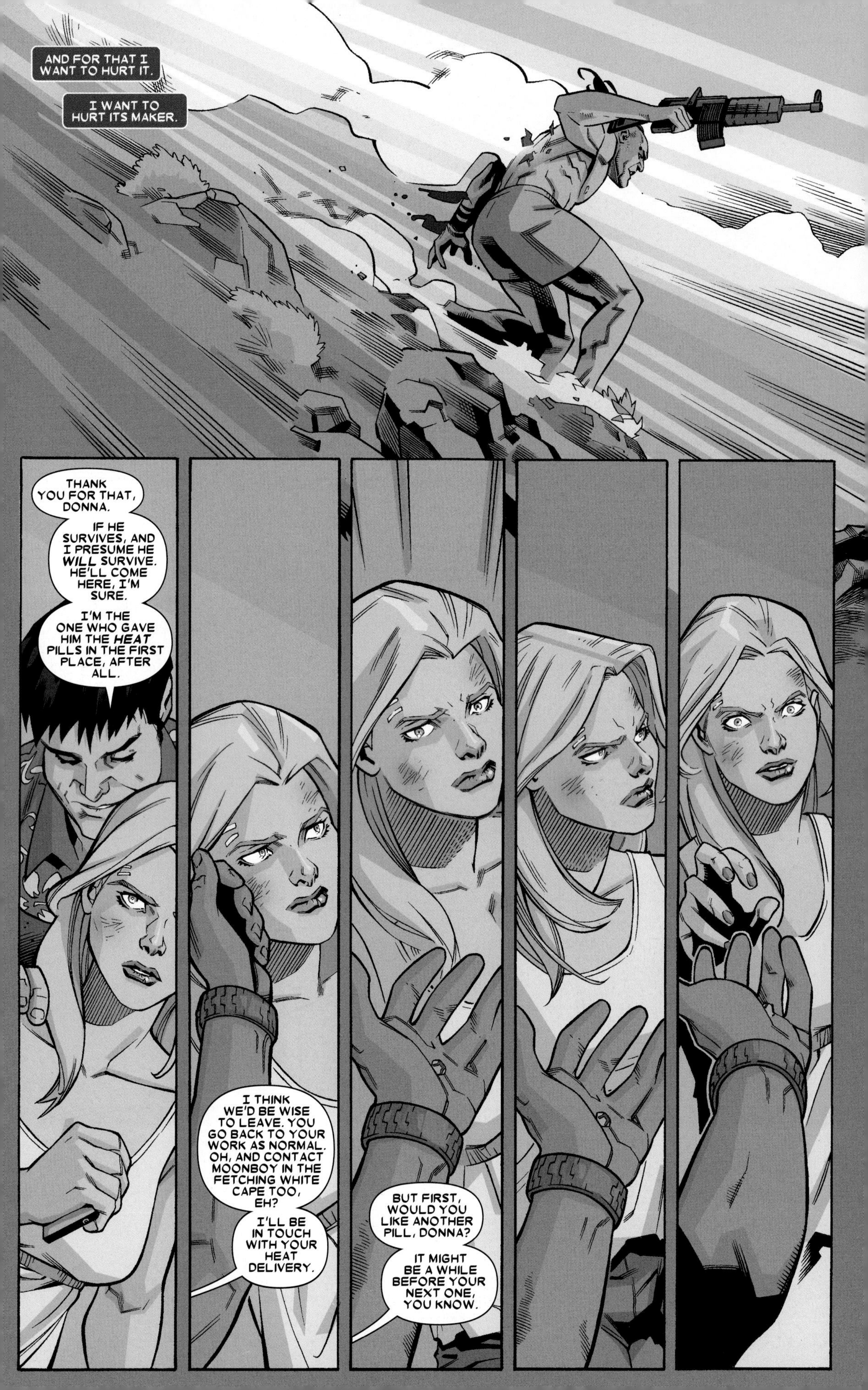
AND FOR THAT I WANT TO HURT IT.
I WANT TO HURT ITS MAKER.
THANK YOU FOR THAT, DONNA.
IF HE SURVIVES, AND I PRESUME HE WILL SURVIVE. HE'LL COME HERE, I'M SURE.
I'M THE ONE WHO GAVE HIM THE HEAT PILLS IN THE FIRST PLACE, AFTER ALL.
I THINK WE'D BE WISE TO LEAVE. YOU GO BACK TO YOUR WORK AS NORMAL. OH, AND CONTACT MOONBOY IN THE FETCHING WHITE CAPE TOO, EH?
I'LL BE IN TOUCH WITH YOUR HEAT DELIVERY.
BUT FIRST, WOULD YOU LIKE ANOTHER PILL, DONNA?
IT MIGHT BE A WHILE BEFORE YOUR NEXT ONE, YOU KNOW.

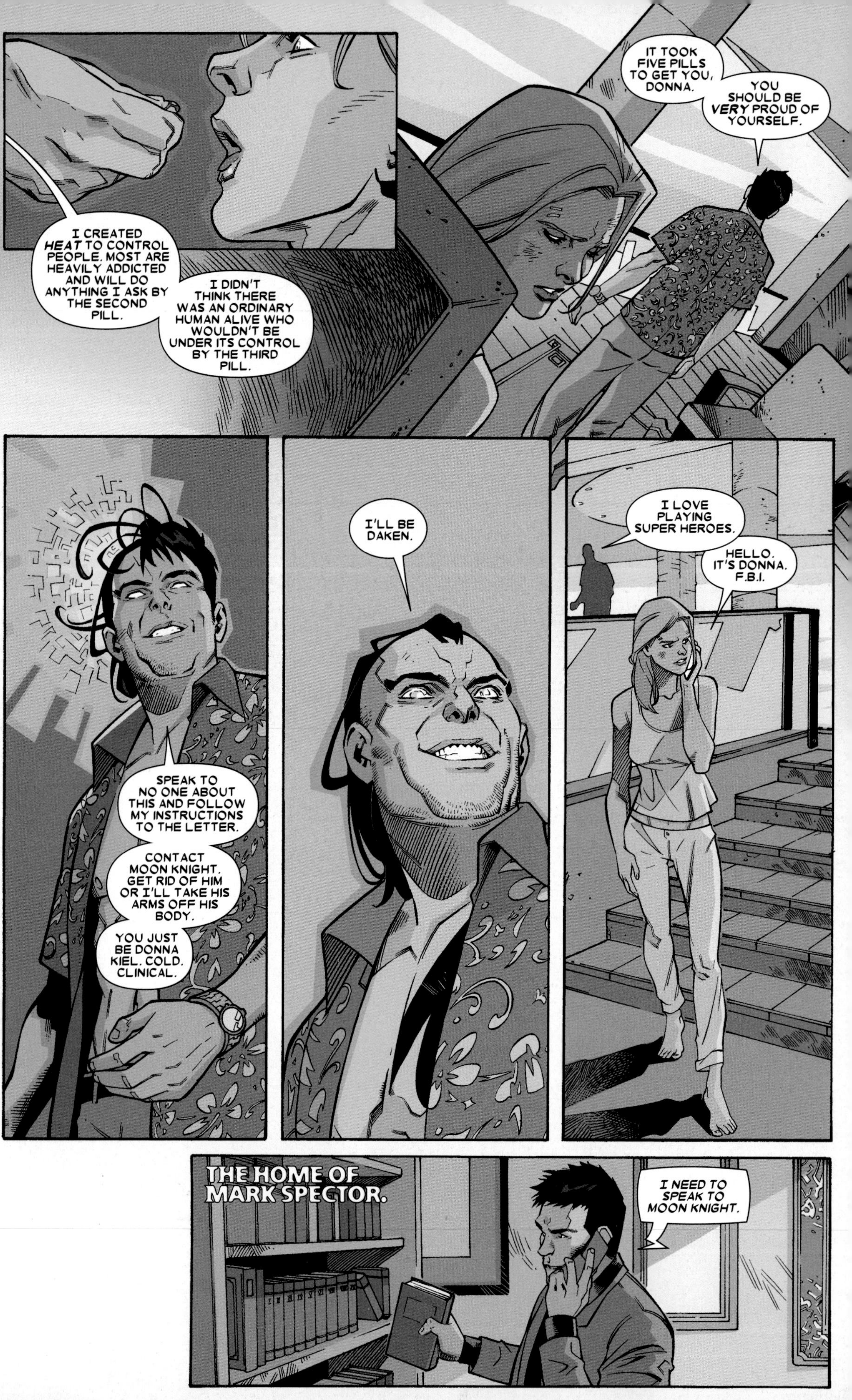
I CREATED HEAT TO CONTROL PEOPLE. MOST ARE HEAVILY ADDICTED AND WILL DO ANYTHING I ASK BY THE SECOND PILL.
I DIDN'T THINK THERE WAS AN ORDINARY HUMAN ALIVE WHO WOULDN'T BE UNDER ITS CONTROL BY THE THIRD PILL.
IT TOOK FIVE PILLS TO GET YOU, DONNA.
YOU SHOULD BE VERY PROUD OF YOURSELF.
SPEAK TO NO ONE ABOUT THIS AND FOLLOW MY INSTRUCTIONS TO THE LETTER.
CONTACT MOON KNIGHT. GET RID OF HIM OR I'LL TAKE HIS ARMS OFF HIS BODY.
YOU JUST BE DONNA KIEL. COLD. CLINICAL.
I'LL BE DAKEN.
I LOVE PLAYING SUPER HEROES.
HELLO. IT'S DONNA. F.B.I.
THE HOME OF MARK SPECTOR.
I NEED TO SPEAK TO MOON KNIGHT.

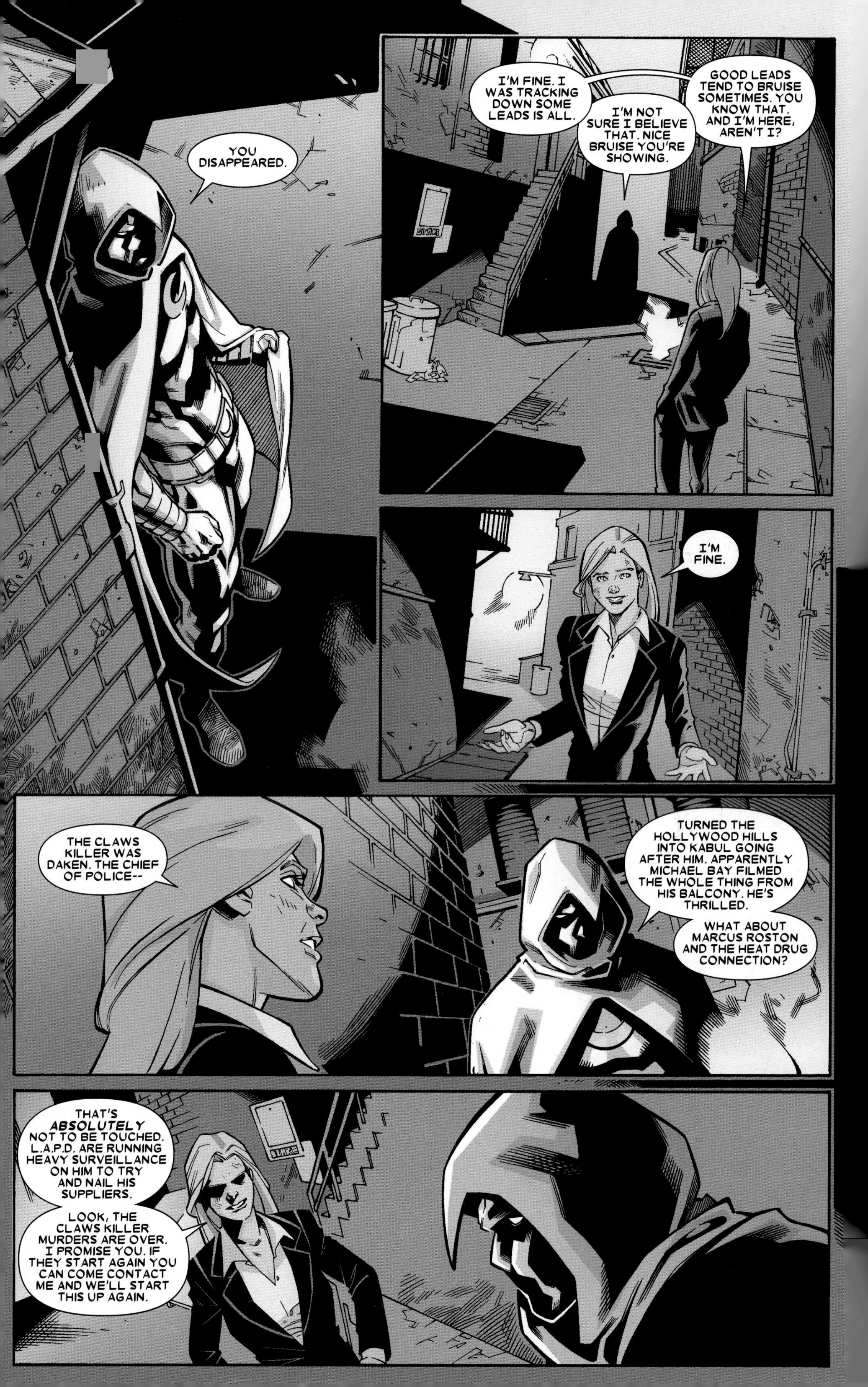
YOU DISAPPEARED.
I'M FINE. I WAS TRACKING DOWN SOME LEADS IS ALL.
I'M NOT SURE I BELIEVE THAT. NICE BRUISE YOU'RE SHOWING.
GOOD LEADS TEND TO BRUISE SOMETIMES. YOU KNOW THAT. AND I'M HERE, AREN'T I?
I'M FINE.
THE CLAWS KILLER WAS DAKEN. THE CHIEF OF POLICE--
TURNED THE HOLLYWOOD HILLS INTO KABUL GOING AFTER HIM. APPARENTLY MICHAEL BAY FILMED THE WHOLE THING FROM HIS BALCONY. HE'S THRILLED.
WHAT ABOUT MARCUS ROSTON AND THE HEAT DRUG CONNECTION?
THAT'S *ABSOLUTELY* NOT TO BE TOUCHED. L.A.P.D. ARE RUNNING HEAVY SURVEILLANCE ON HIM TO TRY AND NAIL HIS SUPPLIERS.
LOOK, THE CLAWS KILLER MURDERS ARE OVER. I PROMISE YOU. IF THEY START AGAIN YOU CAN COME CONTACT ME AND WE'LL START THIS UP AGAIN.

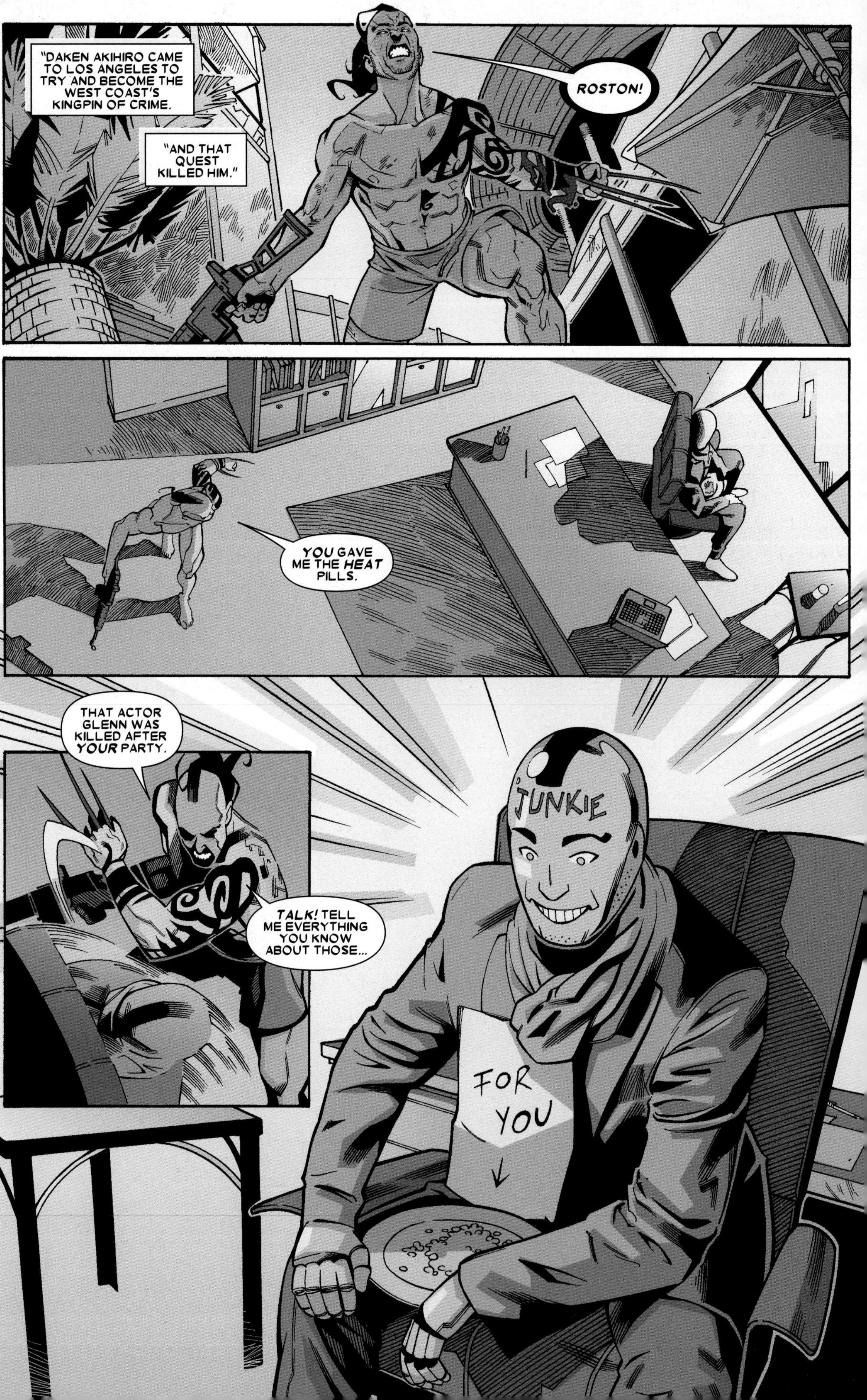
"DAKEN AKIHIRO CAME TO LOS ANGELES TO TRY AND BECOME THE WEST COAST'S KINGPIN OF CRIME.
"AND THAT QUEST KILLED HIM."
ROSTON!
YOU GAVE ME THE HEAT PILLS.
THAT ACTOR GLENN WAS KILLED AFTER YOUR PARTY.
TALK! TELL ME EVERYTHING YOU KNOW ABOUT THOSE...
JUNKIE
FOR YOU

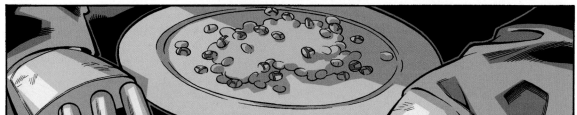

BREEP
BREEEP

BREEP
BREEEP

THIS IS ROSTON. GO AFTER THE BEEP.

BEEP

TAKE THE PILLS, DAKEN.

YOU'VE HAD A TOUGH TIME LATELY. YOU DESERVE IT.

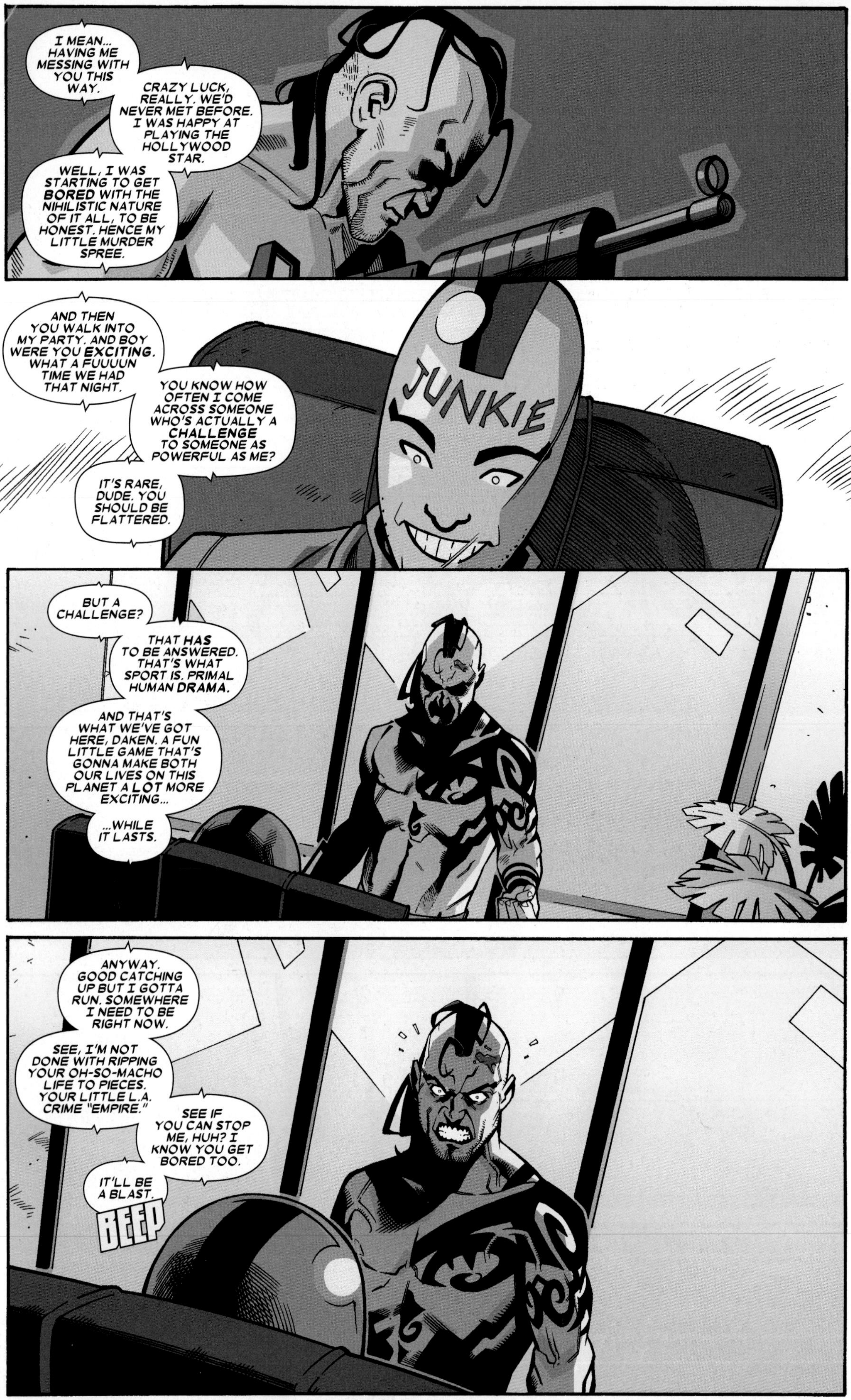

I MEAN... HAVING ME MESSING WITH YOU THIS WAY.
CRAZY LUCK, REALLY. WE'D NEVER MET BEFORE. I WAS HAPPY AT PLAYING THE HOLLYWOOD STAR.
WELL, I WAS STARTING TO GET BORED WITH THE NIHILISTIC NATURE OF IT ALL, TO BE HONEST. HENCE MY LITTLE MURDER SPREE.
AND THEN YOU WALK INTO MY PARTY. AND BOY WERE YOU EXCITING. WHAT A FUUUUN TIME WE HAD THAT NIGHT.
JUNKIE
YOU KNOW HOW OFTEN I COME ACROSS SOMEONE WHO'S ACTUALLY A CHALLENGE TO SOMEONE AS POWERFUL AS ME?
IT'S RARE, DUDE. YOU SHOULD BE FLATTERED.
BUT A CHALLENGE?
THAT HAS TO BE ANSWERED. THAT'S WHAT SPORT IS. PRIMAL HUMAN DRAMA.
AND THAT'S WHAT WE'VE GOT HERE, DAKEN. A FUN LITTLE GAME THAT'S GONNA MAKE BOTH OUR LIVES ON THIS PLANET A LOT MORE EXCITING...
...WHILE IT LASTS.
ANYWAY. GOOD CATCHING UP BUT I GOTTA RUN. SOMEWHERE I NEED TO BE RIGHT NOW.
SEE, I'M NOT DONE WITH RIPPING YOUR OH-SO-MACHO LIFE TO PIECES. YOUR LITTLE L.A. CRIME "EMPIRE."
SEE IF YOU CAN STOP ME, HUH? I KNOW YOU GET BORED TOO.
IT'LL BE A BLAST.
BEEP

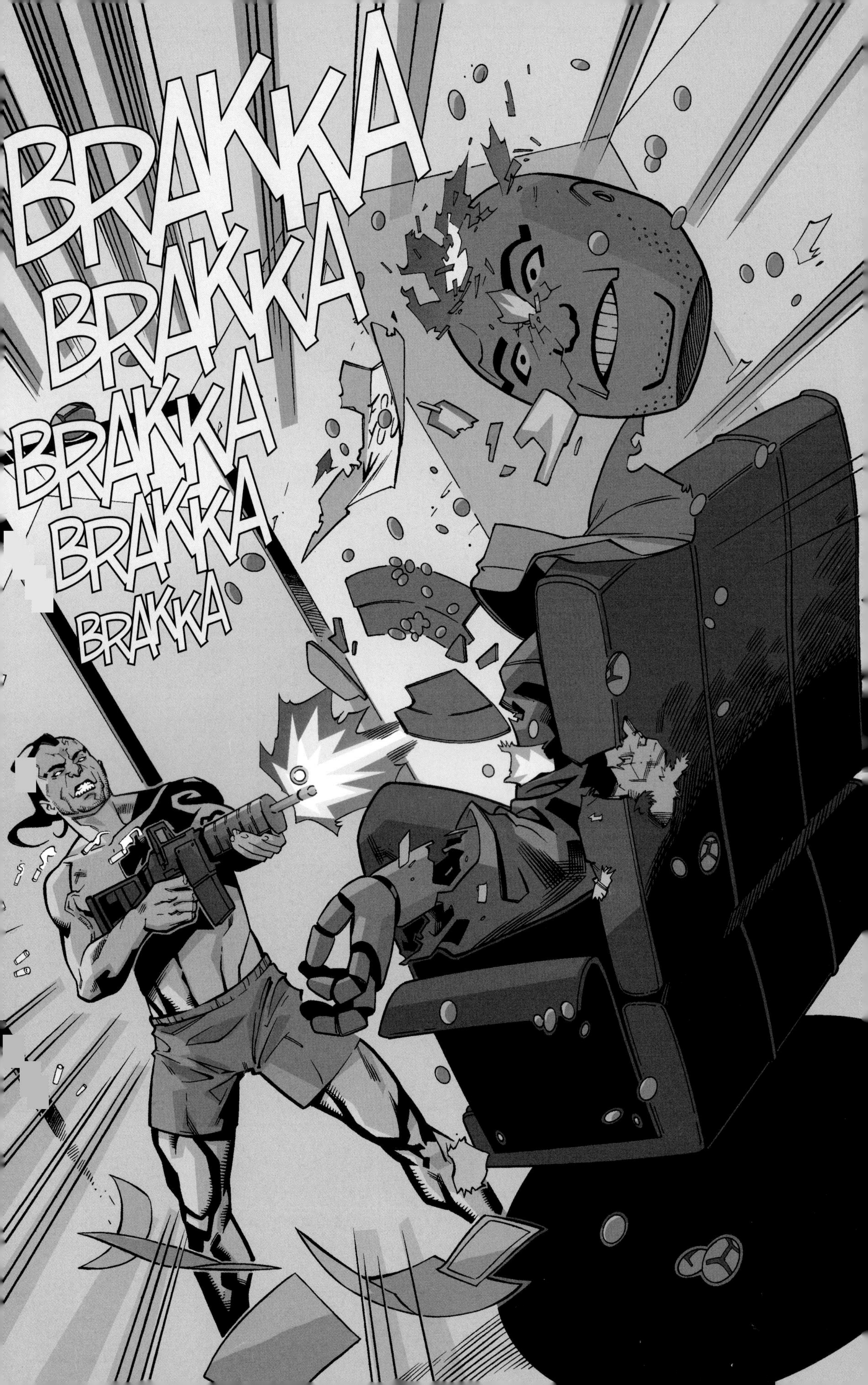
BRAKKA
BRAKKA
BRAKKA
BRAKKA
BRAKKA
BRAKKA

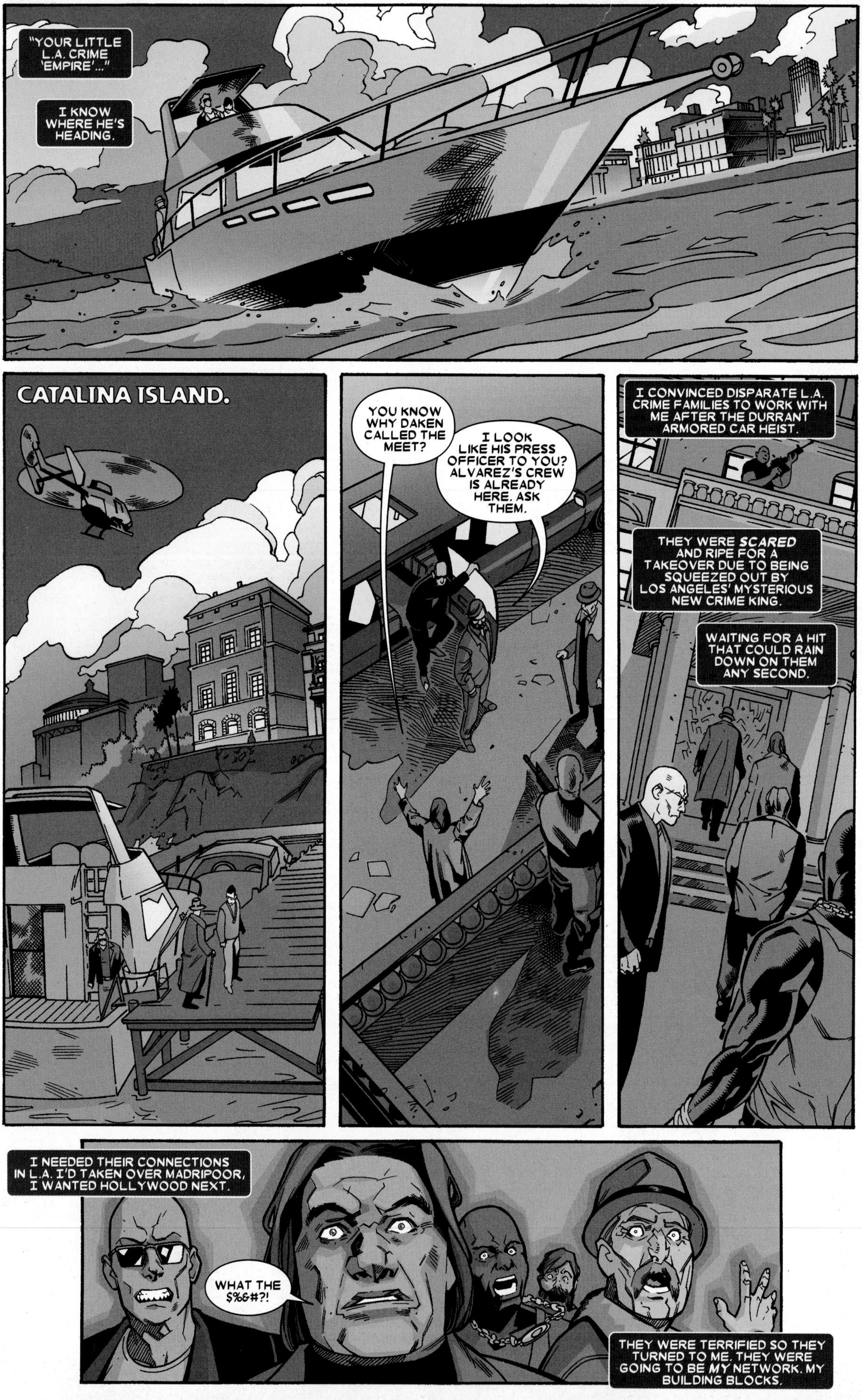
"YOUR LITTLE L.A. CRIME 'EMPIRE'..."
I KNOW WHERE HE'S HEADING.
CATALINA ISLAND.
YOU KNOW WHY DAKEN CALLED THE MEET?
I LOOK LIKE HIS PRESS OFFICER TO YOU? ALVAREZ'S CREW IS ALREADY HERE. ASK THEM.
I CONVINCED DISPARATE L.A. CRIME FAMILIES TO WORK WITH ME AFTER THE DURRANT ARMORED CAR HEIST.
THEY WERE SCARED AND RIPE FOR A TAKEOVER DUE TO BEING SQUEEZED OUT BY LOS ANGELES' MYSTERIOUS NEW CRIME KING.
WAITING FOR A HIT THAT COULD RAIN DOWN ON THEM ANY SECOND.
I NEEDED THEIR CONNECTIONS IN L.A. I'D TAKEN OVER MADRIPOOR, I WANTED HOLLYWOOD NEXT.
WHAT THE $%&#?!
THEY WERE TERRIFIED SO THEY TURNED TO ME. THEY WERE GOING TO BE MY NETWORK. MY BUILDING BLOCKS.

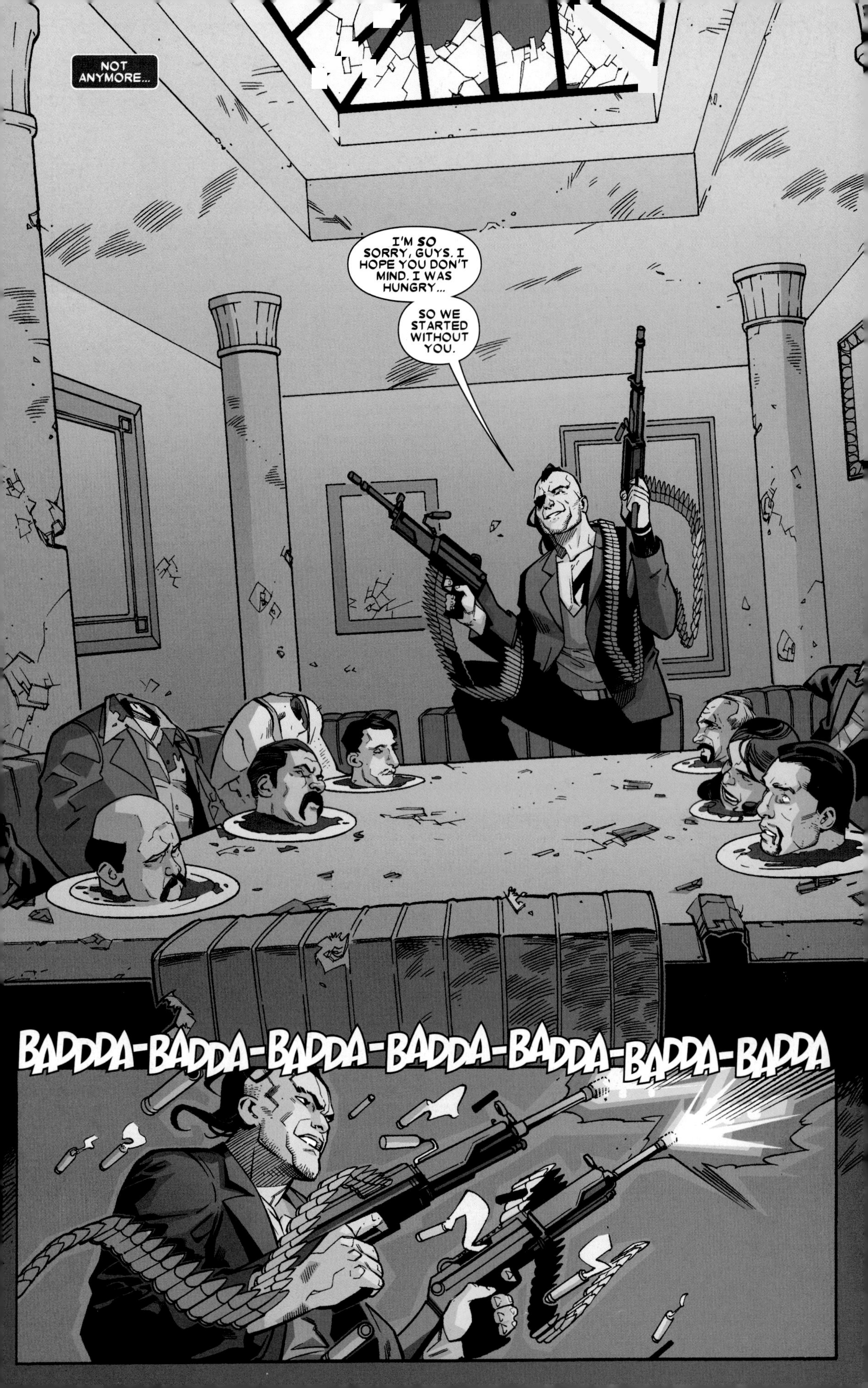
NOT ANYMORE...
I'M SO SORRY, GUYS. I HOPE YOU DON'T MIND. I WAS HUNGRY...
SO WE STARTED WITHOUT YOU.
BADDDA-BADDA-BADDA-BADDA-BADDA-BADDA-BADDA

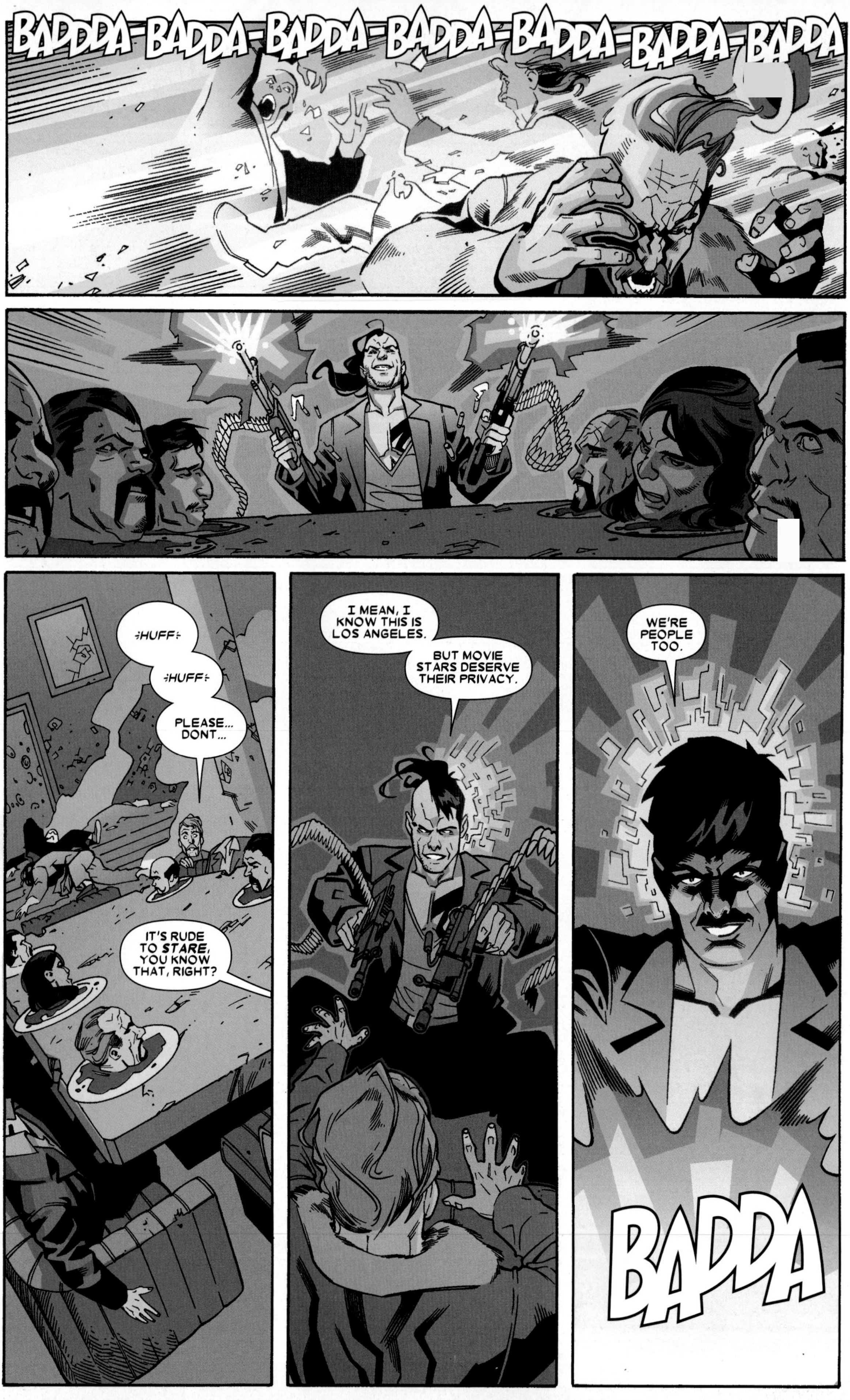

BADDA-BADDA-BADDA-BADDA-BADDA-BADDA-BADDA
≠HUFF≠
≠HUFF≠
PLEASE... DONT...
IT'S RUDE TO STARE, YOU KNOW THAT, RIGHT?
I MEAN, I KNOW THIS IS LOS ANGELES.
BUT MOVIE STARS DESERVE THEIR PRIVACY.
WE'RE PEOPLE TOO.
BADDA

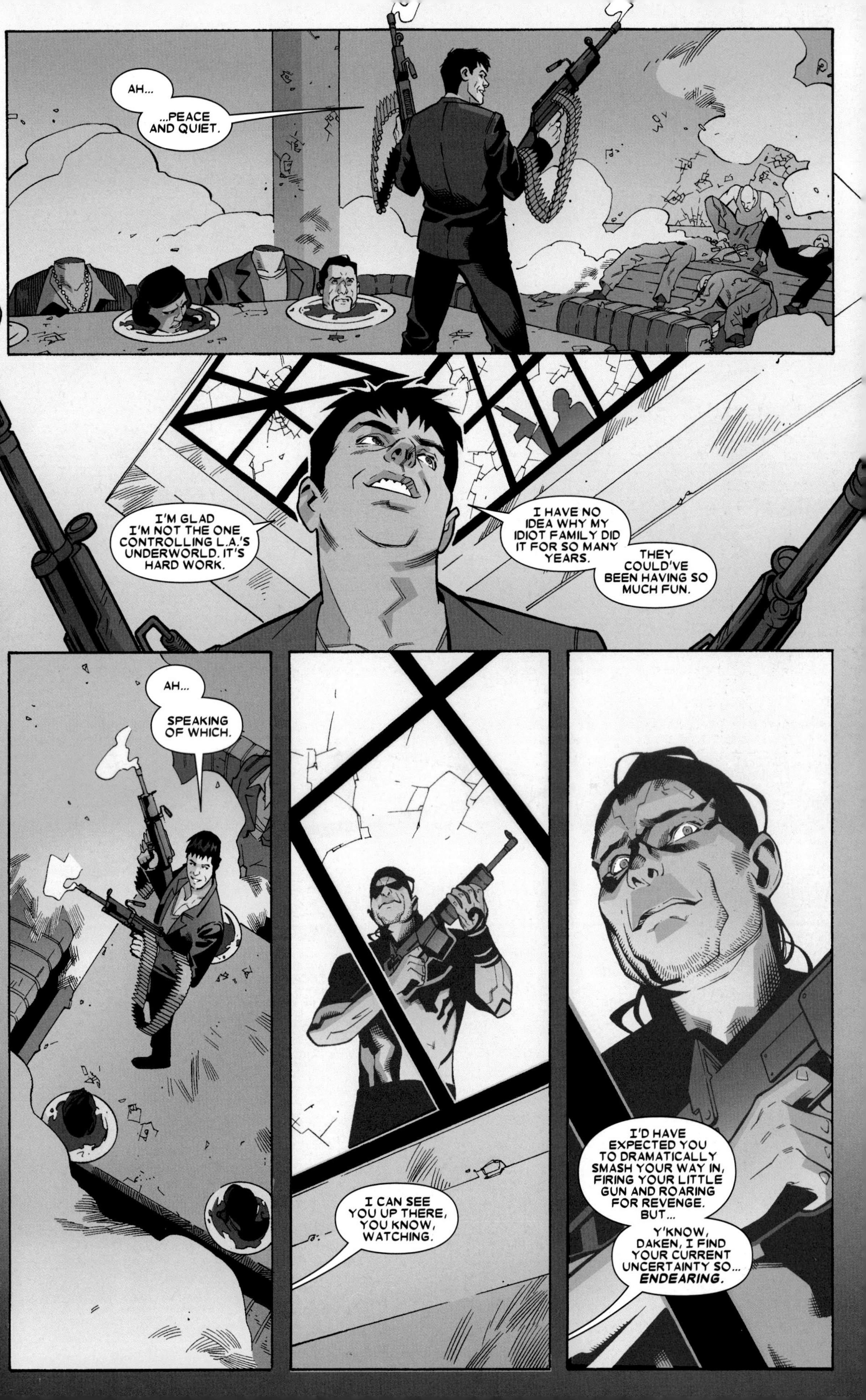
AH...
...PEACE AND QUIET.
I'M GLAD I'M NOT THE ONE CONTROLLING L.A.'S UNDERWORLD. IT'S HARD WORK.
I HAVE NO IDEA WHY MY IDIOT FAMILY DID IT FOR SO MANY YEARS.
THEY COULD'VE BEEN HAVING SO MUCH FUN.
AH...
SPEAKING OF WHICH.
I CAN SEE YOU UP THERE, YOU KNOW, WATCHING.
I'D HAVE EXPECTED YOU TO DRAMATICALLY SMASH YOUR WAY IN, FIRING YOUR LITTLE GUN AND ROARING FOR REVENGE. BUT...
Y'KNOW, DAKEN, I FIND YOUR CURRENT UNCERTAINTY SO... *ENDEARING.*

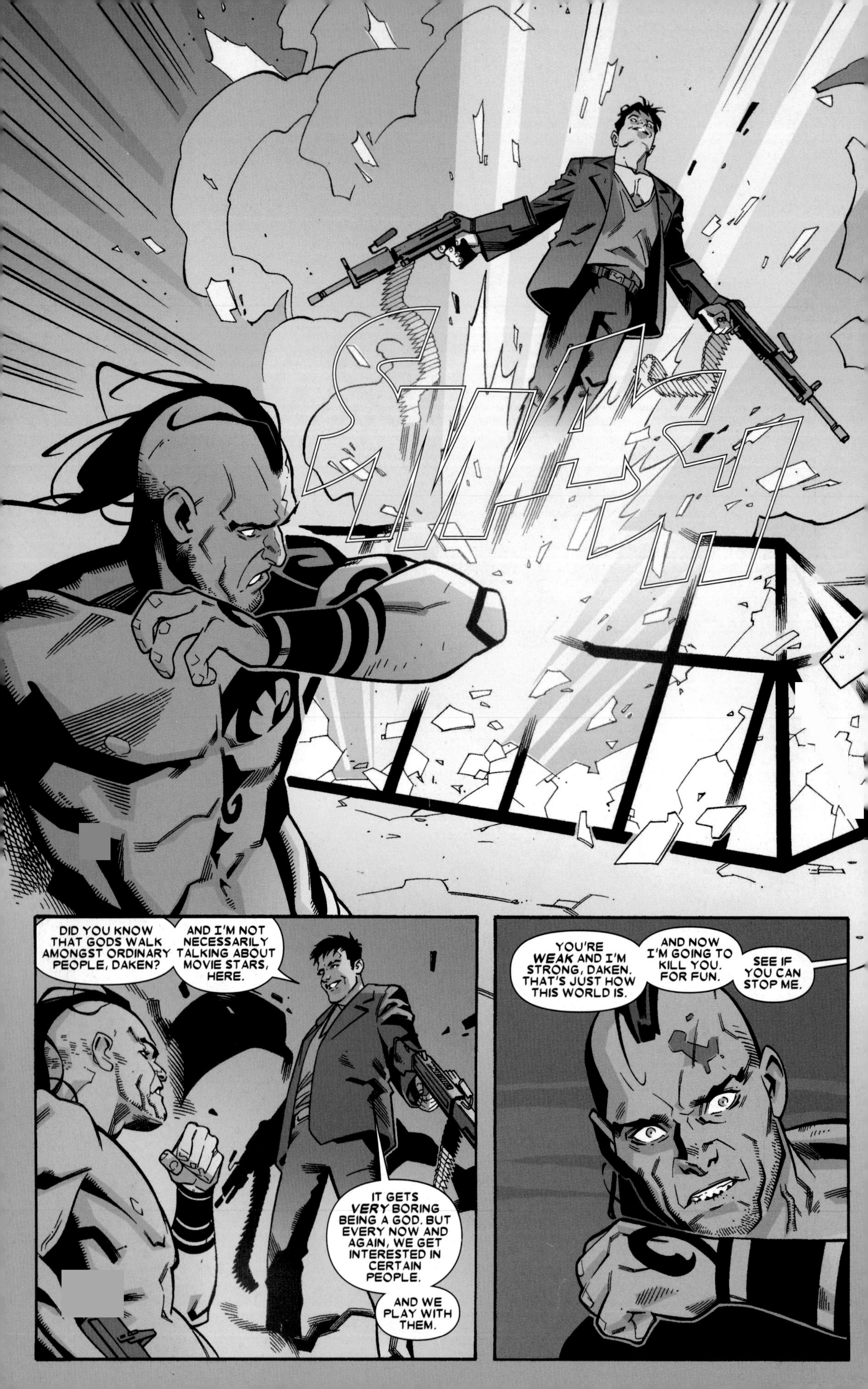
DID YOU KNOW THAT GODS WALK AMONGST ORDINARY PEOPLE, DAKEN?
AND I'M NOT NECESSARILY TALKING ABOUT MOVIE STARS, HERE.
IT GETS *VERY* BORING BEING A GOD. BUT EVERY NOW AND AGAIN, WE GET INTERESTED IN CERTAIN PEOPLE.
AND WE PLAY WITH THEM.
YOU'RE *WEAK* AND I'M STRONG, DAKEN. THAT'S JUST HOW THIS WORLD IS.
AND NOW I'M GOING TO KILL YOU. FOR FUN.
SEE IF YOU CAN STOP ME.

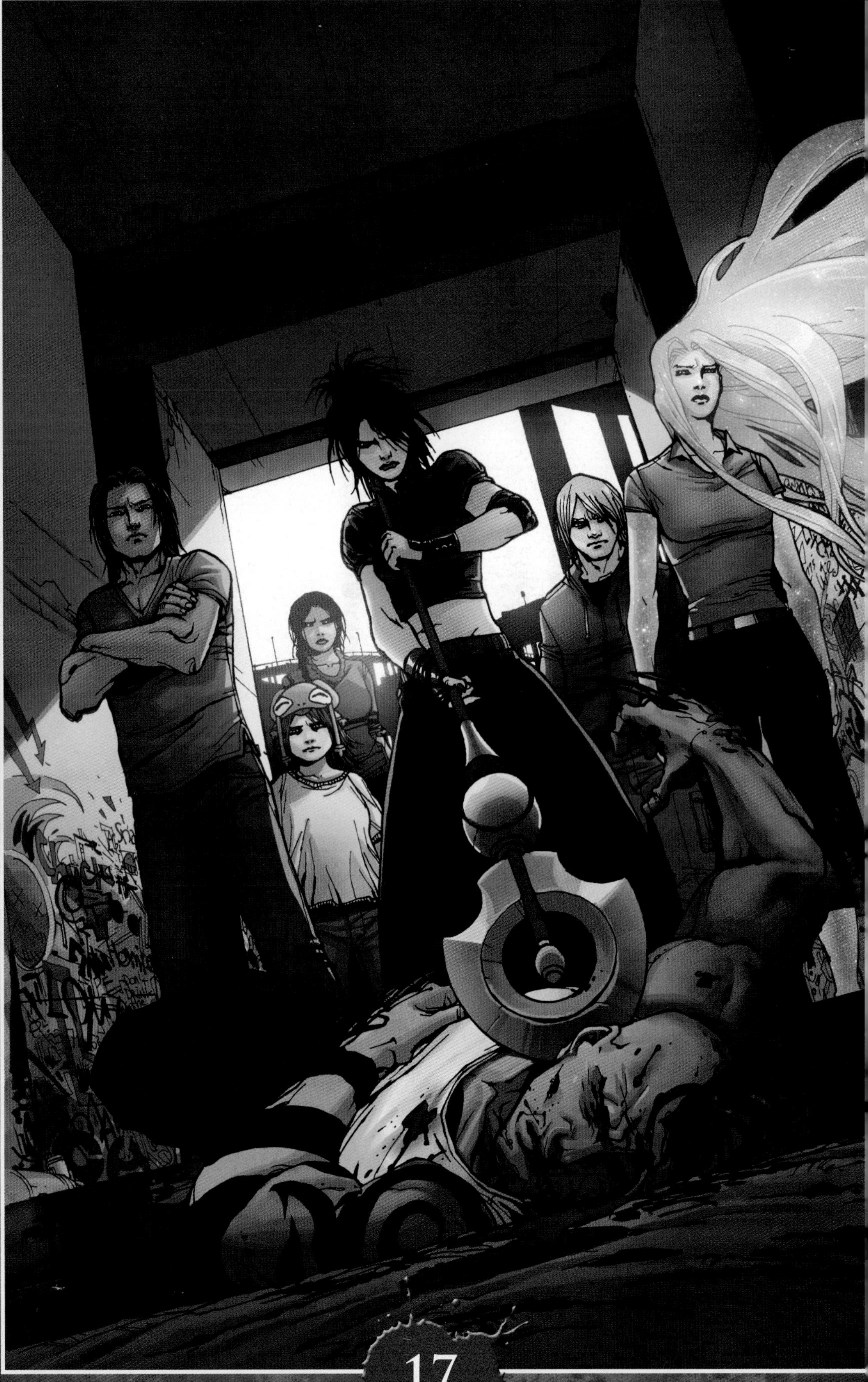

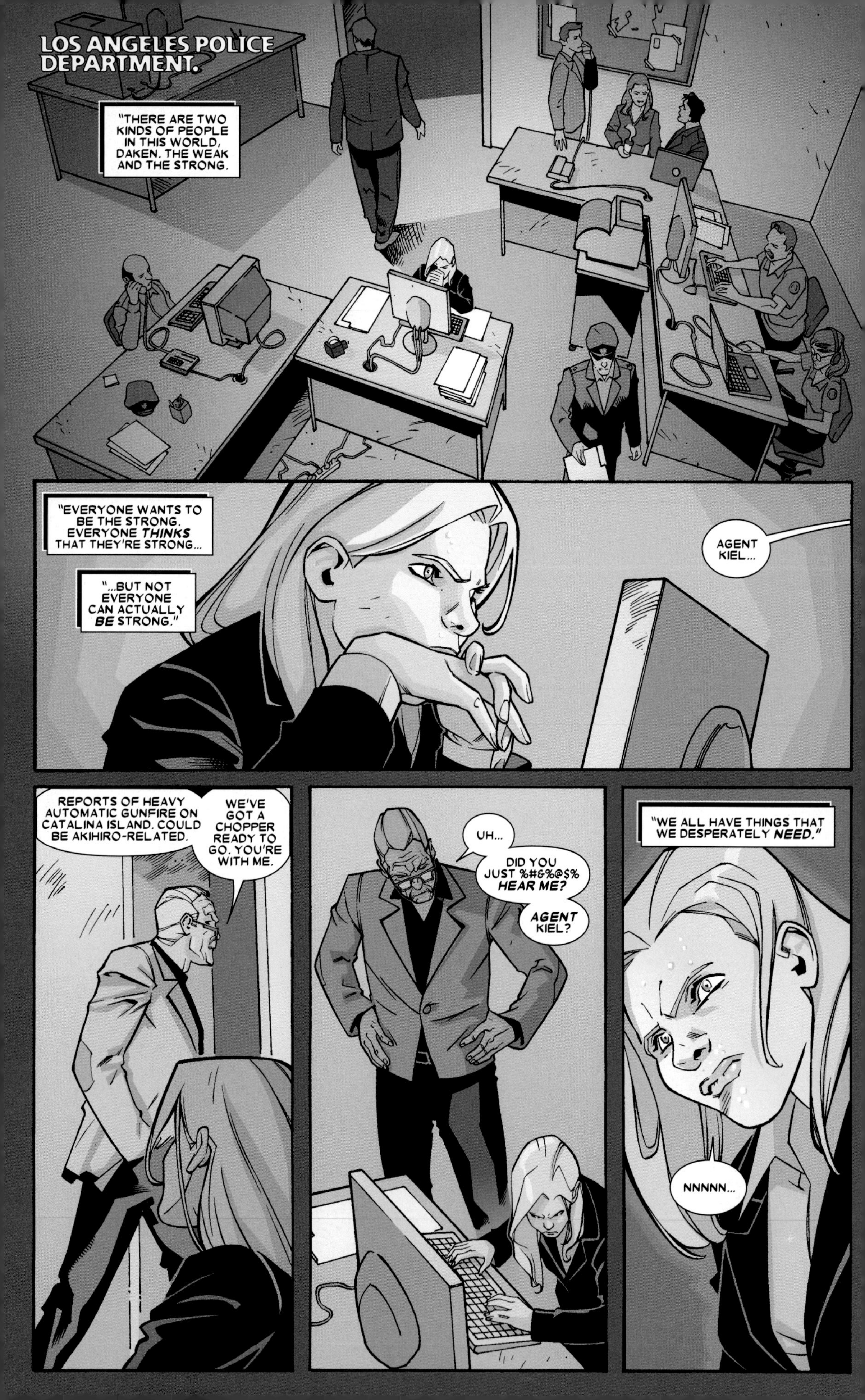
LOS ANGELES POLICE DEPARTMENT.
"THERE ARE TWO KINDS OF PEOPLE IN THIS WORLD, DAKEN. THE WEAK AND THE STRONG.
"EVERYONE WANTS TO BE THE STRONG. EVERYONE THINKS THAT THEY'RE STRONG...
"...BUT NOT EVERYONE CAN ACTUALLY BE STRONG."
AGENT KIEL...
REPORTS OF HEAVY AUTOMATIC GUNFIRE ON CATALINA ISLAND. COULD BE AKIHIRO-RELATED.
WE'VE GOT A CHOPPER READY TO GO. YOU'RE WITH ME.
UH...
DID YOU JUST %#&%@$% HEAR ME?
AGENT KIEL?
"WE ALL HAVE THINGS THAT WE DESPERATELY NEED."
NNNNN...

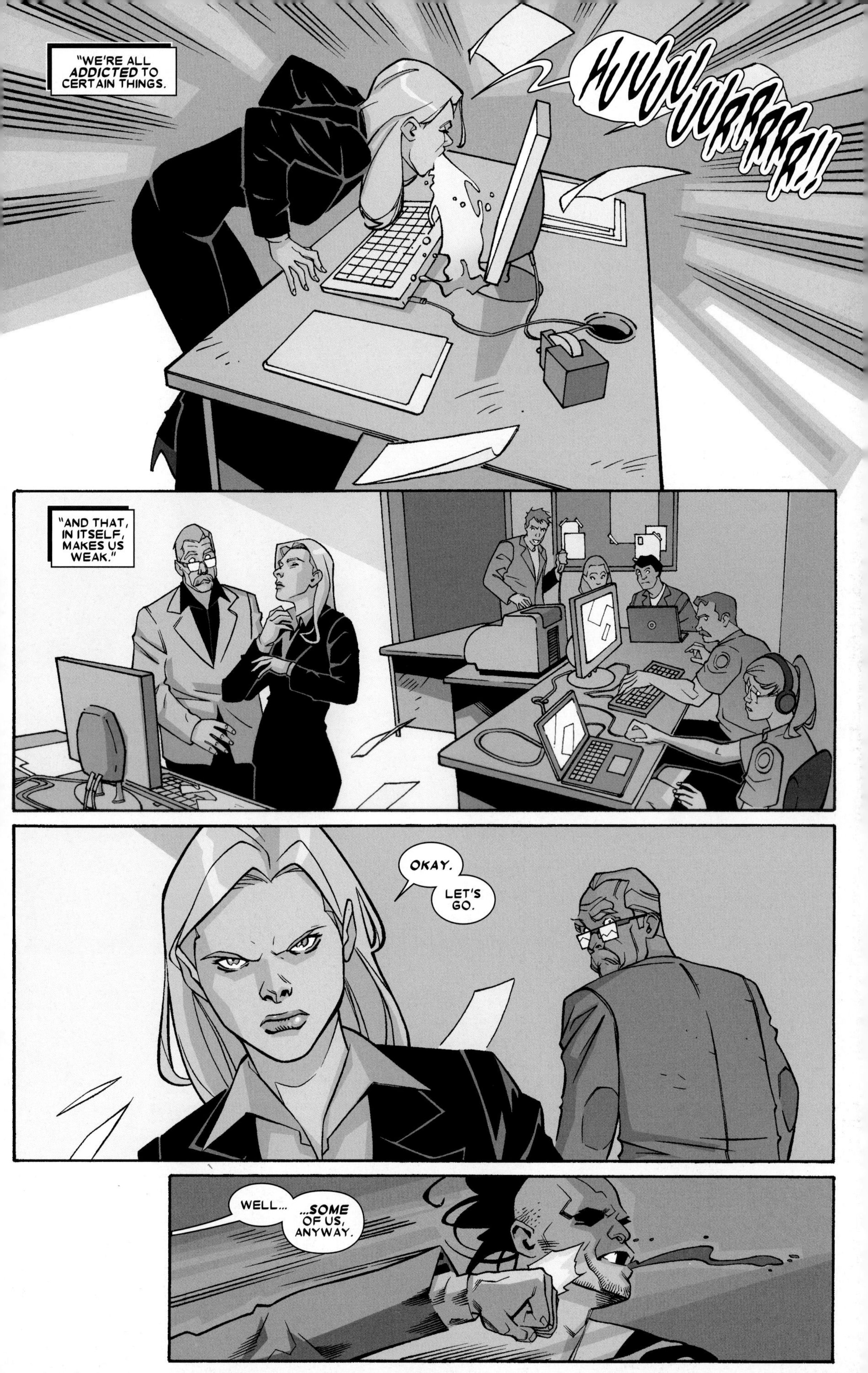
"WE'RE ALL ADDICTED TO CERTAIN THINGS.
HUUUUURRRRR!!
"AND THAT, IN ITSELF, MAKES US WEAK."
OKAY.
LET'S GO.
WELL...
...SOME OF US, ANYWAY.

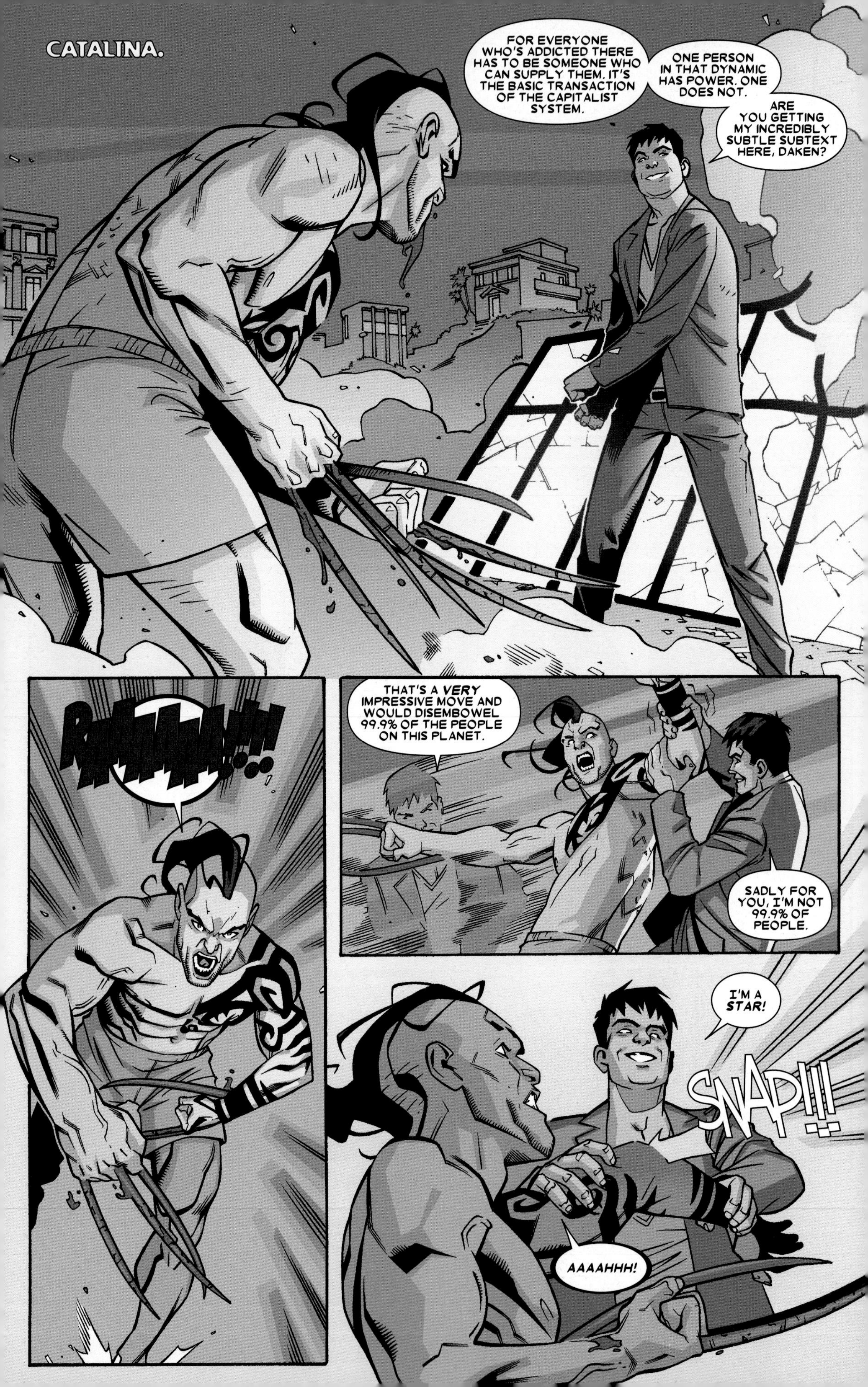
CATALINA.
FOR EVERYONE WHO'S ADDICTED THERE HAS TO BE SOMEONE WHO CAN SUPPLY THEM. IT'S THE BASIC TRANSACTION OF THE CAPITALIST SYSTEM.
ONE PERSON IN THAT DYNAMIC HAS POWER. ONE DOES NOT.
ARE YOU GETTING MY INCREDIBLY SUBTLE SUBTEXT HERE, DAKEN?
THAT'S A VERY IMPRESSIVE MOVE AND WOULD DISEMBOWEL 99.9% OF THE PEOPLE ON THIS PLANET.
SADLY FOR YOU, I'M NOT 99.9% OF PEOPLE.
I'M A STAR!
SNAP!!!
AAAAHHH!

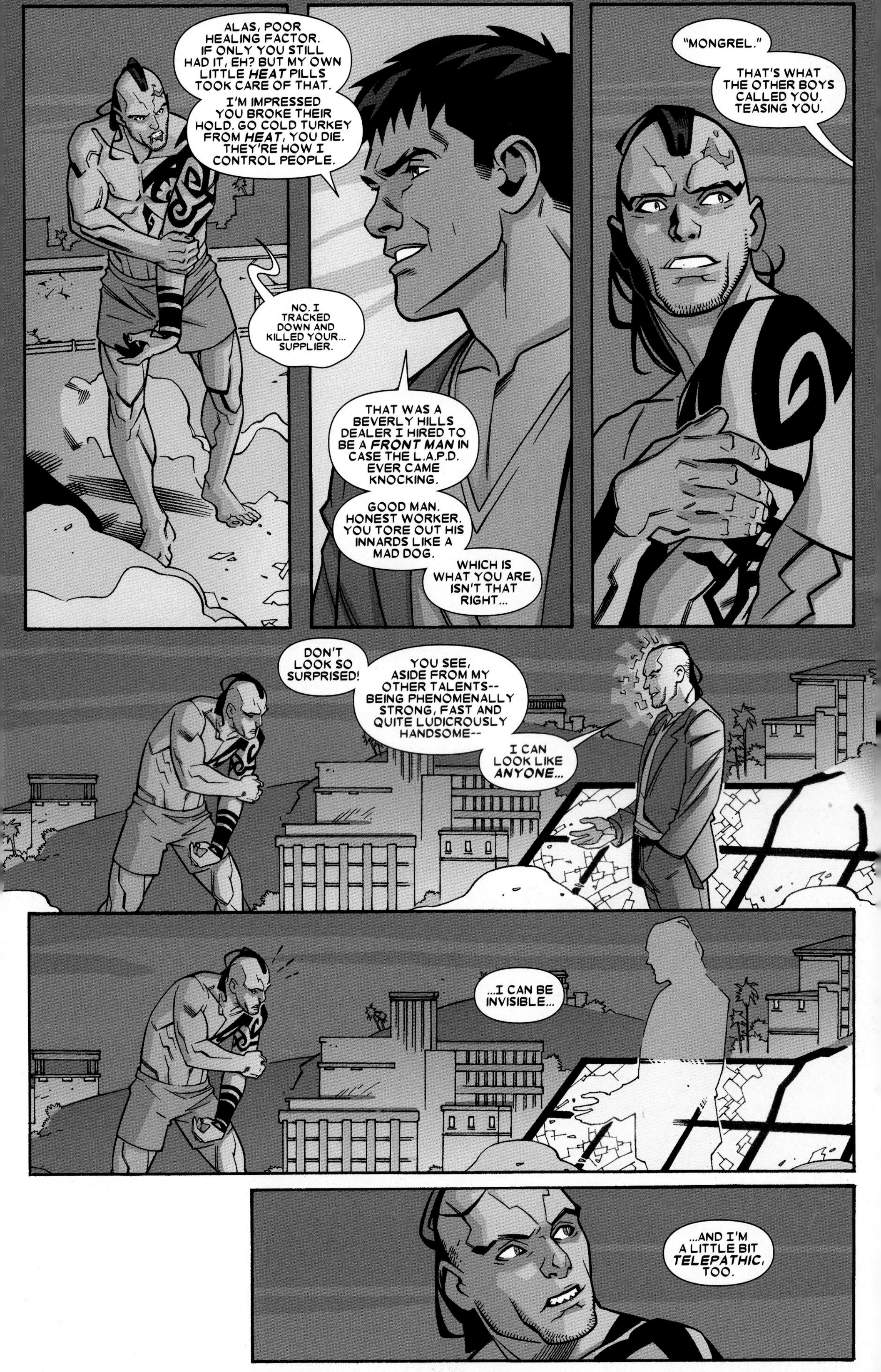
ALAS, POOR HEALING FACTOR. IF ONLY YOU STILL HAD IT, EH? BUT MY OWN LITTLE HEAT PILLS TOOK CARE OF THAT.
I'M IMPRESSED YOU BROKE THEIR HOLD. GO COLD TURKEY FROM HEAT, YOU DIE. THEY'RE HOW I CONTROL PEOPLE.
NO. I TRACKED DOWN AND KILLED YOUR... SUPPLIER.
THAT WAS A BEVERLY HILLS DEALER I HIRED TO BE A FRONT MAN IN CASE THE L.A.P.D. EVER CAME KNOCKING.
GOOD MAN. HONEST WORKER. YOU TORE OUT HIS INNARDS LIKE A MAD DOG.
WHICH IS WHAT YOU ARE, ISN'T THAT RIGHT...
"MONGREL."
THAT'S WHAT THE OTHER BOYS CALLED YOU. TEASING YOU.
DON'T LOOK SO SURPRISED!
YOU SEE, ASIDE FROM MY OTHER TALENTS-- BEING PHENOMENALLY STRONG, FAST AND QUITE LUDICROUSLY HANDSOME--
I CAN LOOK LIKE ANYONE...
...I CAN BE INVISIBLE...
...AND I'M A LITTLE BIT TELEPATHIC, TOO.

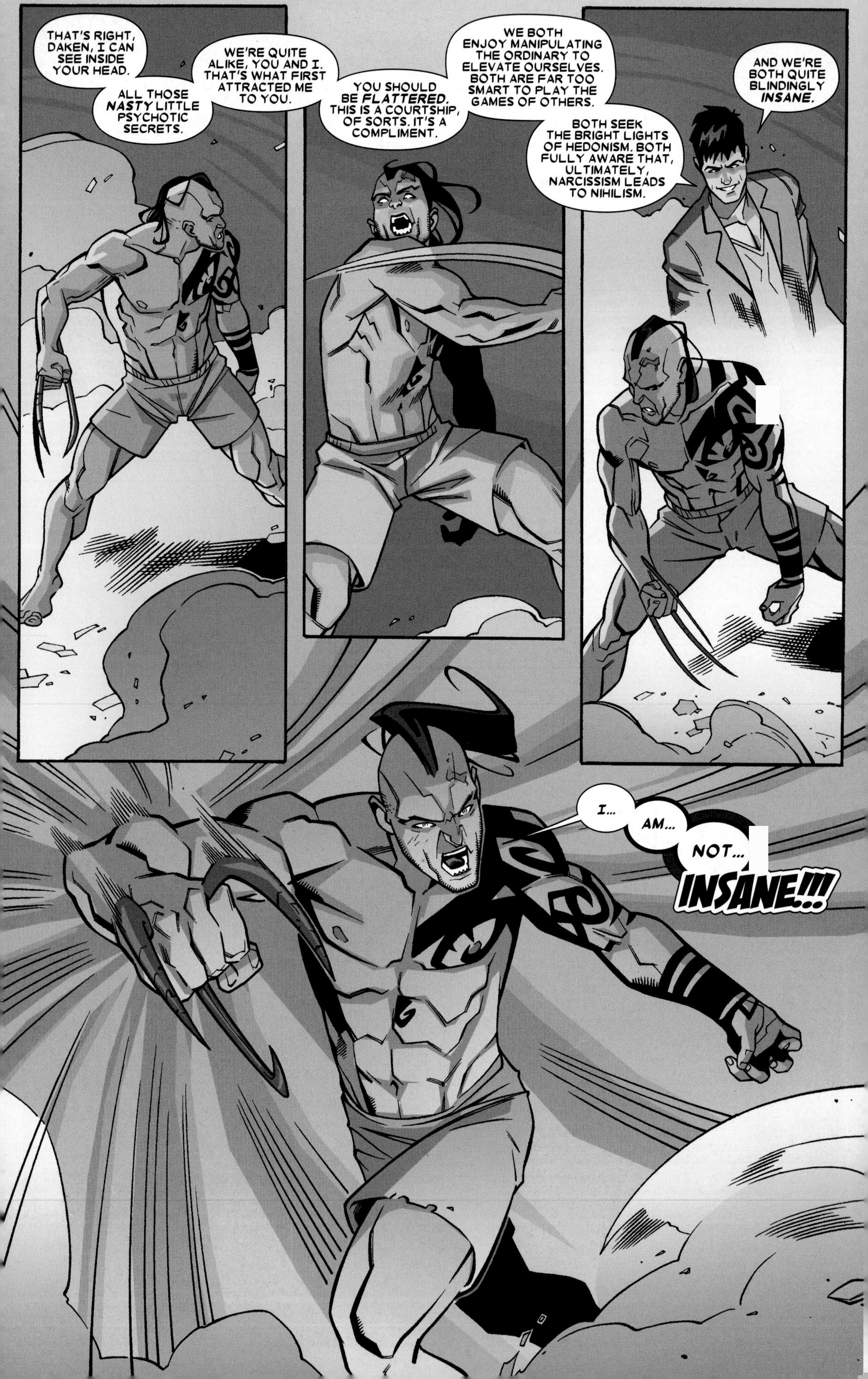
THAT'S RIGHT, DAKEN, I CAN SEE INSIDE YOUR HEAD.
ALL THOSE NASTY LITTLE PSYCHOTIC SECRETS.
WE'RE QUITE ALIKE, YOU AND I. THAT'S WHAT FIRST ATTRACTED ME TO YOU.
YOU SHOULD BE FLATTERED. THIS IS A COURTSHIP, OF SORTS. IT'S A COMPLIMENT.
WE BOTH ENJOY MANIPULATING THE ORDINARY TO ELEVATE OURSELVES. BOTH ARE FAR TOO SMART TO PLAY THE GAMES OF OTHERS.
BOTH SEEK THE BRIGHT LIGHTS OF HEDONISM. BOTH FULLY AWARE THAT, ULTIMATELY, NARCISSISM LEADS TO NIHILISM.
AND WE'RE BOTH QUITE BLINDINGLY INSANE.
I...
AM...
NOT...
INSANE!!!

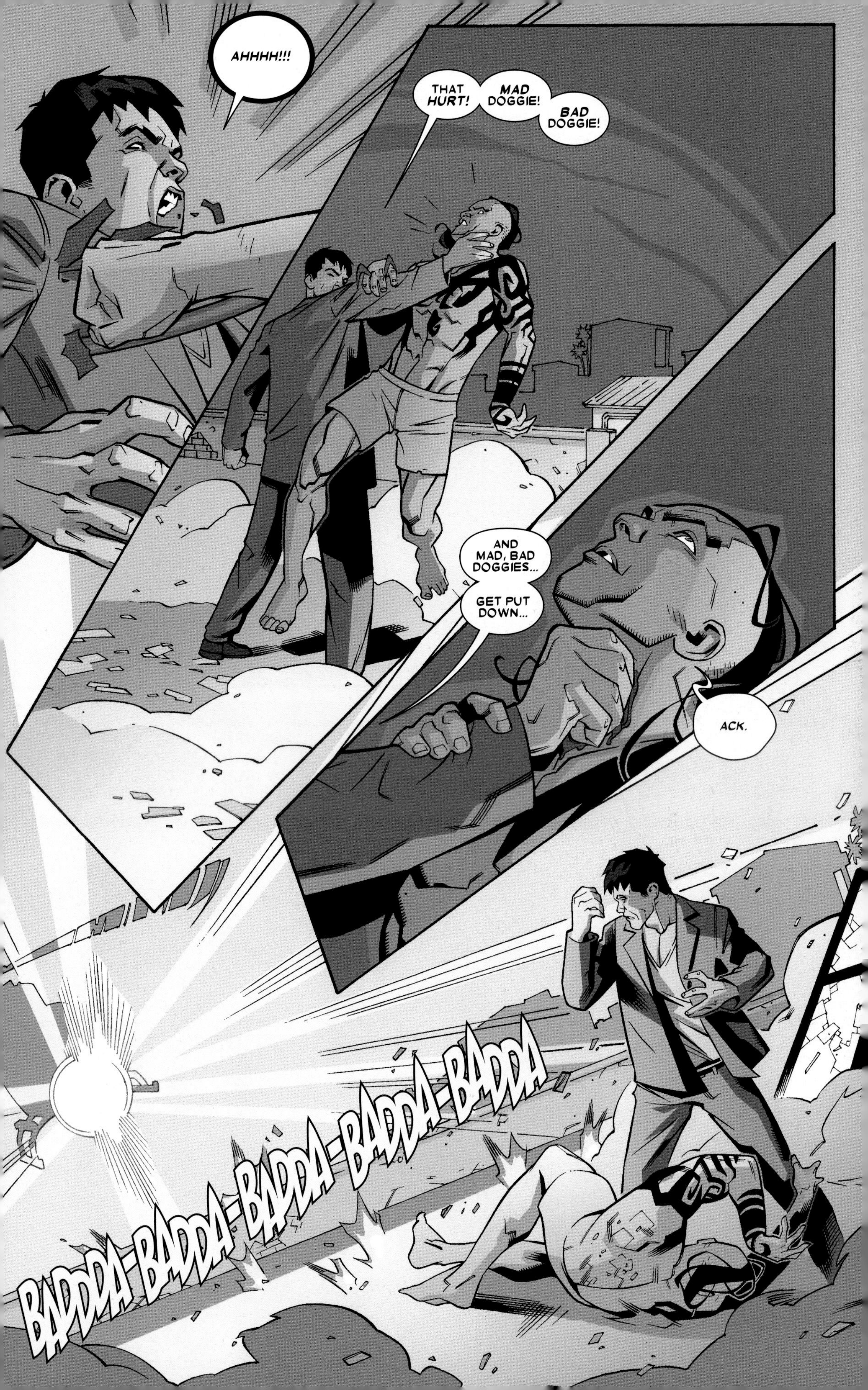
AHHHH!!!
THAT HURT!
MAD DOGGIE!
BAD DOGGIE!
AND MAD, BAD DOGGIES...
GET PUT DOWN...
ACK.
BADDDA-BADDA-BADDA-BADDA-BADDA-BADDA

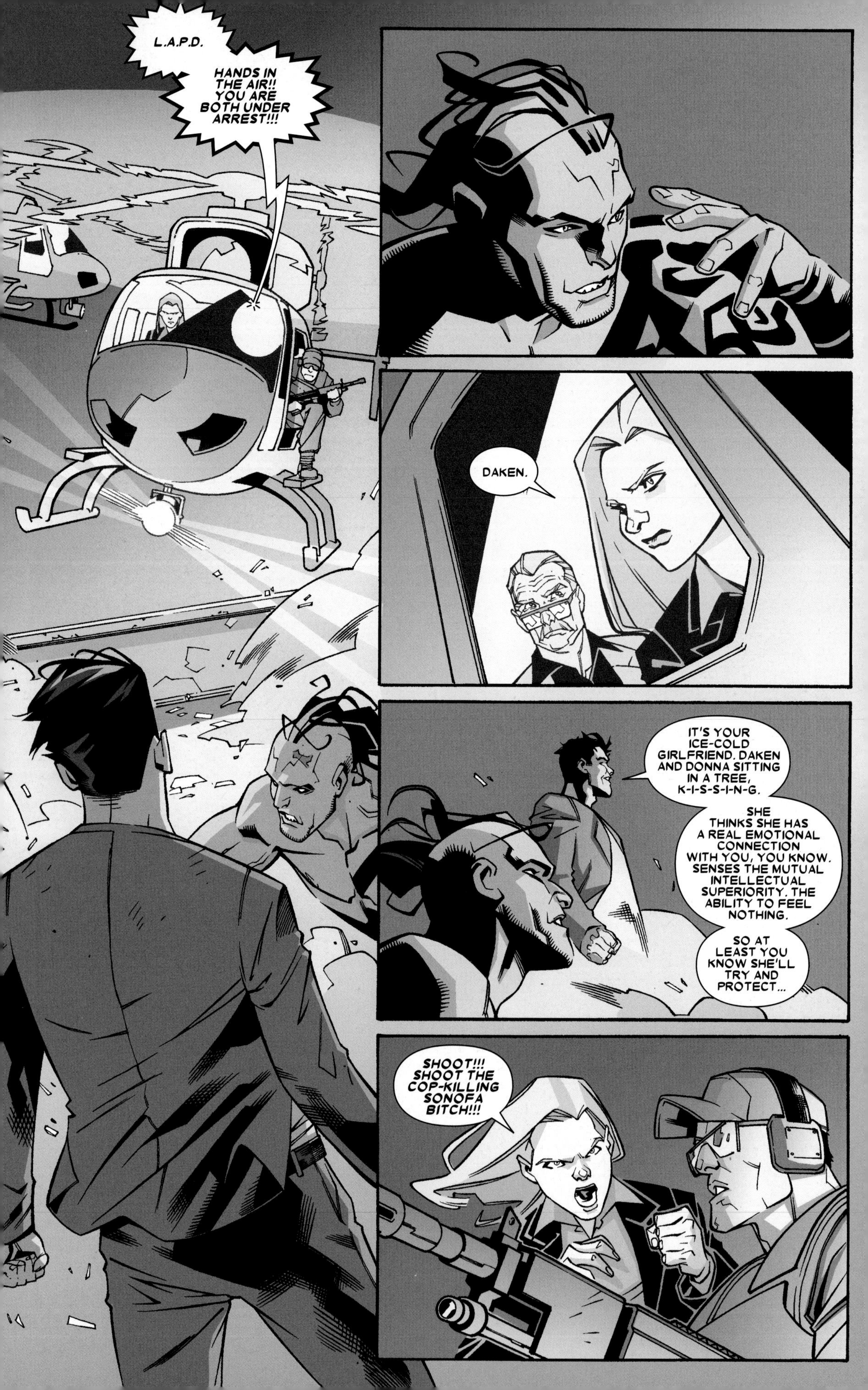
L.A.P.D.
HANDS IN THE AIR!! YOU ARE BOTH UNDER ARREST!!!
DAKEN.
IT'S YOUR ICE-COLD GIRLFRIEND. DAKEN AND DONNA SITTING IN A TREE, K-I-S-S-I-N-G.
SHE THINKS SHE HAS A REAL EMOTIONAL CONNECTION WITH YOU, YOU KNOW. SENSES THE MUTUAL INTELLECTUAL SUPERIORITY. THE ABILITY TO FEEL NOTHING.
SO AT LEAST YOU KNOW SHE'LL TRY AND PROTECT...
SHOOT!!! SHOOT THE COP-KILLING SONOFA BITCH!!!

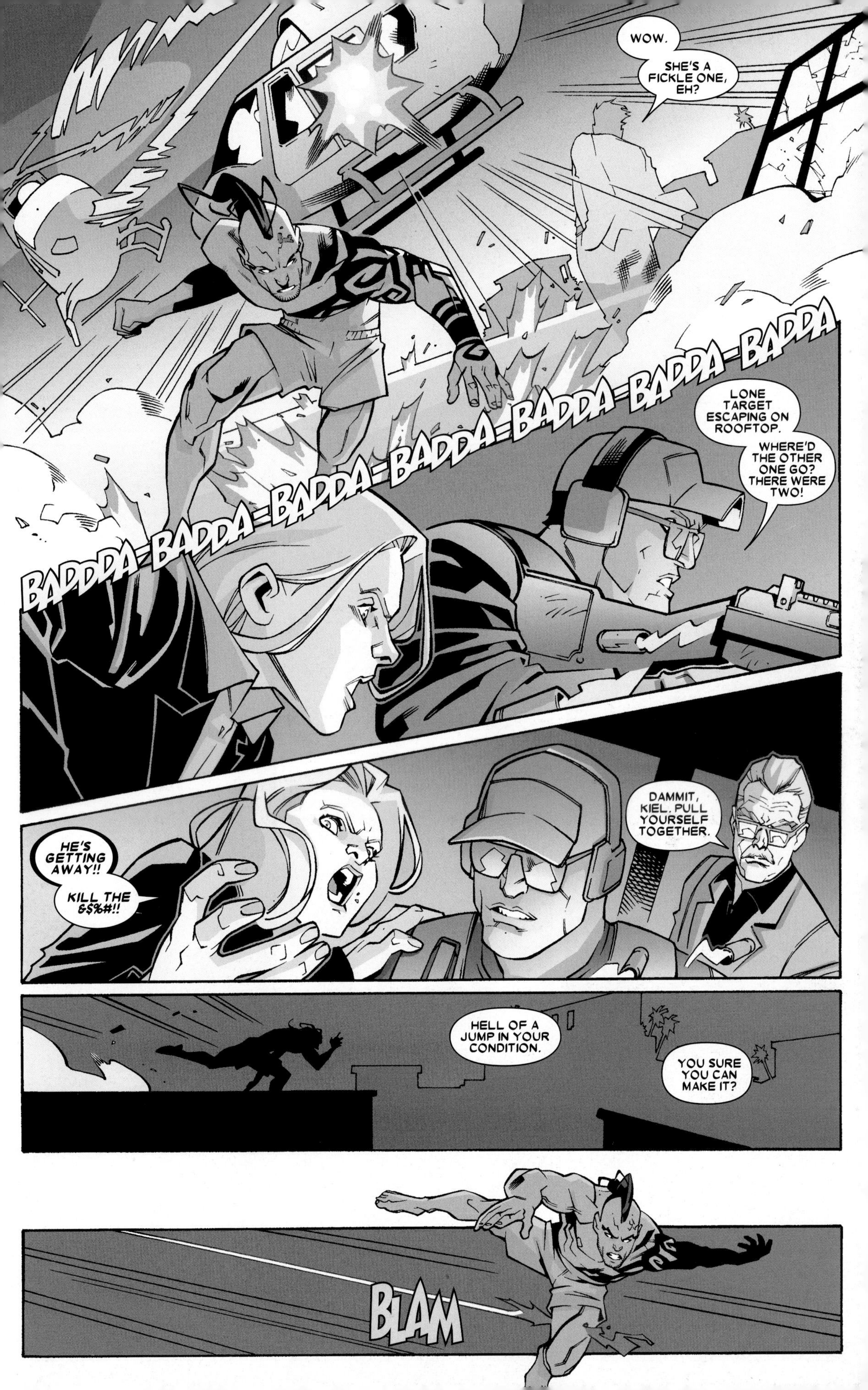
WOW.
SHE'S A FICKLE ONE, EH?
BADDDA-BADDA-BADDA-BADDA-BADDA-BADDA-BADDA-BADDA
LONE TARGET ESCAPING ON ROOFTOP.
WHERE'D THE OTHER ONE GO? THERE WERE TWO!
HE'S GETTING AWAY!!
KILL THE &$%#!!
DAMMIT, KIEL. PULL YOURSELF TOGETHER.
HELL OF A JUMP IN YOUR CONDITION.
YOU SURE YOU CAN MAKE IT?
BLAM

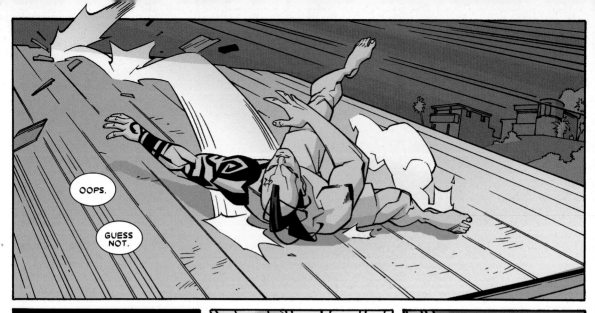

OOPS.

GUESS NOT.

GOT HIM.

WHEN YOU CAME TO LOS ANGELES YOU WANTED TO CREATE SOMETHING, DIDN'T YOU, DAKEN?

SOMETHING TANGIBLE THAT YOU COULD BE PROUD OF.

SOMETHING THAT WOULD *DISTINGUISH* YOU.

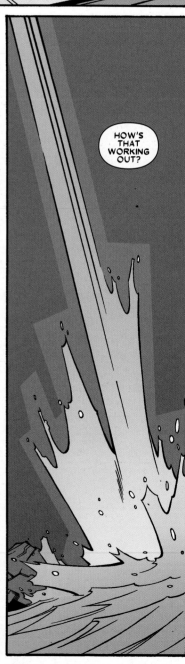

HOW'S THAT WORKING OUT?

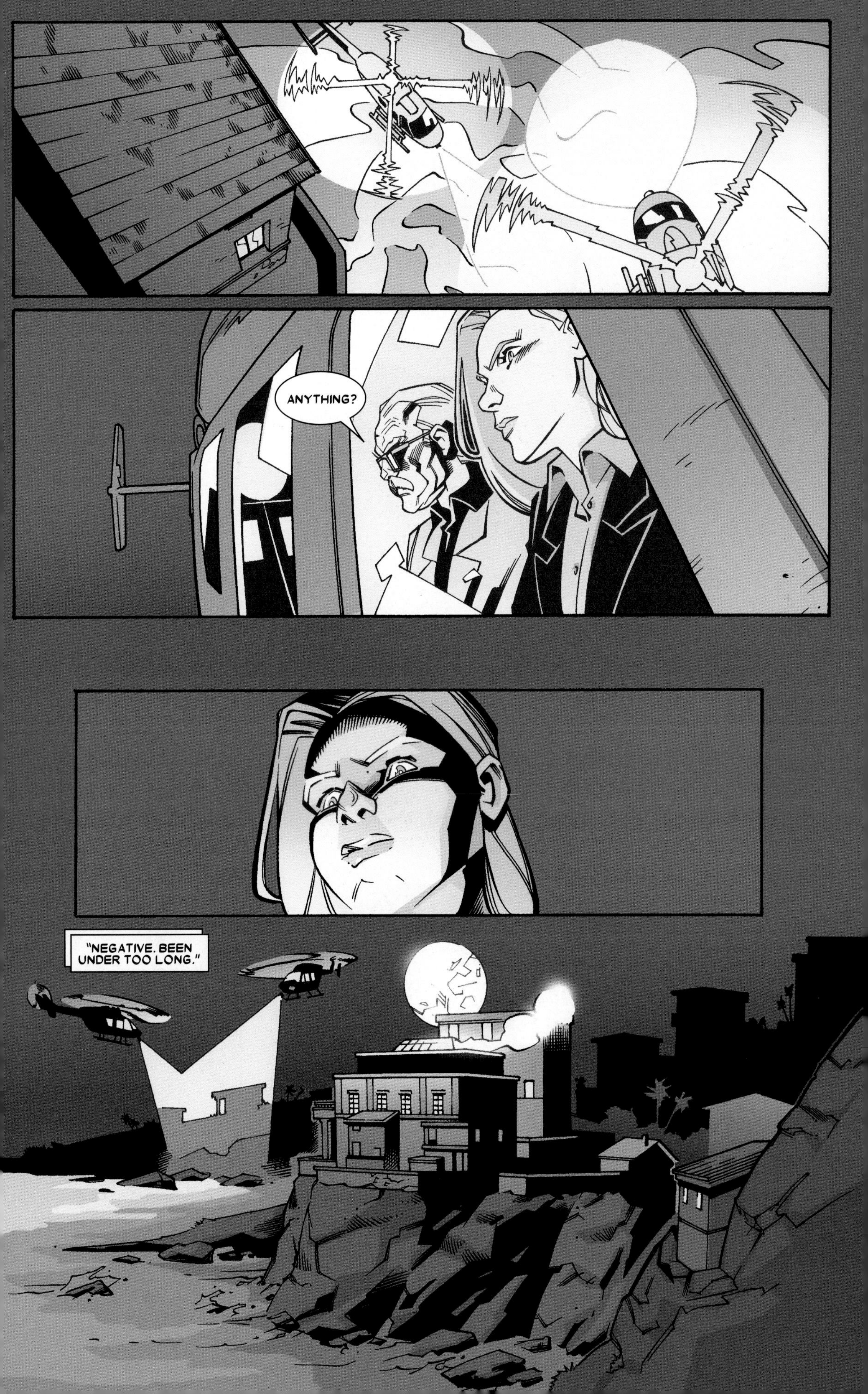
ANYTHING?
"NEGATIVE. BEEN UNDER TOO LONG."

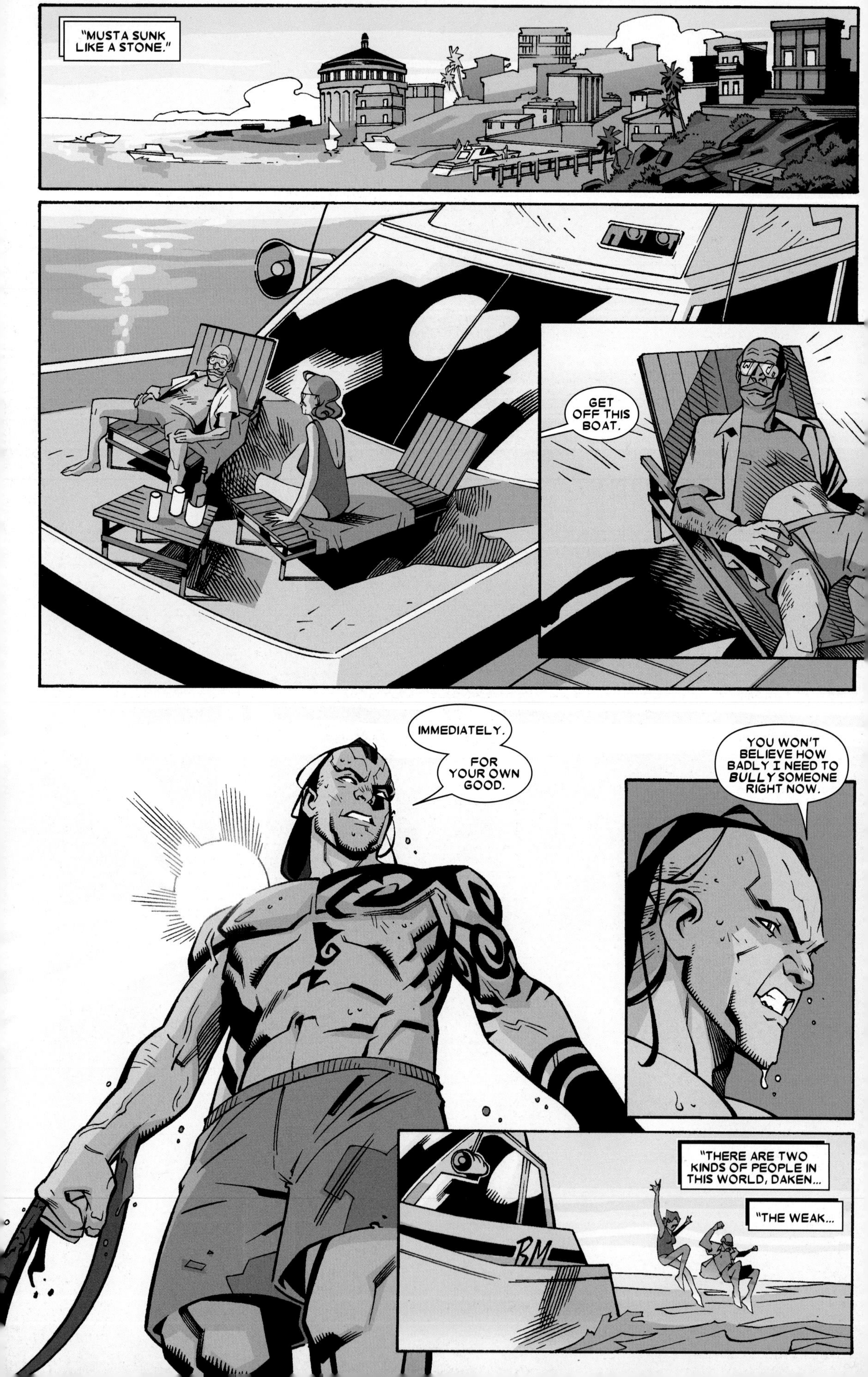
"MUSTA SUNK LIKE A STONE."
GET OFF THIS BOAT.
IMMEDIATELY.
FOR YOUR OWN GOOD.
YOU WON'T BELIEVE HOW BADLY I NEED TO BULLY SOMEONE RIGHT NOW.
"THERE ARE TWO KINDS OF PEOPLE IN THIS WORLD, DAKEN...
"THE WEAK...
BM

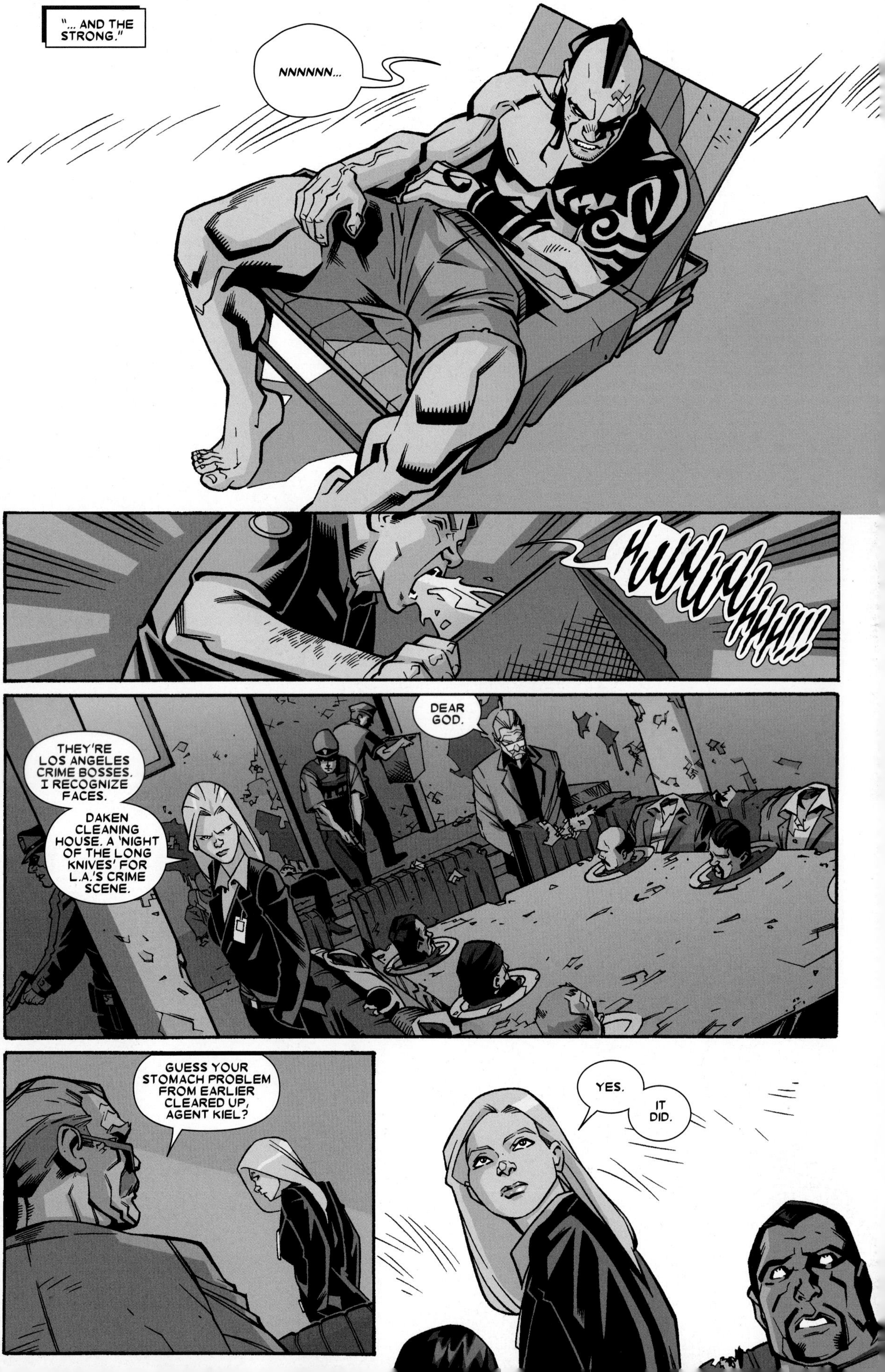
"... AND THE STRONG."
NNNNNN...
DEAR GOD.
THEY'RE LOS ANGELES CRIME BOSSES. I RECOGNIZE FACES.
DAKEN CLEANING HOUSE. A 'NIGHT OF THE LONG KNIVES' FOR L.A.'S CRIME SCENE.
GUESS YOUR STOMACH PROBLEM FROM EARLIER CLEARED UP, AGENT KIEL?
YES.
IT DID.

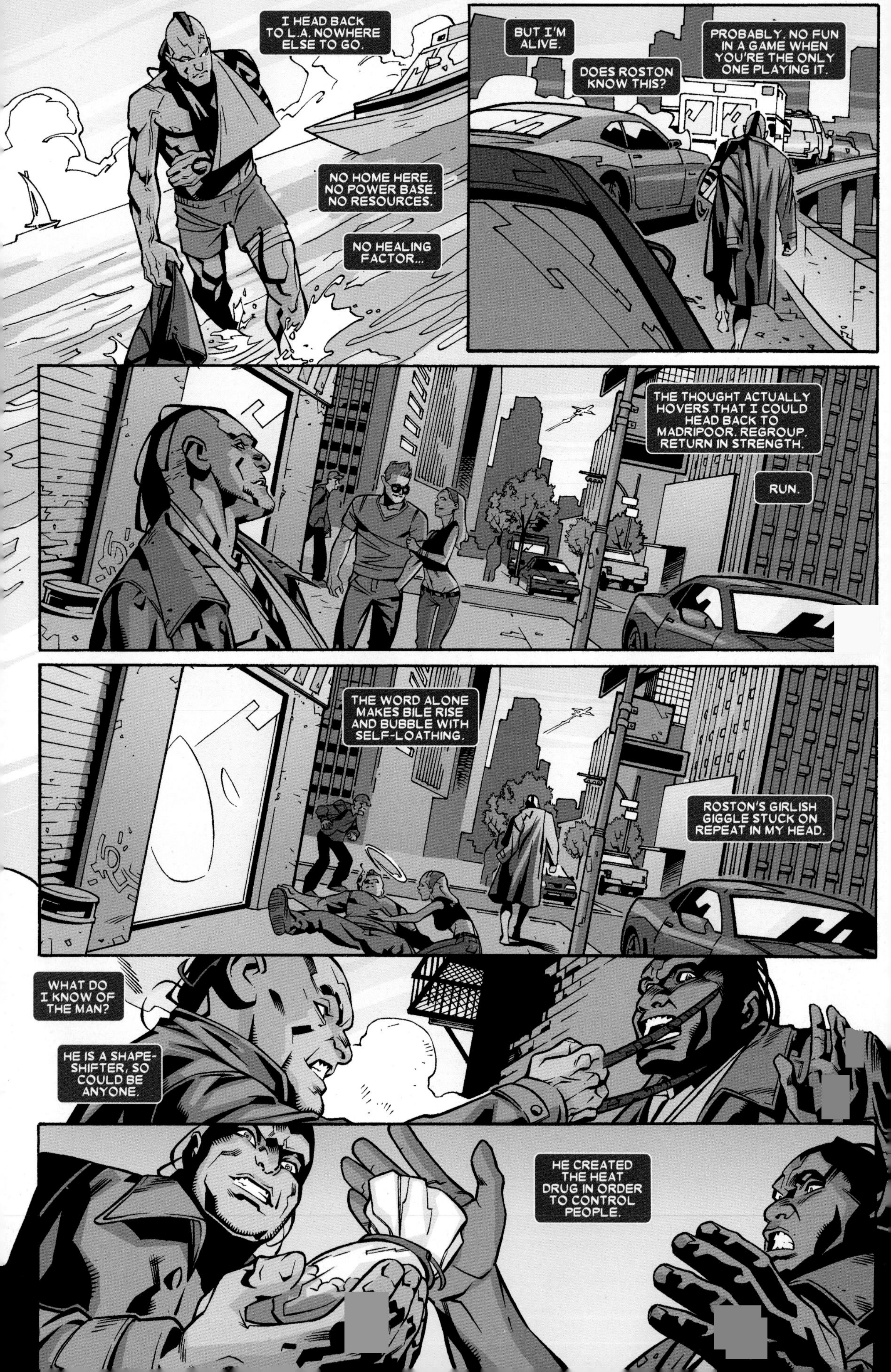
I HEAD BACK TO L.A. NOWHERE ELSE TO GO.
NO HOME HERE. NO POWER BASE. NO RESOURCES.
NO HEALING FACTOR...
BUT I'M ALIVE.
DOES ROSTON KNOW THIS?
PROBABLY. NO FUN IN A GAME WHEN YOU'RE THE ONLY ONE PLAYING IT.
THE THOUGHT ACTUALLY HOVERS THAT I COULD HEAD BACK TO MADRIPOOR. REGROUP. RETURN IN STRENGTH.
RUN.
THE WORD ALONE MAKES BILE RISE AND BUBBLE WITH SELF-LOATHING.
ROSTON'S GIRLISH GIGGLE STUCK ON REPEAT IN MY HEAD.
WHAT DO I KNOW OF THE MAN?
HE IS A SHAPE-SHIFTER, SO COULD BE ANYONE.
HE CREATED THE HEAT DRUG IN ORDER TO CONTROL PEOPLE.

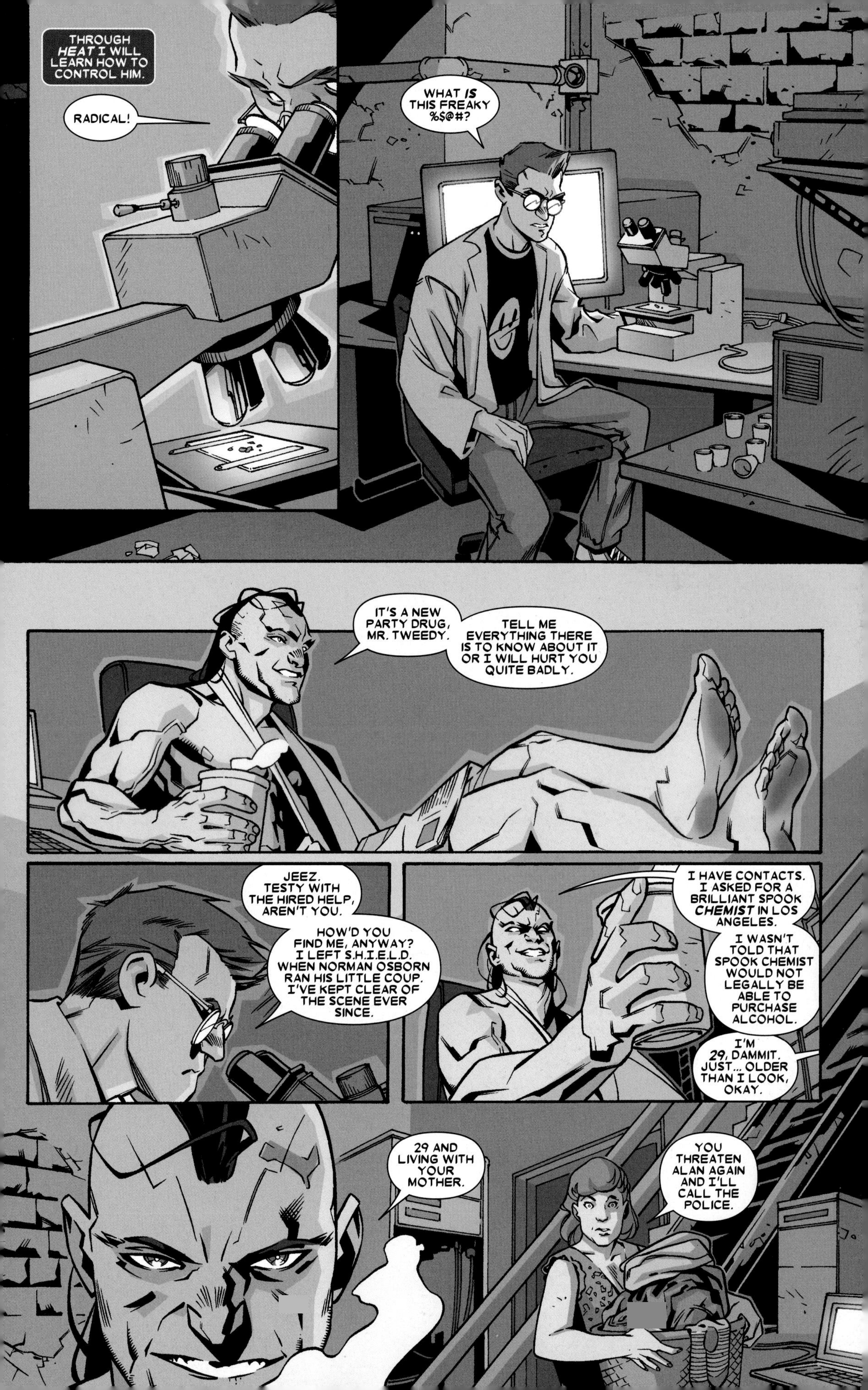
THROUGH HEAT I WILL LEARN HOW TO CONTROL HIM.
RADICAL!
WHAT IS THIS FREAKY %$@#?
IT'S A NEW PARTY DRUG, MR. TWEEDY.
TELL ME EVERYTHING THERE IS TO KNOW ABOUT IT OR I WILL HURT YOU QUITE BADLY.
JEEZ. TESTY WITH THE HIRED HELP, AREN'T YOU.
HOW'D YOU FIND ME, ANYWAY? I LEFT S.H.I.E.L.D. WHEN NORMAN OSBORN RAN HIS LITTLE COUP. I'VE KEPT CLEAR OF THE SCENE EVER SINCE.
I HAVE CONTACTS. I ASKED FOR A BRILLIANT SPOOK CHEMIST IN LOS ANGELES.
I WASN'T TOLD THAT SPOOK CHEMIST WOULD NOT LEGALLY BE ABLE TO PURCHASE ALCOHOL.
I'M 29, DAMMIT. JUST... OLDER THAN I LOOK, OKAY.
29 AND LIVING WITH YOUR MOTHER.
YOU THREATEN ALAN AGAIN AND I'LL CALL THE POLICE.

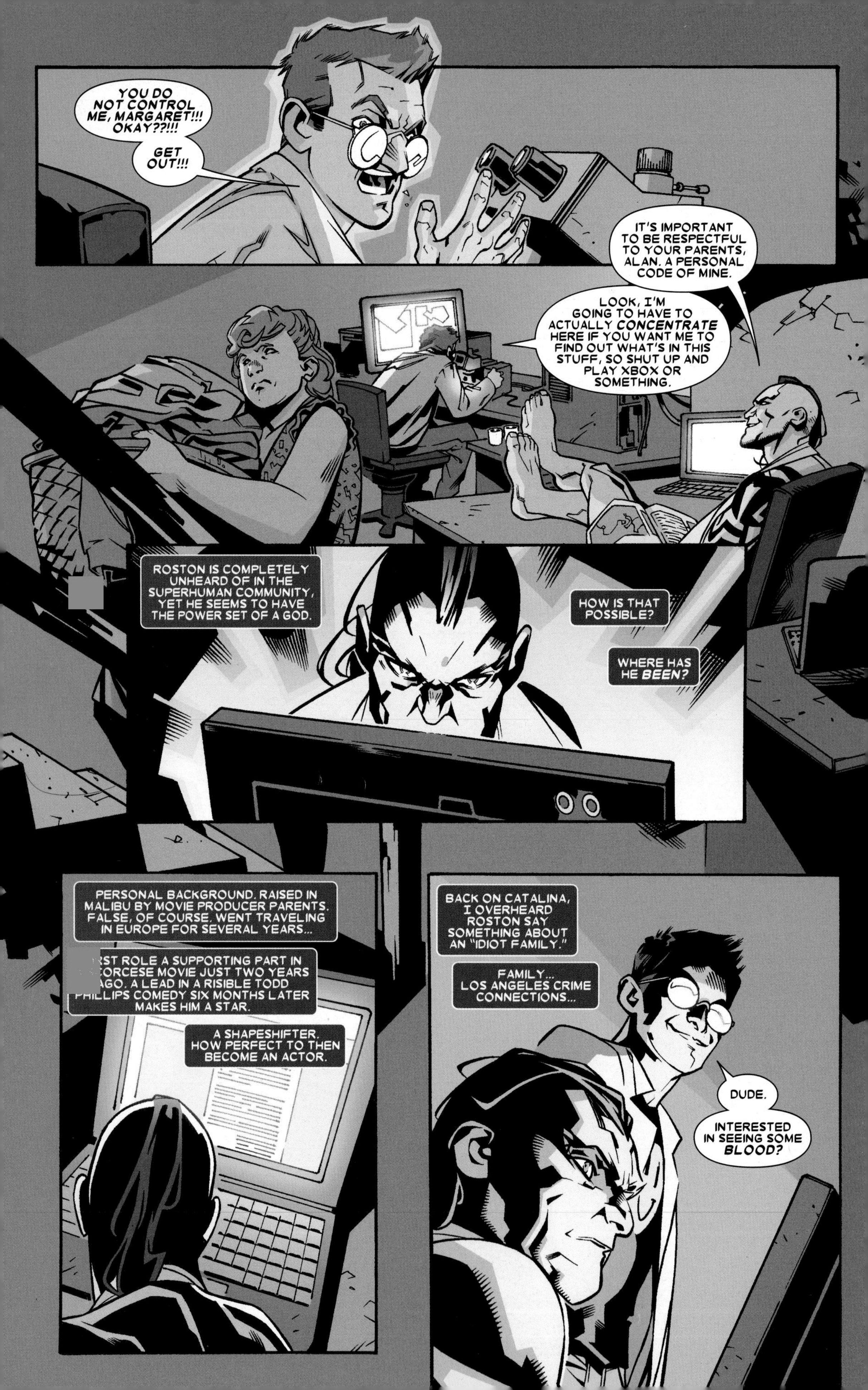
YOU DO NOT CONTROL ME, MARGARET!!! OKAY??!!!
GET OUT!!!
IT'S IMPORTANT TO BE RESPECTFUL TO YOUR PARENTS, ALAN. A PERSONAL CODE OF MINE.
LOOK, I'M GOING TO HAVE TO ACTUALLY CONCENTRATE HERE IF YOU WANT ME TO FIND OUT WHAT'S IN THIS STUFF, SO SHUT UP AND PLAY XBOX OR SOMETHING.
ROSTON IS COMPLETELY UNHEARD OF IN THE SUPERHUMAN COMMUNITY, YET HE SEEMS TO HAVE THE POWER SET OF A GOD.
HOW IS THAT POSSIBLE?
WHERE HAS HE BEEN?
PERSONAL BACKGROUND. RAISED IN MALIBU BY MOVIE PRODUCER PARENTS. FALSE, OF COURSE. WENT TRAVELING IN EUROPE FOR SEVERAL YEARS...
RST ROLE A SUPPORTING PART IN CORCESE MOVIE JUST TWO YEARS AGO. A LEAD IN A RISIBLE TODD PHILLIPS COMEDY SIX MONTHS LATER MAKES HIM A STAR.
A SHAPESHIFTER. HOW PERFECT TO THEN BECOME AN ACTOR.
BACK ON CATALINA, I OVERHEARD ROSTON SAY SOMETHING ABOUT AN "IDIOT FAMILY."
FAMILY... LOS ANGELES CRIME CONNECTIONS...
DUDE.
INTERESTED IN SEEING SOME BLOOD?

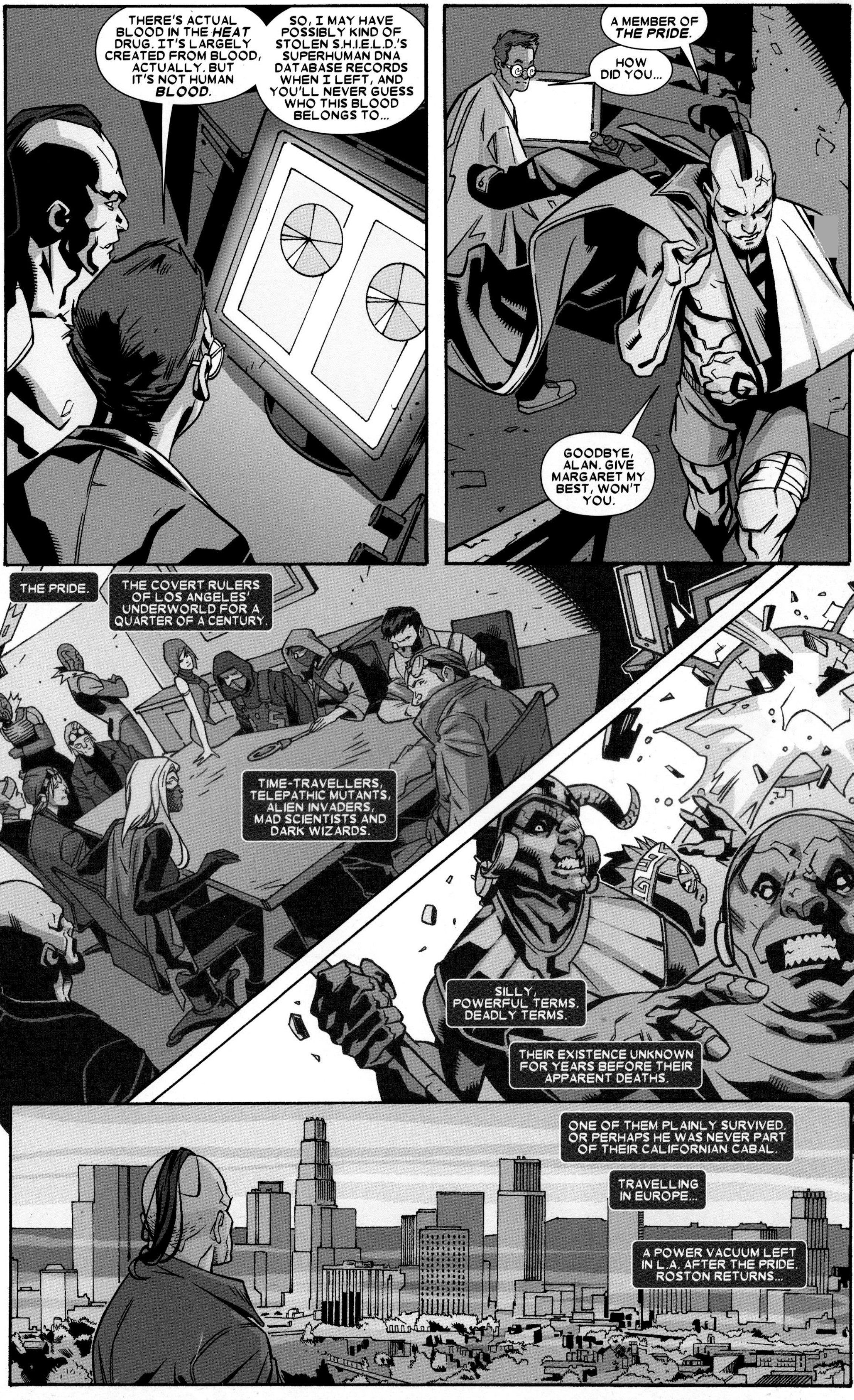
THERE'S ACTUAL BLOOD IN THE HEAT DRUG. IT'S LARGELY CREATED FROM BLOOD, ACTUALLY. BUT IT'S NOT HUMAN BLOOD.
SO, I MAY HAVE POSSIBLY KIND OF STOLEN S.H.I.E.L.D.'S SUPERHUMAN DNA DATABASE RECORDS WHEN I LEFT, AND YOU'LL NEVER GUESS WHO THIS BLOOD BELONGS TO...
A MEMBER OF THE PRIDE.
HOW DID YOU...
GOODBYE, ALAN. GIVE MARGARET MY BEST, WON'T YOU.
THE PRIDE.
THE COVERT RULERS OF LOS ANGELES' UNDERWORLD FOR A QUARTER OF A CENTURY.
TIME-TRAVELLERS, TELEPATHIC MUTANTS, ALIEN INVADERS, MAD SCIENTISTS AND DARK WIZARDS.
SILLY, POWERFUL TERMS. DEADLY TERMS.
THEIR EXISTENCE UNKNOWN FOR YEARS BEFORE THEIR APPARENT DEATHS.
ONE OF THEM PLAINLY SURVIVED. OR PERHAPS HE WAS NEVER PART OF THEIR CALIFORNIAN CABAL.
TRAVELLING IN EUROPE...
A POWER VACUUM LEFT IN L.A. AFTER THE PRIDE. ROSTON RETURNS...

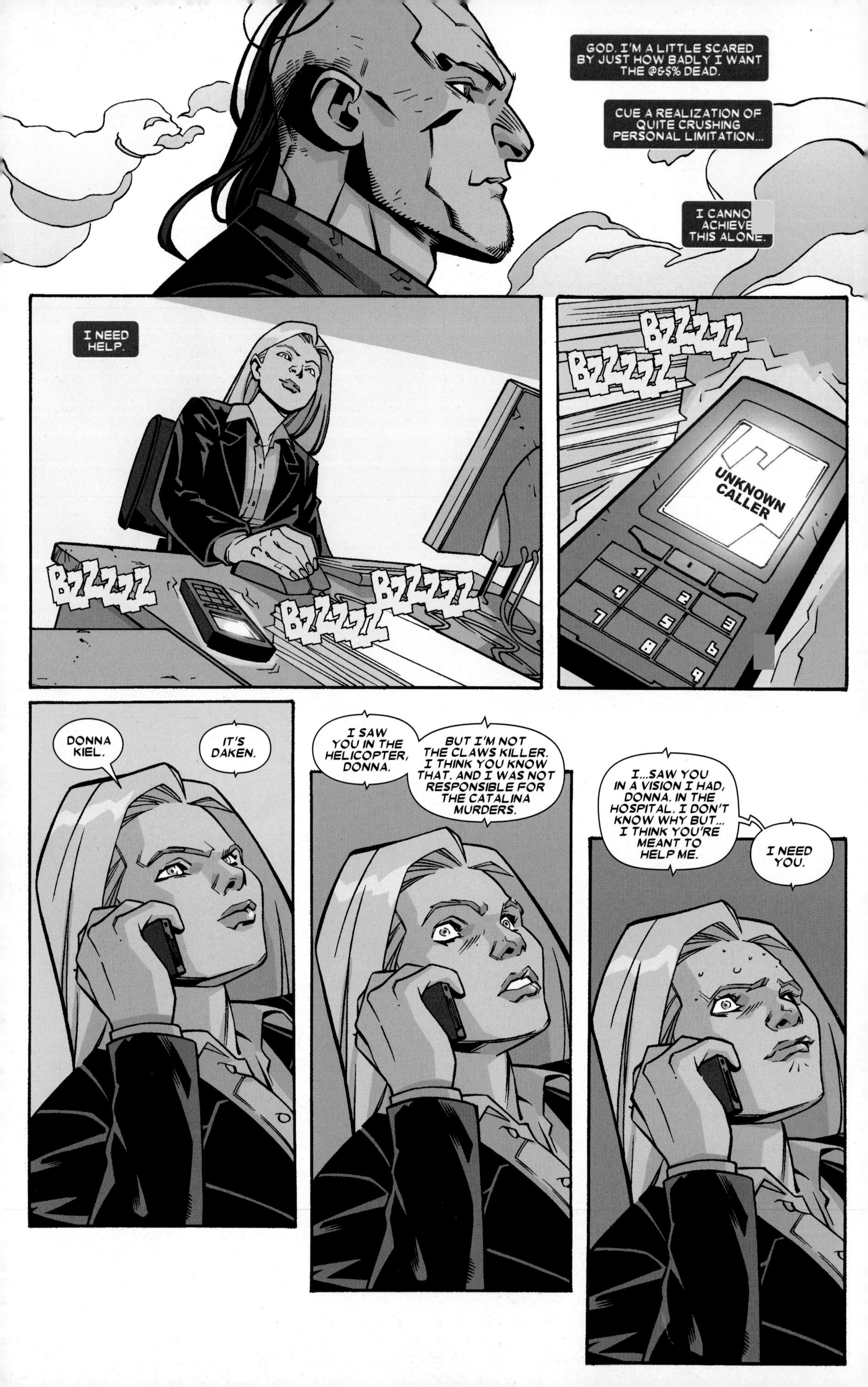
GOD. I'M A LITTLE SCARED BY JUST HOW BADLY I WANT THE @&$% DEAD.
CUE A REALIZATION OF QUITE CRUSHING PERSONAL LIMITATION...
I CANNO ACHIEVE THIS ALONE.
I NEED HELP.
BZZZZZ
BZZZZZ
BZZZZZ
BZZZZZ
BZZZZZ
UNKNOWN CALLER
DONNA KIEL.
IT'S DAKEN.
I SAW YOU IN THE HELICOPTER, DONNA.
BUT I'M NOT THE CLAWS KILLER. I THINK YOU KNOW THAT. AND I WAS NOT RESPONSIBLE FOR THE CATALINA MURDERS.
I...SAW YOU IN A VISION I HAD, DONNA. IN THE HOSPITAL. I DON'T KNOW WHY BUT... I THINK YOU'RE MEANT TO HELP ME.
I NEED YOU.

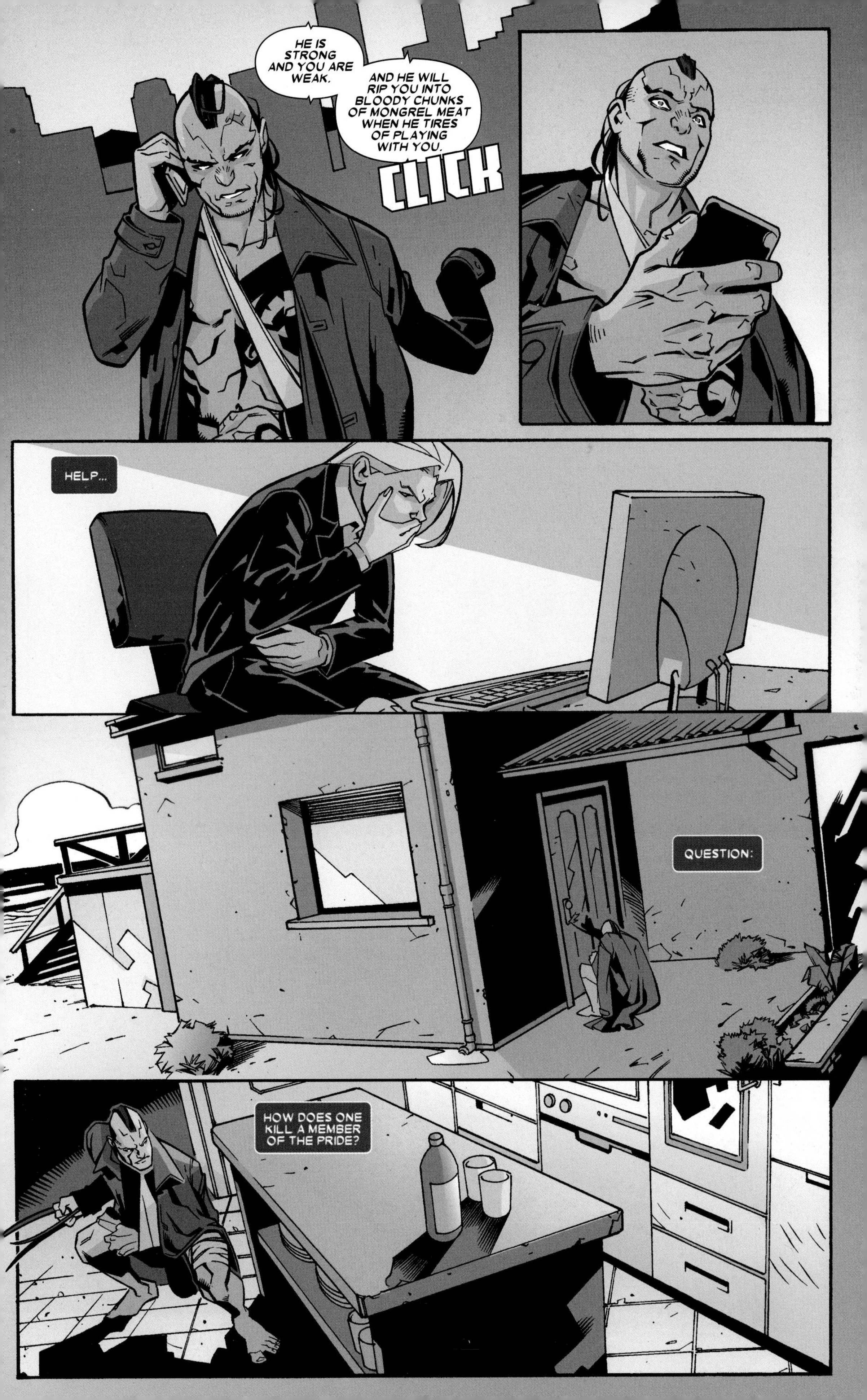
HE IS STRONG AND YOU ARE WEAK.
AND HE WILL RIP YOU INTO BLOODY CHUNKS OF MONGREL MEAT WHEN HE TIRES OF PLAYING WITH YOU.
CLICK
HELP...
QUESTION:
HOW DOES ONE KILL A MEMBER OF THE PRIDE?

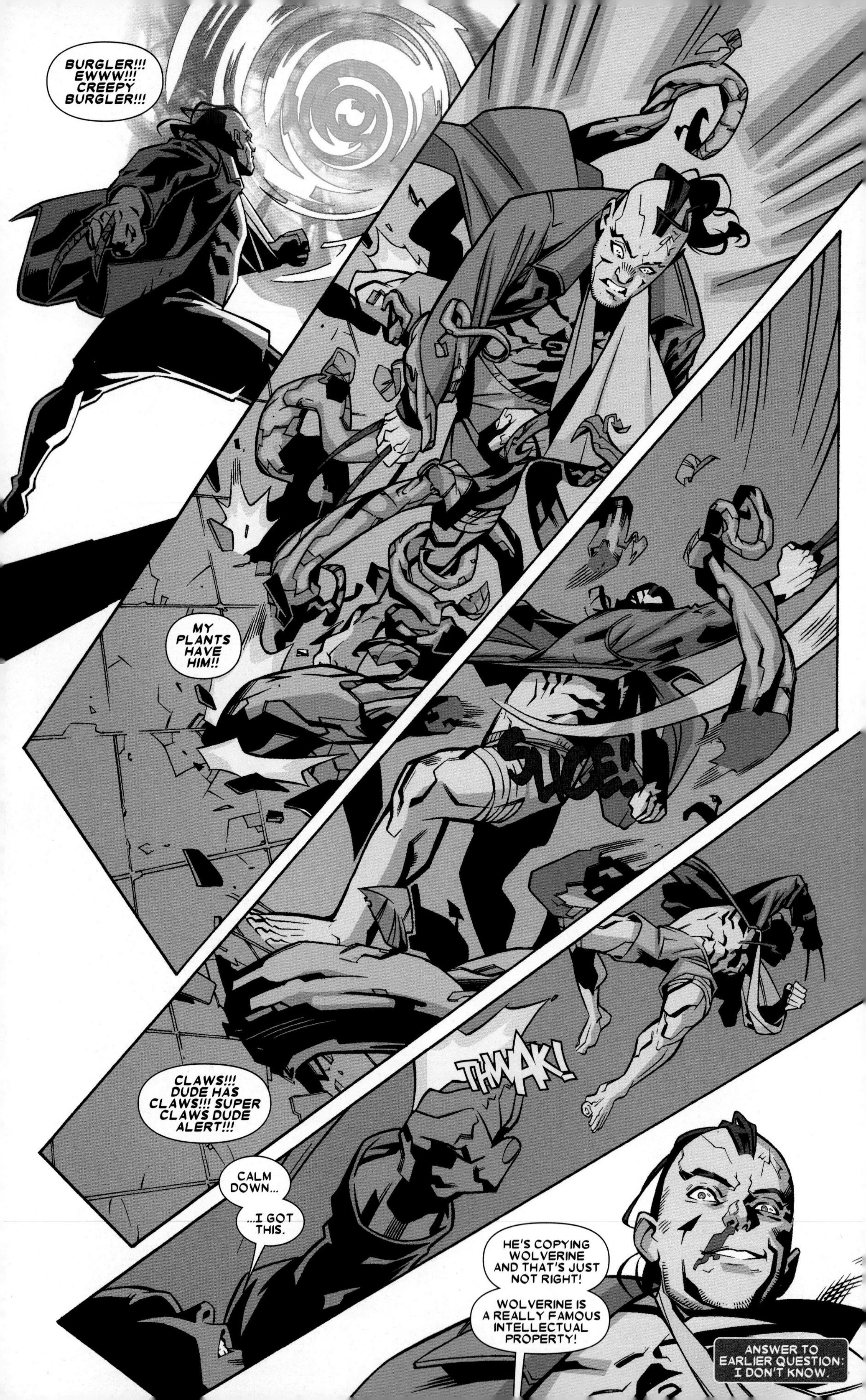
BURGLER!!! EWWW!!! CREEPY BURGLER!!!
MY PLANTS HAVE HIM!!
SLICE!!
CLAWS!!! DUDE HAS CLAWS!!! SUPER CLAWS DUDE ALERT!!!
THWAK!
CALM DOWN...
...I GOT THIS.
HE'S COPYING WOLVERINE AND THAT'S JUST NOT RIGHT!
WOLVERINE IS A REALLY FAMOUS INTELLECTUAL PROPERTY!
ANSWER TO EARLIER QUESTION: I DON'T KNOW.

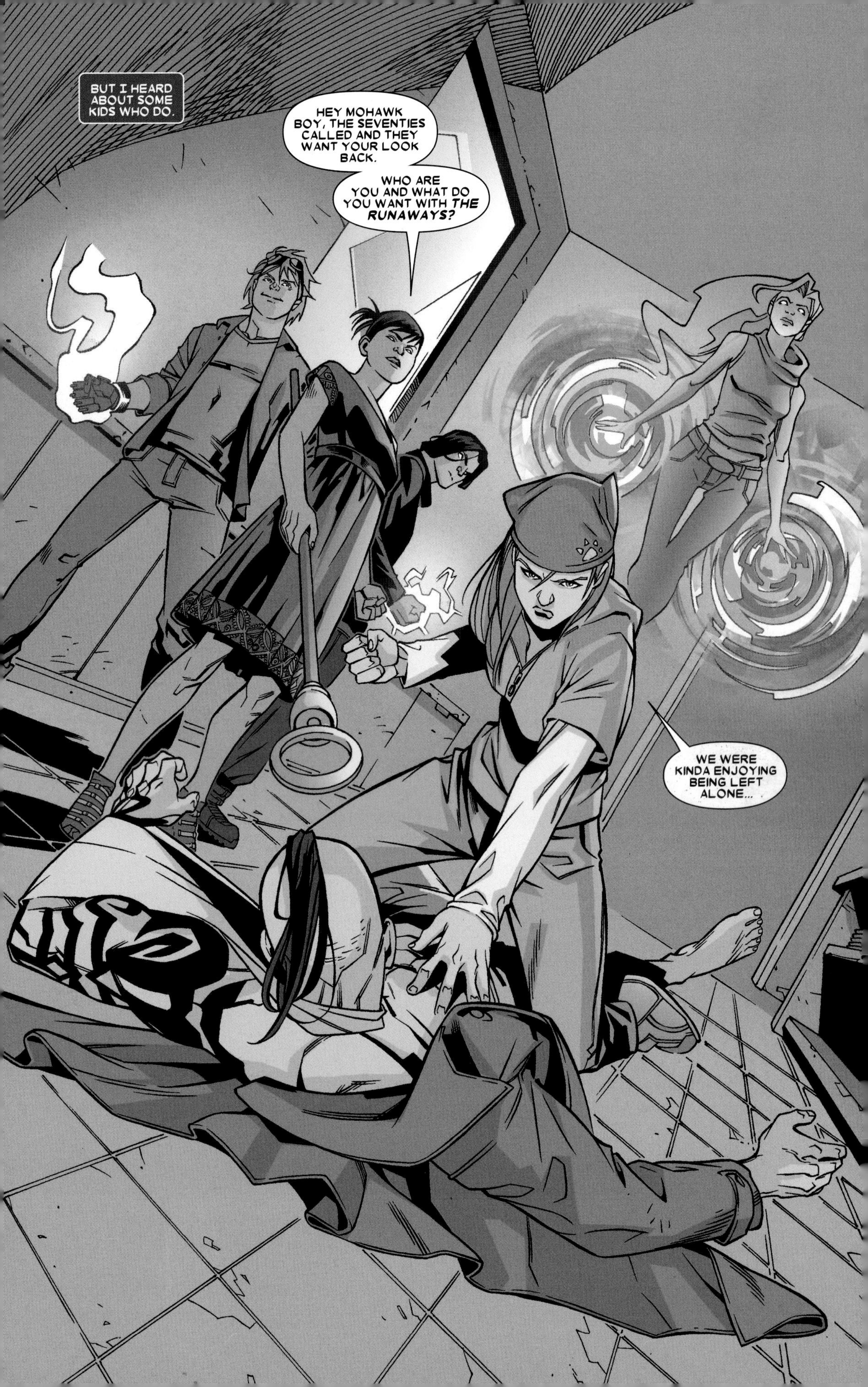
BUT I HEARD ABOUT SOME KIDS WHO DO.
HEY MOHAWK BOY, THE SEVENTIES CALLED AND THEY WANT YOUR LOOK BACK.
WHO ARE YOU AND WHAT DO YOU WANT WITH *THE RUNAWAYS?*
WE WERE KINDA ENJOYING BEING LEFT ALONE...

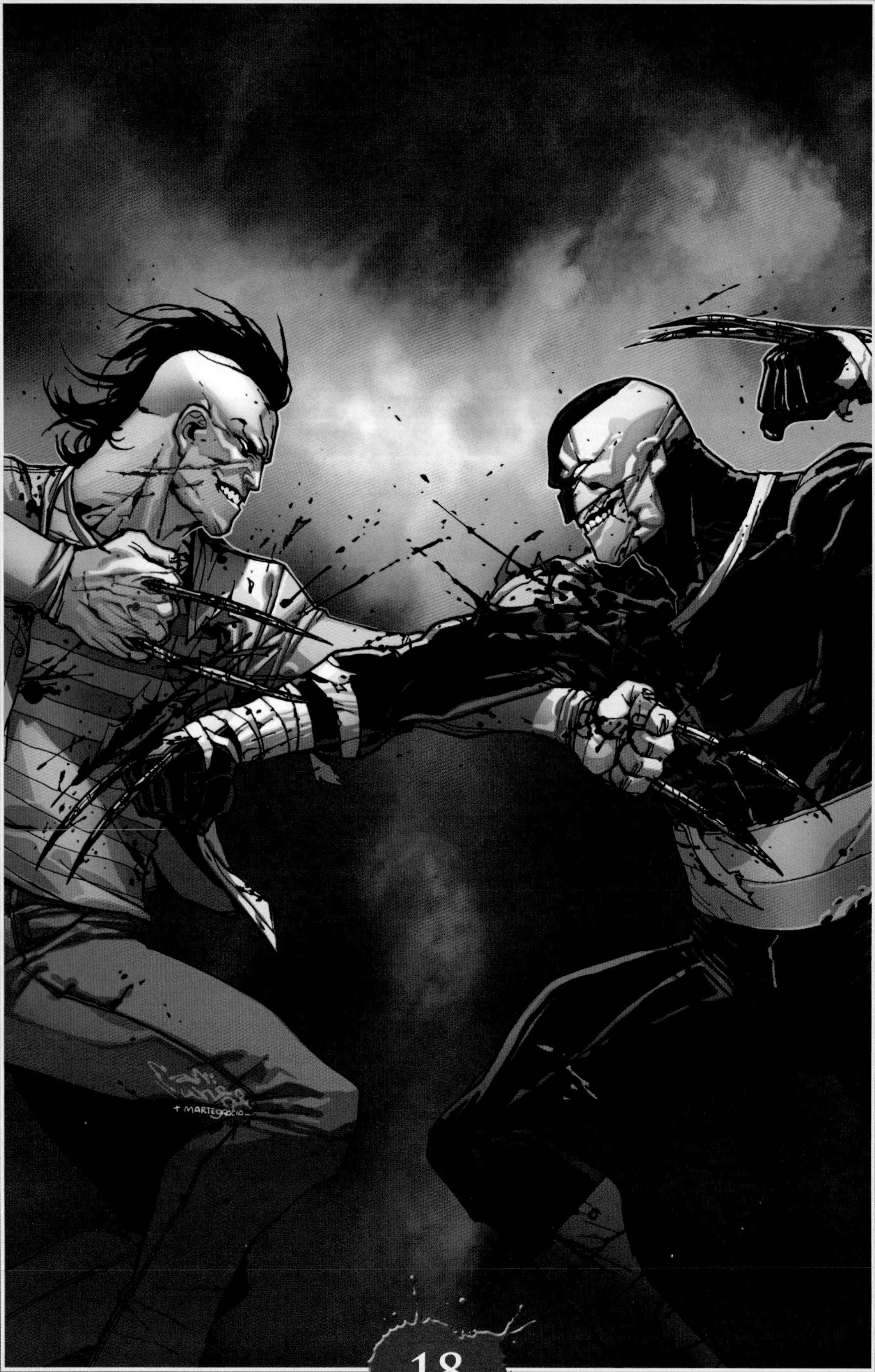

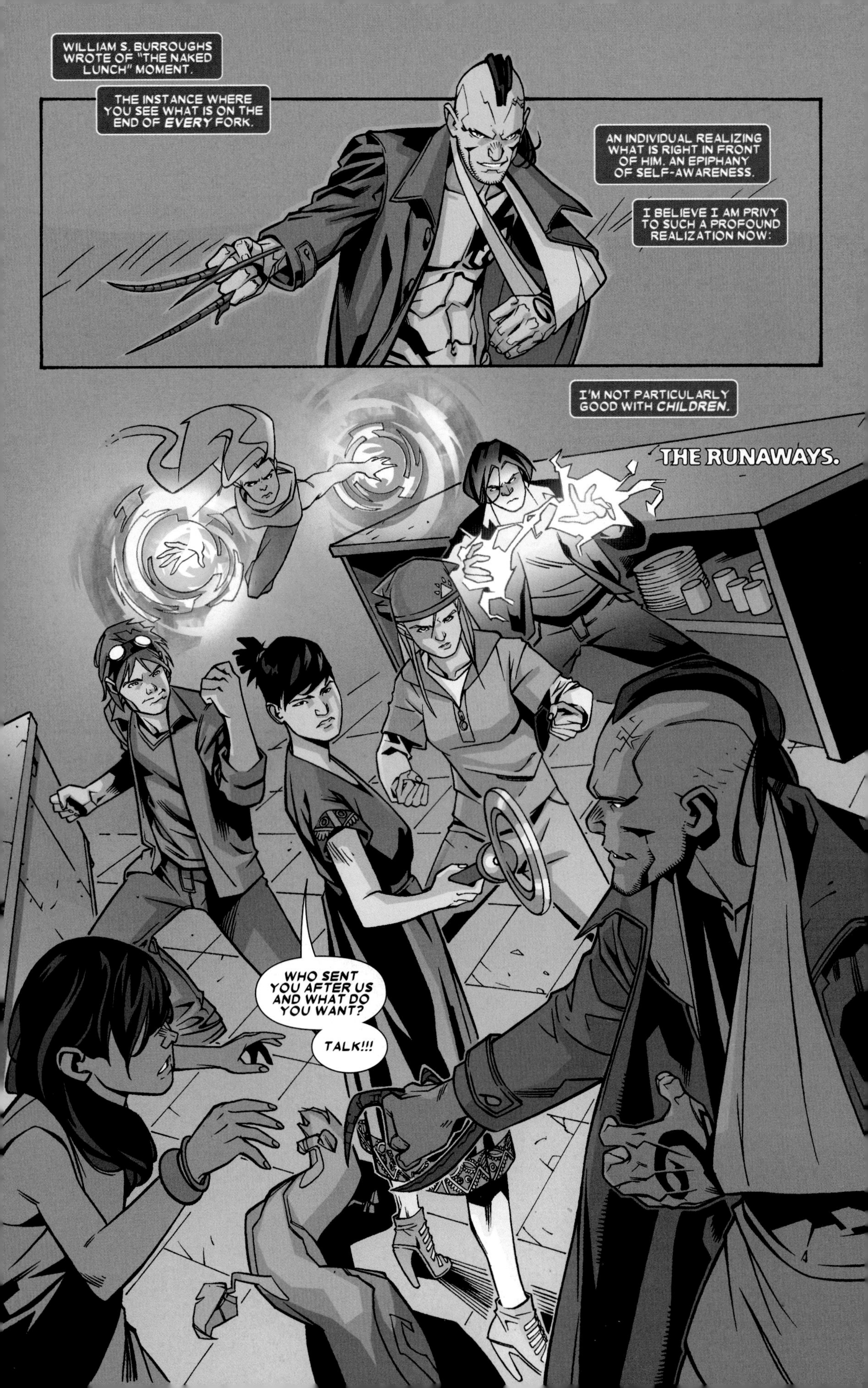
WILLIAM S. BURROUGHS WROTE OF "THE NAKED LUNCH" MOMENT.
THE INSTANCE WHERE YOU SEE WHAT IS ON THE END OF EVERY FORK.
AN INDIVIDUAL REALIZING WHAT IS RIGHT IN FRONT OF HIM. AN EPIPHANY OF SELF-AWARENESS.
I BELIEVE I AM PRIVY TO SUCH A PROFOUND REALIZATION NOW:
I'M NOT PARTICULARLY GOOD WITH CHILDREN.
THE RUNAWAYS.
WHO SENT YOU AFTER US AND WHAT DO YOU WANT?
TALK!!!

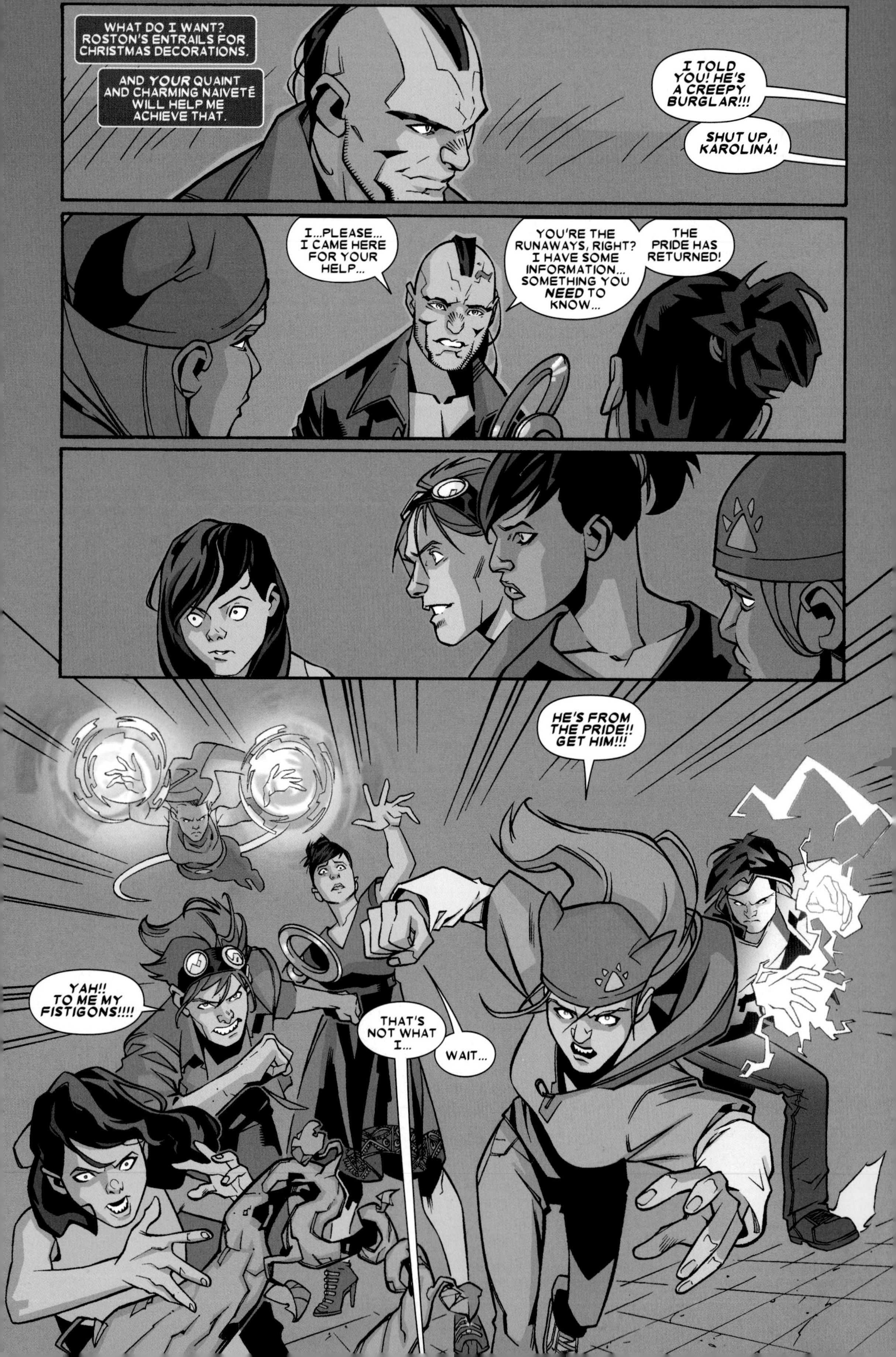
WHAT DO I WANT? ROSTON'S ENTRAILS FOR CHRISTMAS DECORATIONS.
AND YOUR QUAINT AND CHARMING NAIVETÉ WILL HELP ME ACHIEVE THAT.
I TOLD YOU! HE'S A CREEPY BURGLAR!!!
SHUT UP, KAROLINA!
I...PLEASE... I CAME HERE FOR YOUR HELP...
YOU'RE THE RUNAWAYS, RIGHT? I HAVE SOME INFORMATION... SOMETHING YOU NEED TO KNOW...
THE PRIDE HAS RETURNED!
HE'S FROM THE PRIDE!! GET HIM!!!
YAH!! TO ME MY FISTIGONS!!!!
THAT'S NOT WHAT I...
WAIT...

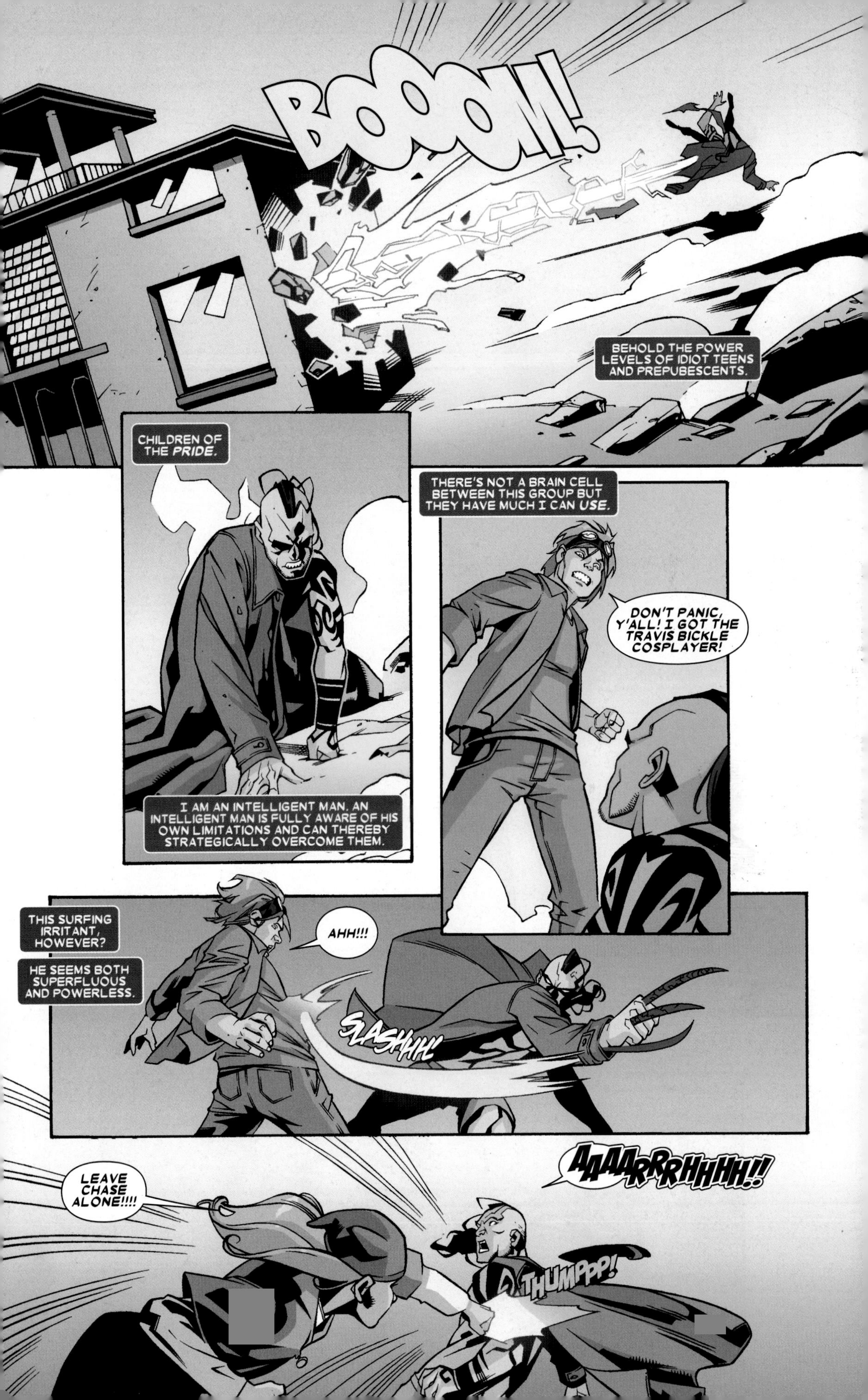
BOOOM!
BEHOLD THE POWER LEVELS OF IDIOT TEENS AND PREPUBESCENTS.
CHILDREN OF THE *PRIDE*.
I AM AN INTELLIGENT MAN. AN INTELLIGENT MAN IS FULLY AWARE OF HIS OWN LIMITATIONS AND CAN THEREBY STRATEGICALLY OVERCOME THEM.
THERE'S NOT A BRAIN CELL BETWEEN THIS GROUP BUT THEY HAVE MUCH I CAN *USE*.
DON'T PANIC, Y'ALL! I GOT THE TRAVIS BICKLE COSPLAYER!
THIS SURFING IRRITANT, HOWEVER?
HE SEEMS BOTH SUPERFLUOUS AND POWERLESS.
AHH!!!
SLASHHH!
LEAVE CHASE ALONE!!!!
AAAARRRHHHH!!
THUMPPP!

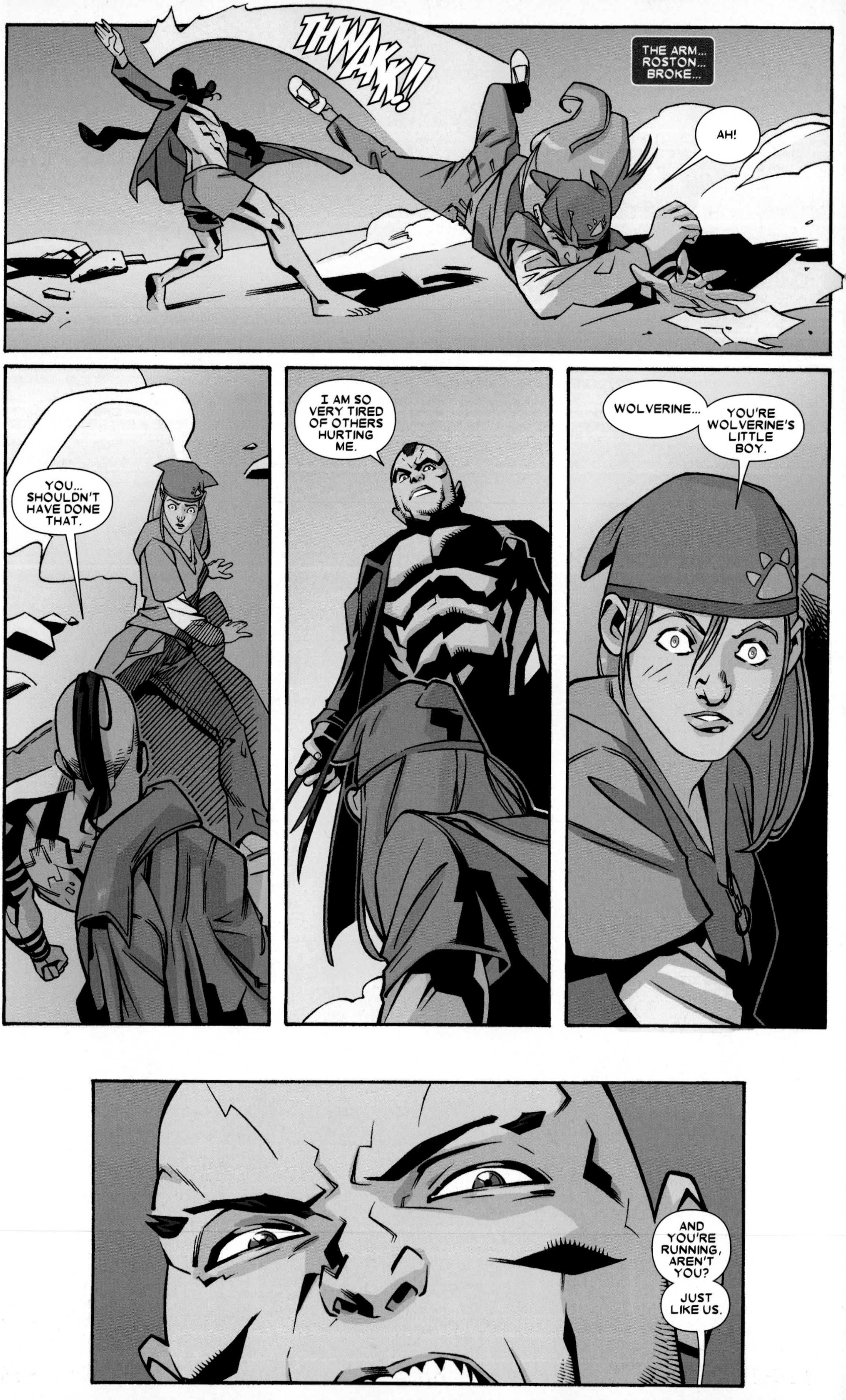
THWAKK!!
THE ARM... ROSTON... BROKE...
AH!
YOU... SHOULDN'T HAVE DONE THAT.
I AM SO VERY TIRED OF OTHERS HURTING ME.
WOLVERINE...
YOU'RE WOLVERINE'S LITTLE BOY.
AND YOU'RE RUNNING, AREN'T YOU?
JUST LIKE US.

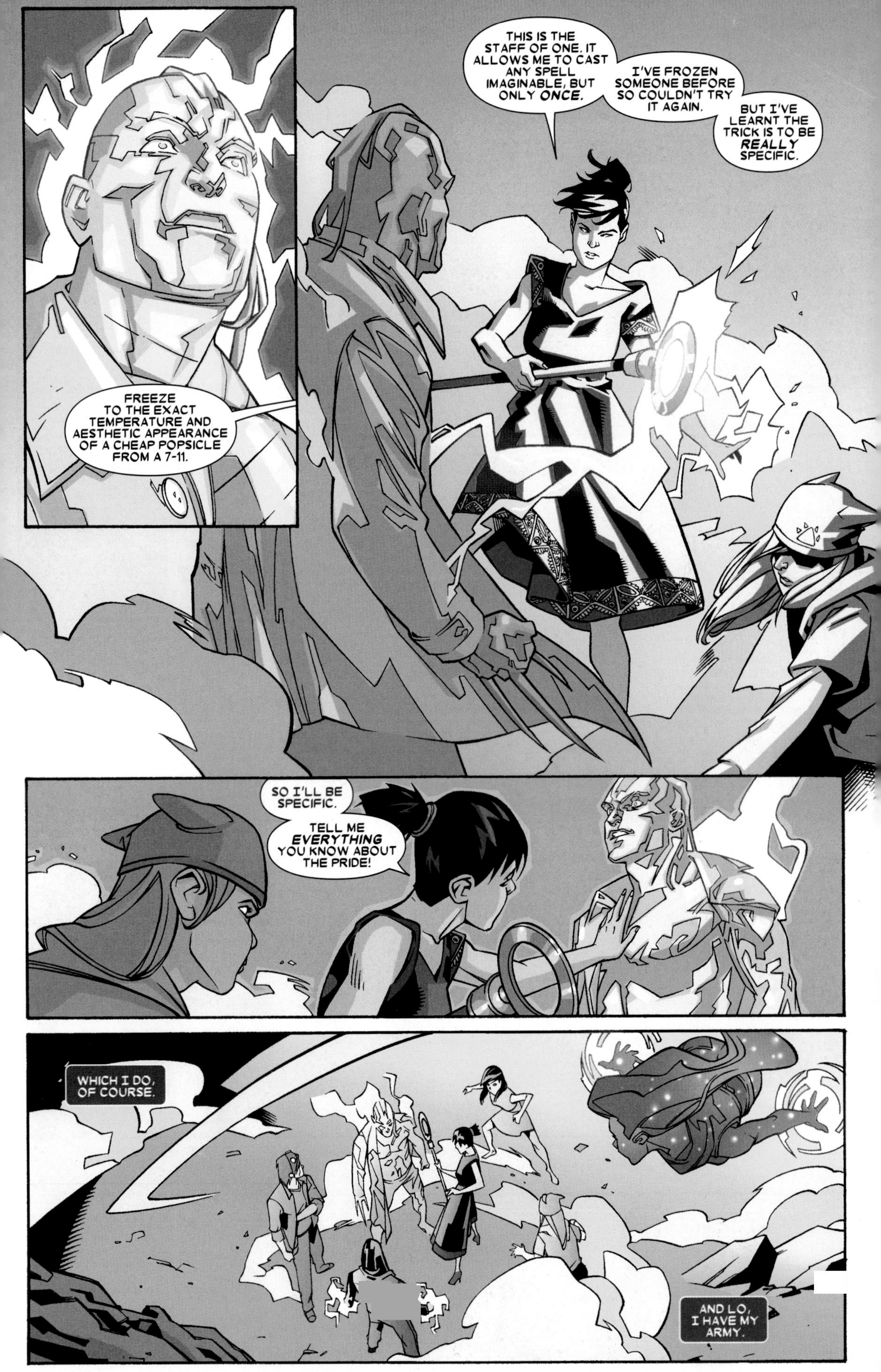
THIS IS THE STAFF OF ONE. IT ALLOWS ME TO CAST ANY SPELL IMAGINABLE, BUT ONLY ONCE.
I'VE FROZEN SOMEONE BEFORE SO COULDN'T TRY IT AGAIN.
BUT I'VE LEARNT THE TRICK IS TO BE REALLY SPECIFIC.
FREEZE TO THE EXACT TEMPERATURE AND AESTHETIC APPEARANCE OF A CHEAP POPSICLE FROM A 7-11.
SO I'LL BE SPECIFIC.
TELL ME EVERYTHING YOU KNOW ABOUT THE PRIDE!
WHICH I DO, OF COURSE.
AND LO, I HAVE MY ARMY.

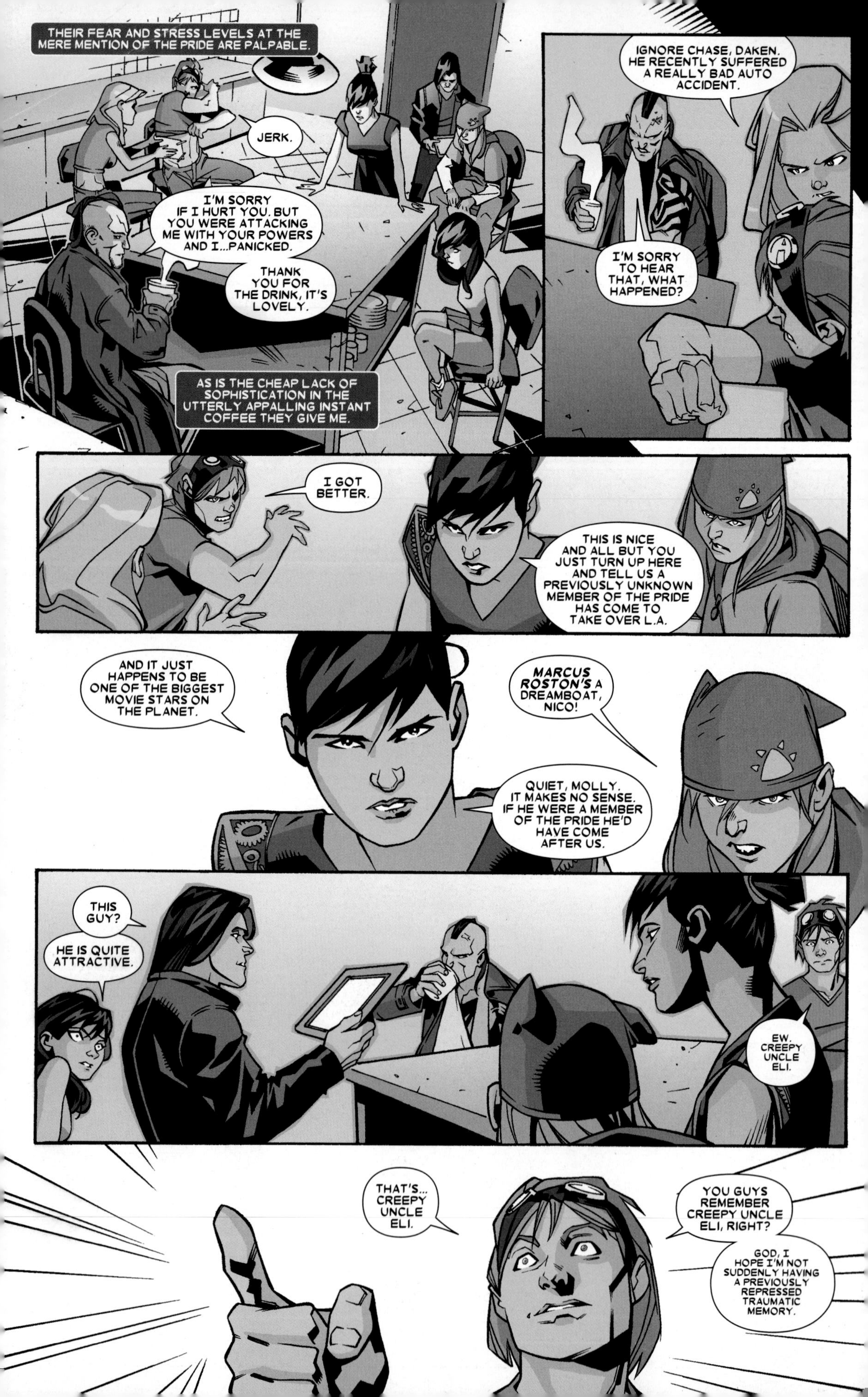
THEIR FEAR AND STRESS LEVELS AT THE MERE MENTION OF THE PRIDE ARE PALPABLE.
JERK.
I'M SORRY IF I HURT YOU. BUT YOU WERE ATTACKING ME WITH YOUR POWERS AND I...PANICKED.
THANK YOU FOR THE DRINK, IT'S LOVELY.
AS IS THE CHEAP LACK OF SOPHISTICATION IN THE UTTERLY APPALLING INSTANT COFFEE THEY GIVE ME.
IGNORE CHASE, DAKEN. HE RECENTLY SUFFERED A REALLY BAD AUTO ACCIDENT.
I'M SORRY TO HEAR THAT, WHAT HAPPENED?
I GOT BETTER.
THIS IS NICE AND ALL BUT YOU JUST TURN UP HERE AND TELL US A PREVIOUSLY UNKNOWN MEMBER OF THE PRIDE HAS COME TO TAKE OVER L.A.
AND IT JUST HAPPENS TO BE ONE OF THE BIGGEST MOVIE STARS ON THE PLANET.
MARCUS ROSTON'S A DREAMBOAT, NICO!
QUIET, MOLLY. IT MAKES NO SENSE. IF HE WERE A MEMBER OF THE PRIDE HE'D HAVE COME AFTER US.
THIS GUY?
HE IS QUITE ATTRACTIVE.
EW. CREEPY UNCLE ELI.
THAT'S... CREEPY UNCLE ELI.
YOU GUYS REMEMBER CREEPY UNCLE ELI, RIGHT?
GOD, I HOPE I'M NOT SUDDENLY HAVING A PREVIOUSLY REPRESSED TRAUMATIC MEMORY.

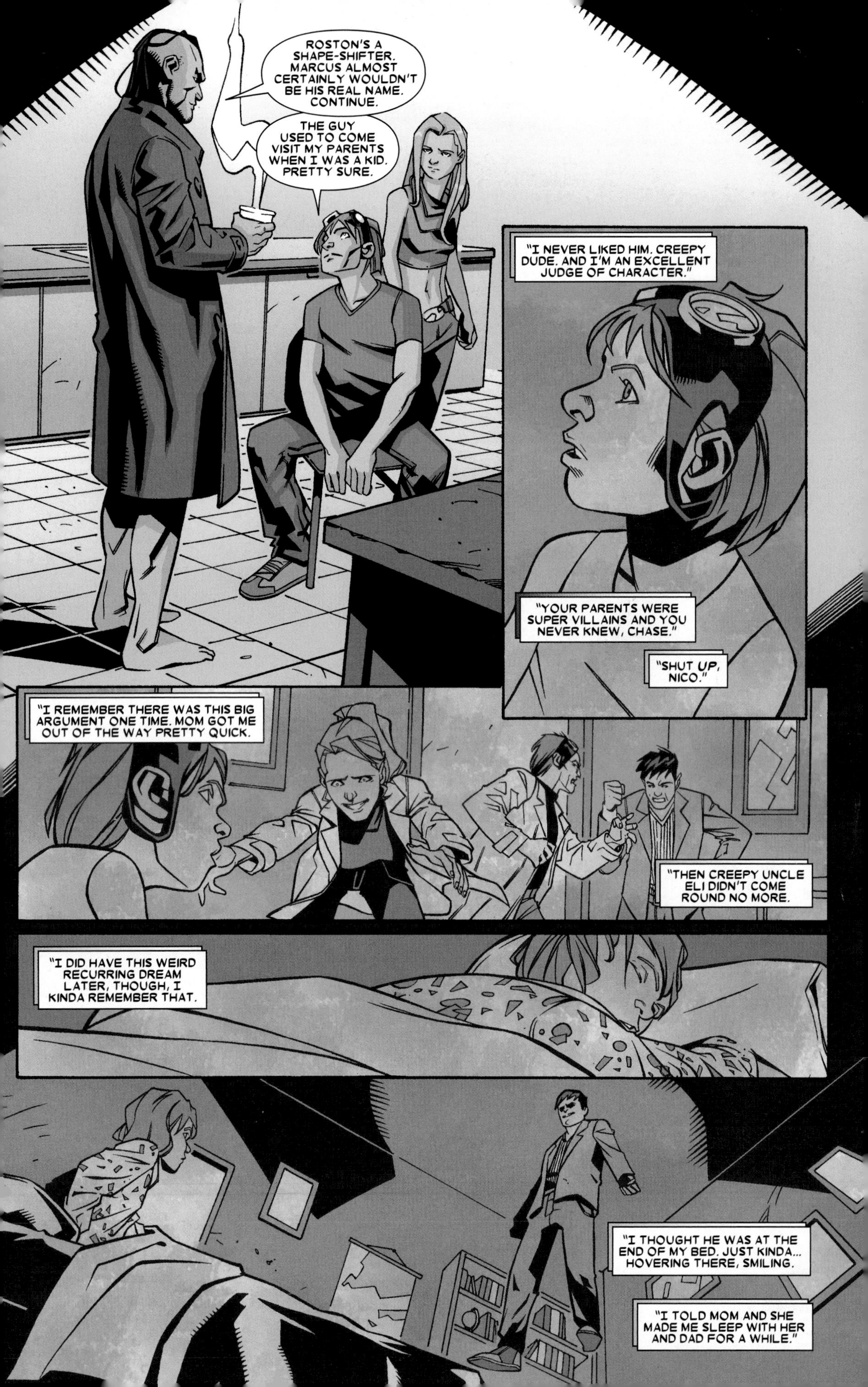

ROSTON'S A SHAPE-SHIFTER. MARCUS ALMOST CERTAINLY WOULDN'T BE HIS REAL NAME. CONTINUE.
THE GUY USED TO COME VISIT MY PARENTS WHEN I WAS A KID. PRETTY SURE.
"I NEVER LIKED HIM. CREEPY DUDE. AND I'M AN EXCELLENT JUDGE OF CHARACTER."
"YOUR PARENTS WERE SUPER VILLAINS AND YOU NEVER KNEW, CHASE."
"SHUT *UP*, NICO."
"I REMEMBER THERE WAS THIS BIG ARGUMENT ONE TIME. MOM GOT ME OUT OF THE WAY PRETTY QUICK.
"THEN CREEPY UNCLE ELI DIDN'T COME ROUND NO MORE.
"I DID HAVE THIS WEIRD RECURRING DREAM LATER, THOUGH, I KINDA REMEMBER THAT.
"I THOUGHT HE WAS AT THE END OF MY BED. JUST KINDA... HOVERING THERE, SMILING.
"I TOLD MOM AND SHE MADE ME SLEEP WITH HER AND DAD FOR A WHILE."

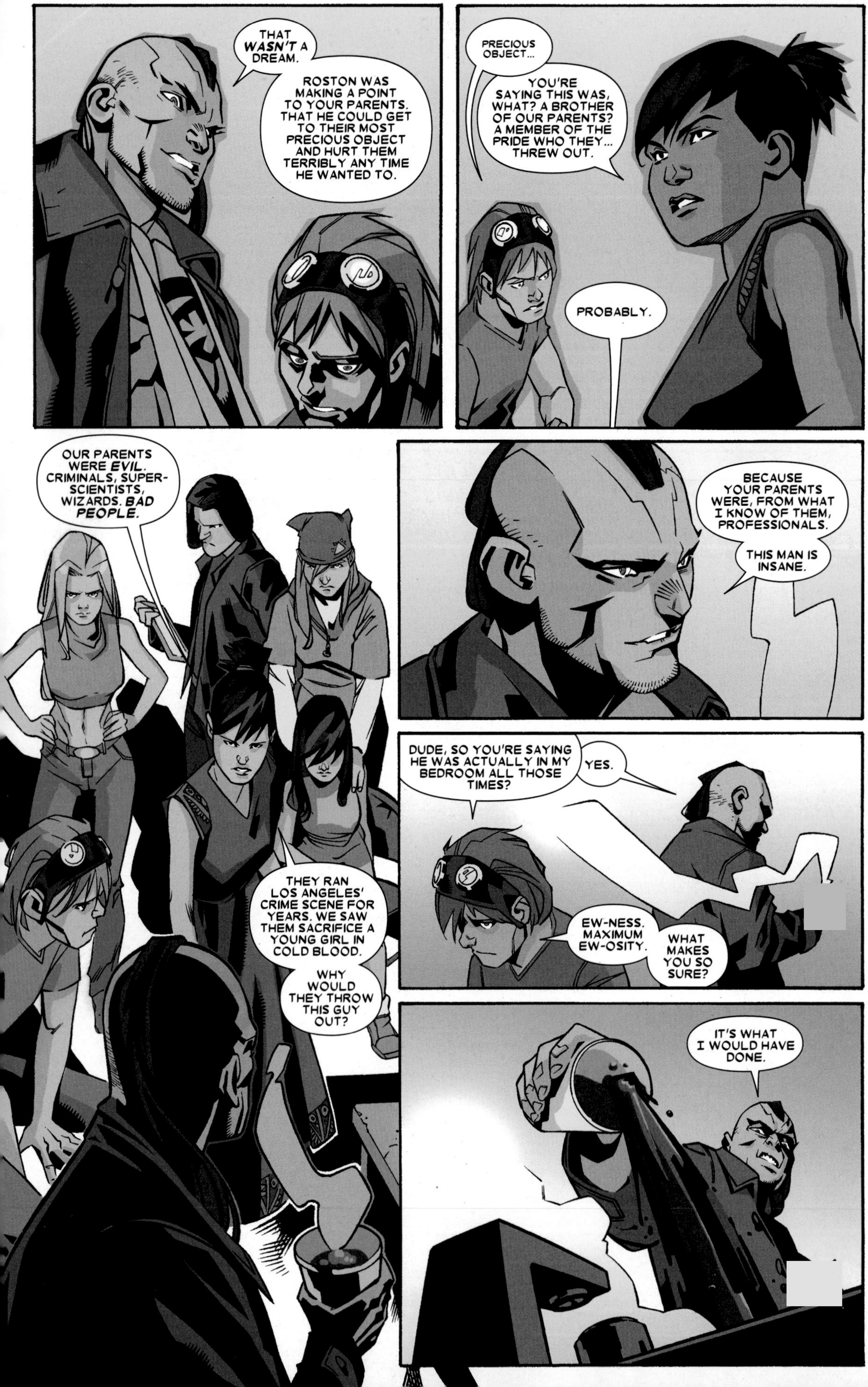
THAT WASN'T A DREAM.
ROSTON WAS MAKING A POINT TO YOUR PARENTS. THAT HE COULD GET TO THEIR MOST PRECIOUS OBJECT AND HURT THEM TERRIBLY ANY TIME HE WANTED TO.
PRECIOUS OBJECT...
YOU'RE SAYING THIS WAS, WHAT? A BROTHER OF OUR PARENTS? A MEMBER OF THE PRIDE WHO THEY... THREW OUT.
PROBABLY.
OUR PARENTS WERE EVIL. CRIMINALS, SUPER-SCIENTISTS, WIZARDS. BAD PEOPLE.
THEY RAN LOS ANGELES' CRIME SCENE FOR YEARS. WE SAW THEM SACRIFICE A YOUNG GIRL IN COLD BLOOD.
WHY WOULD THEY THROW THIS GUY OUT?
BECAUSE YOUR PARENTS WERE, FROM WHAT I KNOW OF THEM, PROFESSIONALS.
THIS MAN IS INSANE.
DUDE, SO YOU'RE SAYING HE WAS ACTUALLY IN MY BEDROOM ALL THOSE TIMES?
YES.
EW-NESS. MAXIMUM EW-OSITY.
WHAT MAKES YOU SO SURE?
IT'S WHAT I WOULD HAVE DONE.

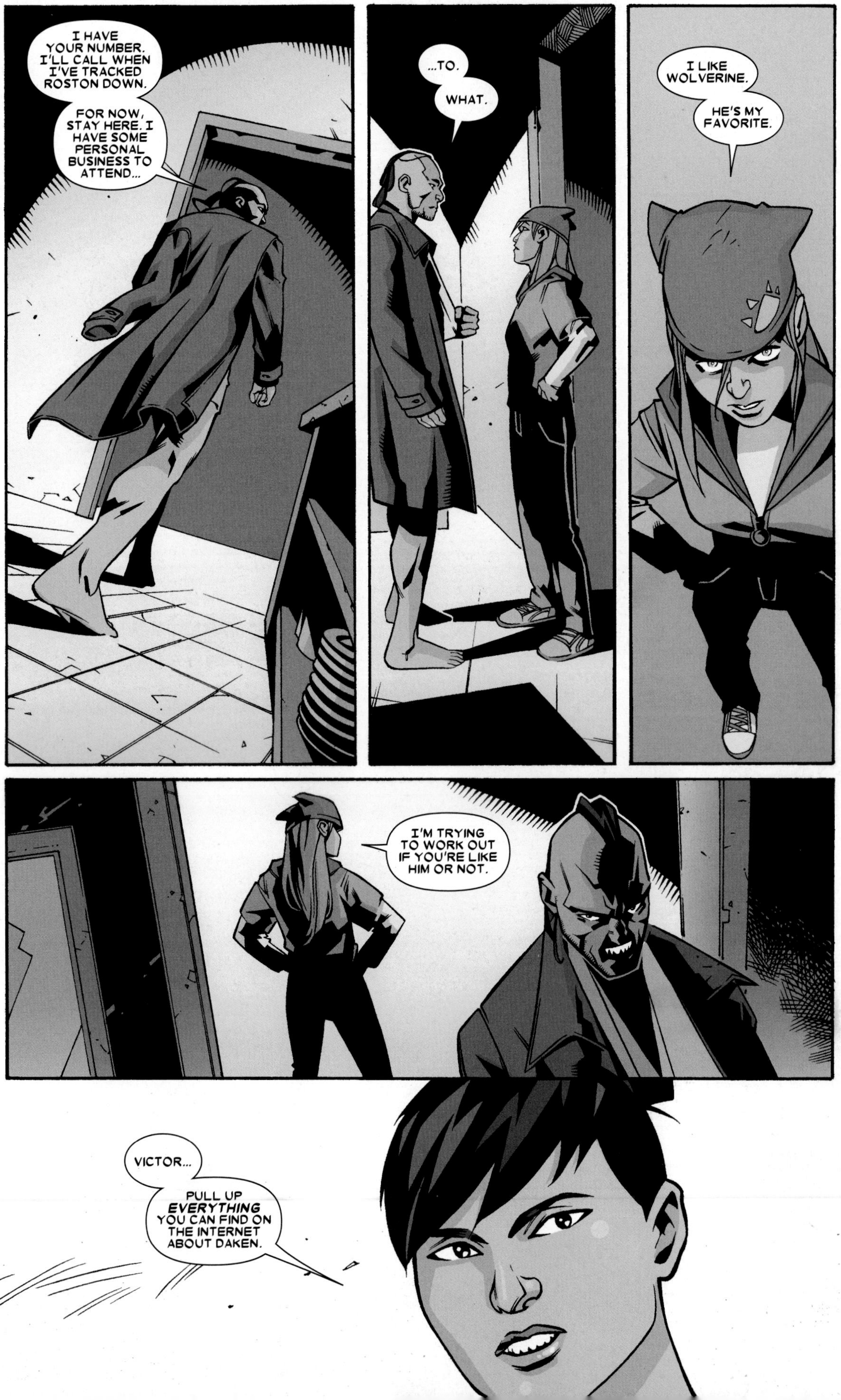

I HAVE YOUR NUMBER. I'LL CALL WHEN I'VE TRACKED ROSTON DOWN.
FOR NOW, STAY HERE. I HAVE SOME PERSONAL BUSINESS TO ATTEND...
...TO.
WHAT.
I LIKE WOLVERINE.
HE'S MY FAVORITE.
I'M TRYING TO WORK OUT IF YOU'RE LIKE HIM OR NOT.
VICTOR...
PULL UP *EVERYTHING* YOU CAN FIND ON THE INTERNET ABOUT DAKEN.

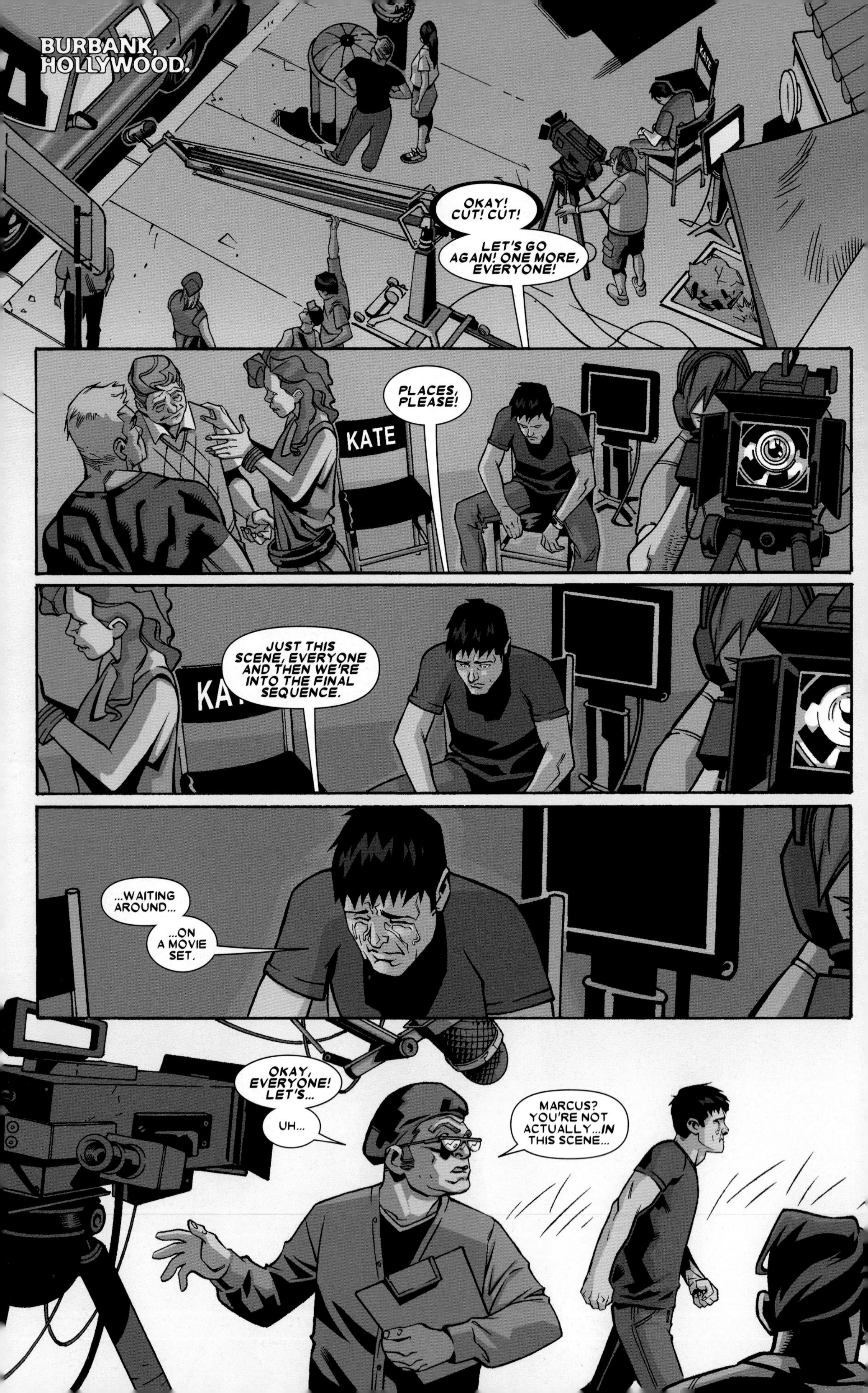
BURBANK, HOLLYWOOD.
OKAY! CUT! CUT!
LET'S GO AGAIN! ONE MORE, EVERYONE!
KATE
PLACES, PLEASE!
KATE
JUST THIS SCENE, EVERYONE AND THEN WE'RE INTO THE FINAL SEQUENCE.
...WAITING AROUND...
...ON A MOVIE SET.
OKAY, EVERYONE! LET'S...
UH...
MARCUS? YOU'RE NOT ACTUALLY...*IN* THIS SCENE...

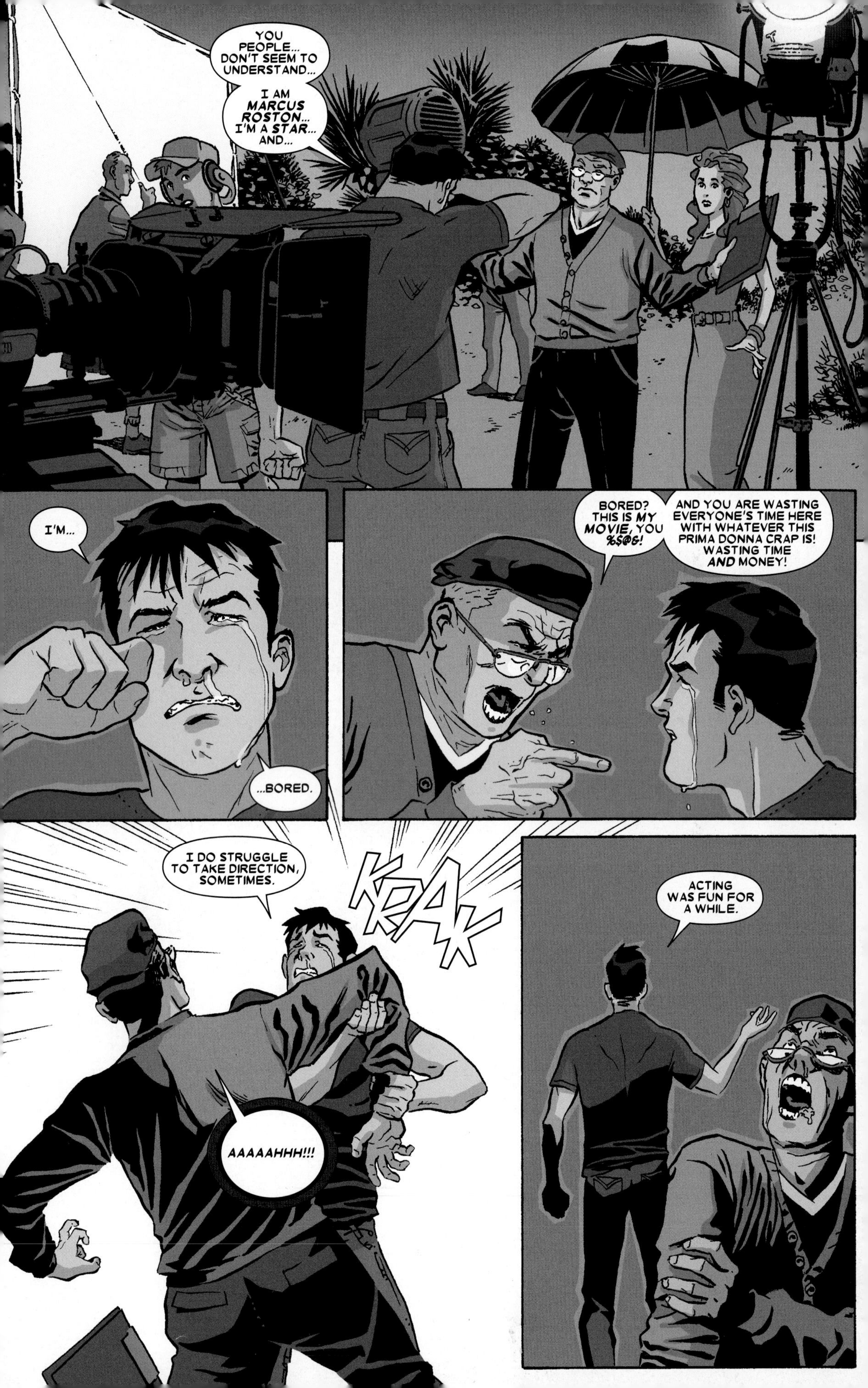

YOU PEOPLE... DON'T SEEM TO UNDERSTAND...
I AM *MARCUS ROSTON*... I'M A *STAR*... AND...
I'M...
...BORED.
BORED? THIS IS *MY MOVIE*, YOU %$@&!
AND YOU ARE WASTING EVERYONE'S TIME HERE WITH WHATEVER THIS PRIMA DONNA CRAP IS! WASTING TIME *AND* MONEY!
I DO STRUGGLE TO TAKE DIRECTION, SOMETIMES.
KRAK
AAAAAHHH!!!
ACTING WAS FUN FOR A WHILE.

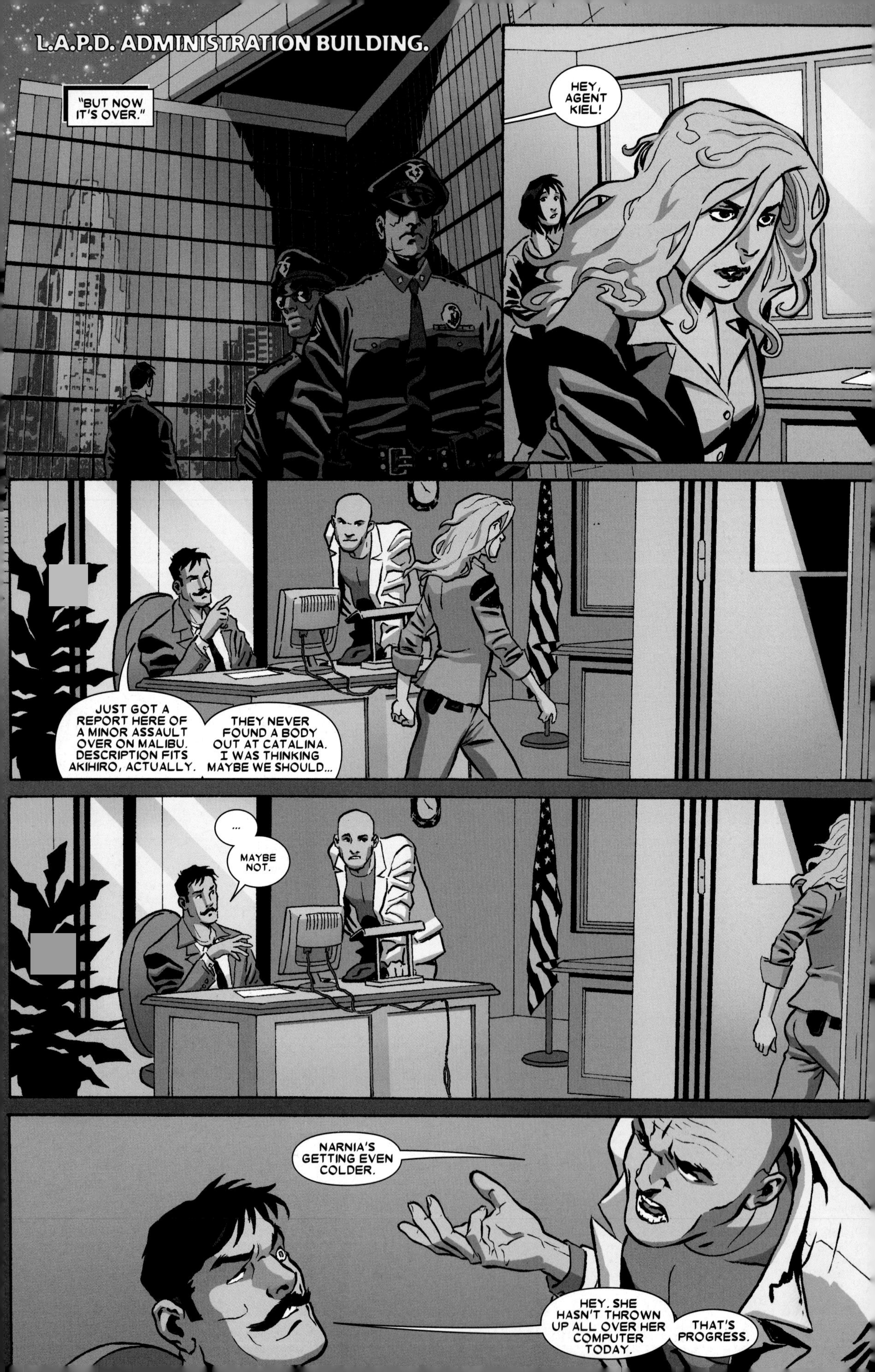
L.A.P.D. ADMINISTRATION BUILDING.
"BUT NOW IT'S OVER."
HEY, AGENT KIEL!
JUST GOT A REPORT HERE OF A MINOR ASSAULT OVER ON MALIBU. DESCRIPTION FITS AKIHIRO, ACTUALLY.
THEY NEVER FOUND A BODY OUT AT CATALINA. I WAS THINKING MAYBE WE SHOULD...
...MAYBE NOT.
NARNIA'S GETTING EVEN COLDER.
HEY. SHE HASN'T THROWN UP ALL OVER HER COMPUTER TODAY.
THAT'S PROGRESS.

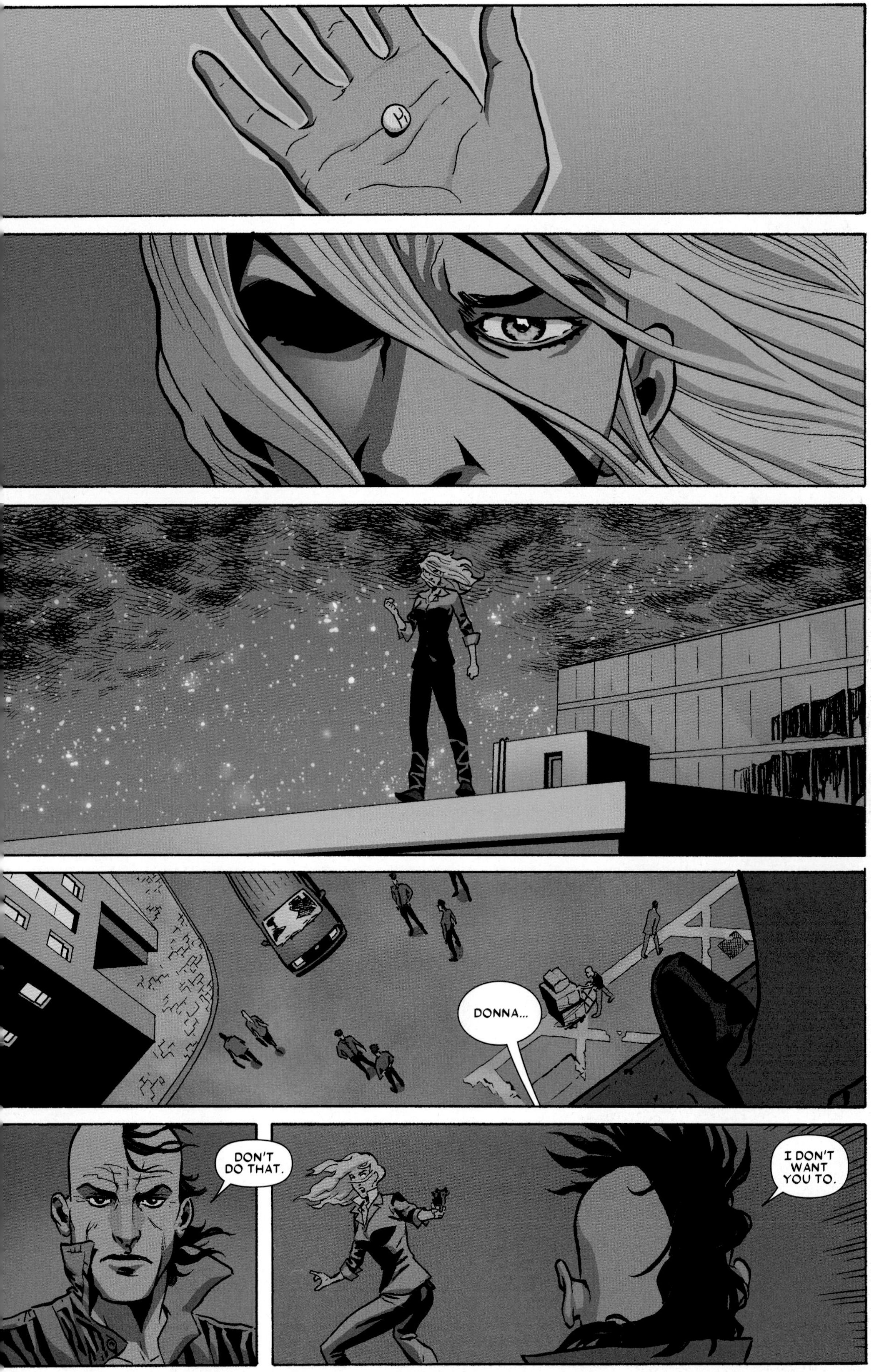
DONNA...
DON'T DO THAT.
I DON'T WANT YOU TO.

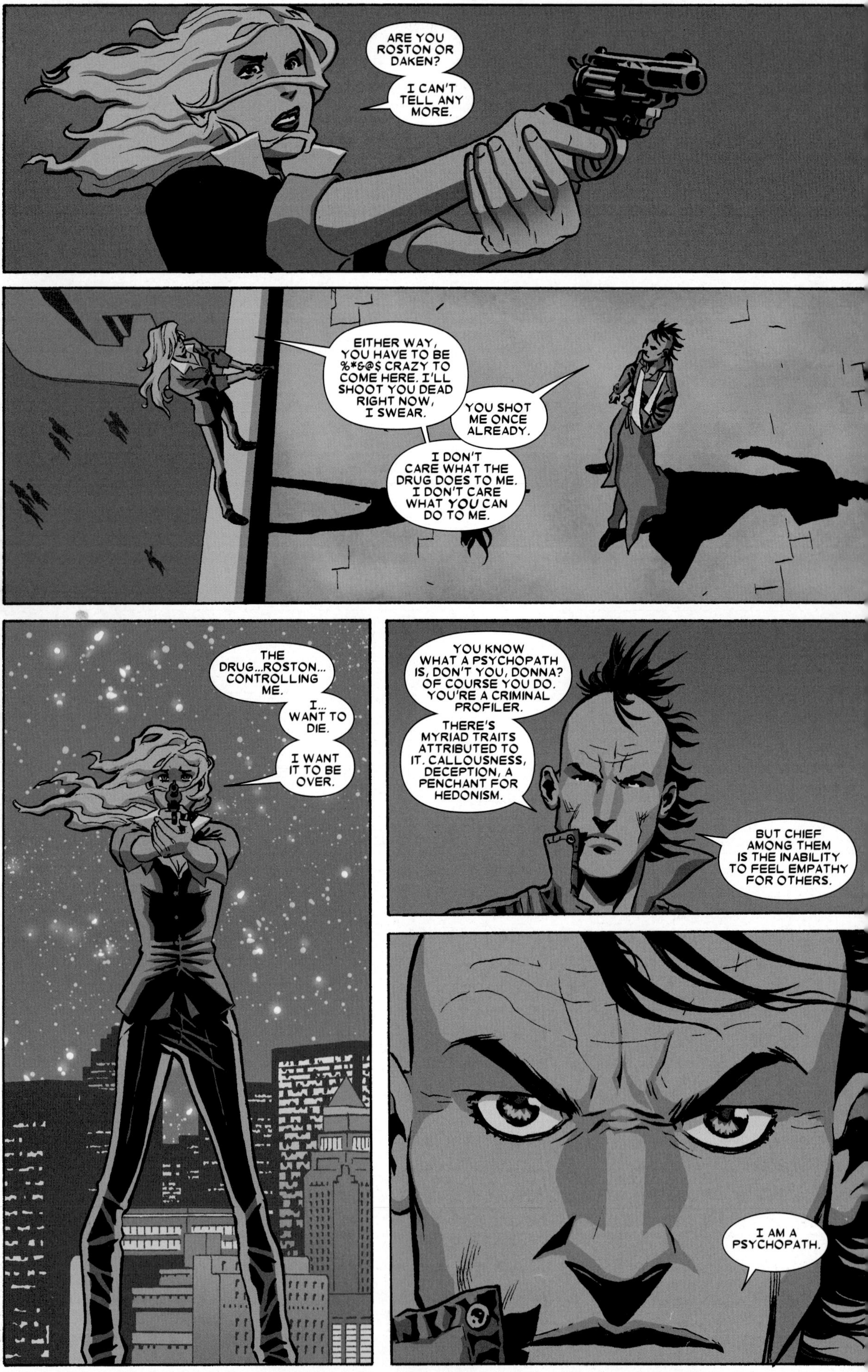
ARE YOU ROSTON OR DAKEN?
I CAN'T TELL ANY MORE.
EITHER WAY, YOU HAVE TO BE %*&@$ CRAZY TO COME HERE. I'LL SHOOT YOU DEAD RIGHT NOW, I SWEAR.
YOU SHOT ME ONCE ALREADY.
I DON'T CARE WHAT THE DRUG DOES TO ME. I DON'T CARE WHAT *YOU* CAN DO TO ME.
THE DRUG...ROSTON... CONTROLLING ME.
I... WANT TO DIE.
I WANT IT TO BE OVER.
YOU KNOW WHAT A PSYCHOPATH IS, DON'T YOU, DONNA? OF COURSE YOU DO. YOU'RE A CRIMINAL PROFILER.
THERE'S MYRIAD TRAITS ATTRIBUTED TO IT. CALLOUSNESS, DECEPTION, A PENCHANT FOR HEDONISM.
BUT CHIEF AMONG THEM IS THE INABILITY TO FEEL EMPATHY FOR OTHERS.
I AM A PSYCHOPATH.

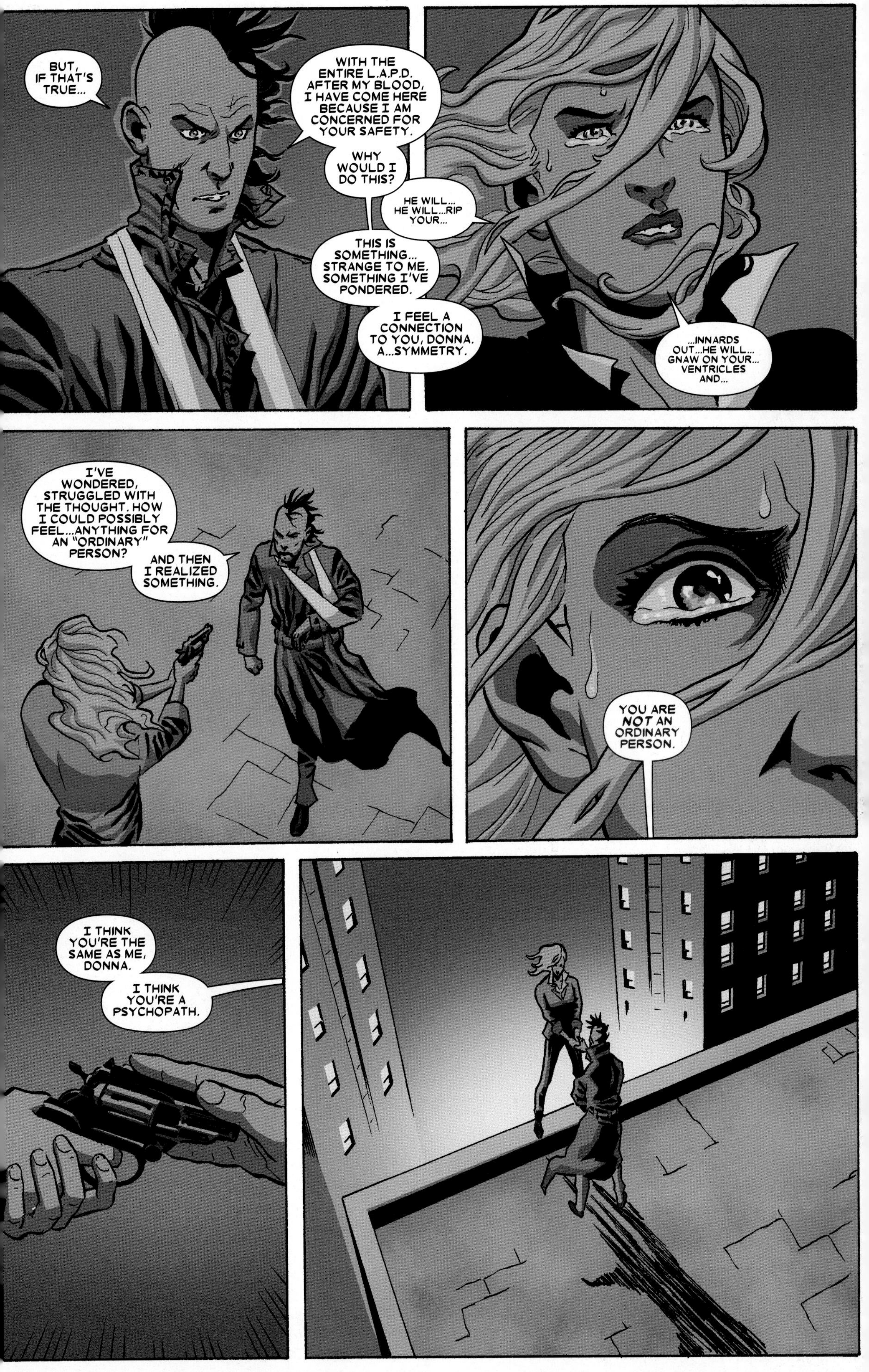
BUT, IF THAT'S TRUE...
WITH THE ENTIRE L.A.P.D. AFTER MY BLOOD, I HAVE COME HERE BECAUSE I AM CONCERNED FOR YOUR SAFETY.
WHY WOULD I DO THIS?
HE WILL... HE WILL...RIP YOUR...
THIS IS SOMETHING... STRANGE TO ME. SOMETHING I'VE PONDERED.
I FEEL A CONNECTION TO YOU, DONNA. A...SYMMETRY.
...INNARDS OUT...HE WILL... GNAW ON YOUR... VENTRICLES AND...
I'VE WONDERED, STRUGGLED WITH THE THOUGHT. HOW I COULD POSSIBLY FEEL...ANYTHING FOR AN "ORDINARY" PERSON?
AND THEN I REALIZED SOMETHING.
YOU ARE *NOT* AN ORDINARY PERSON.
I THINK YOU'RE THE SAME AS ME, DONNA.
I THINK YOU'RE A PSYCHOPATH.

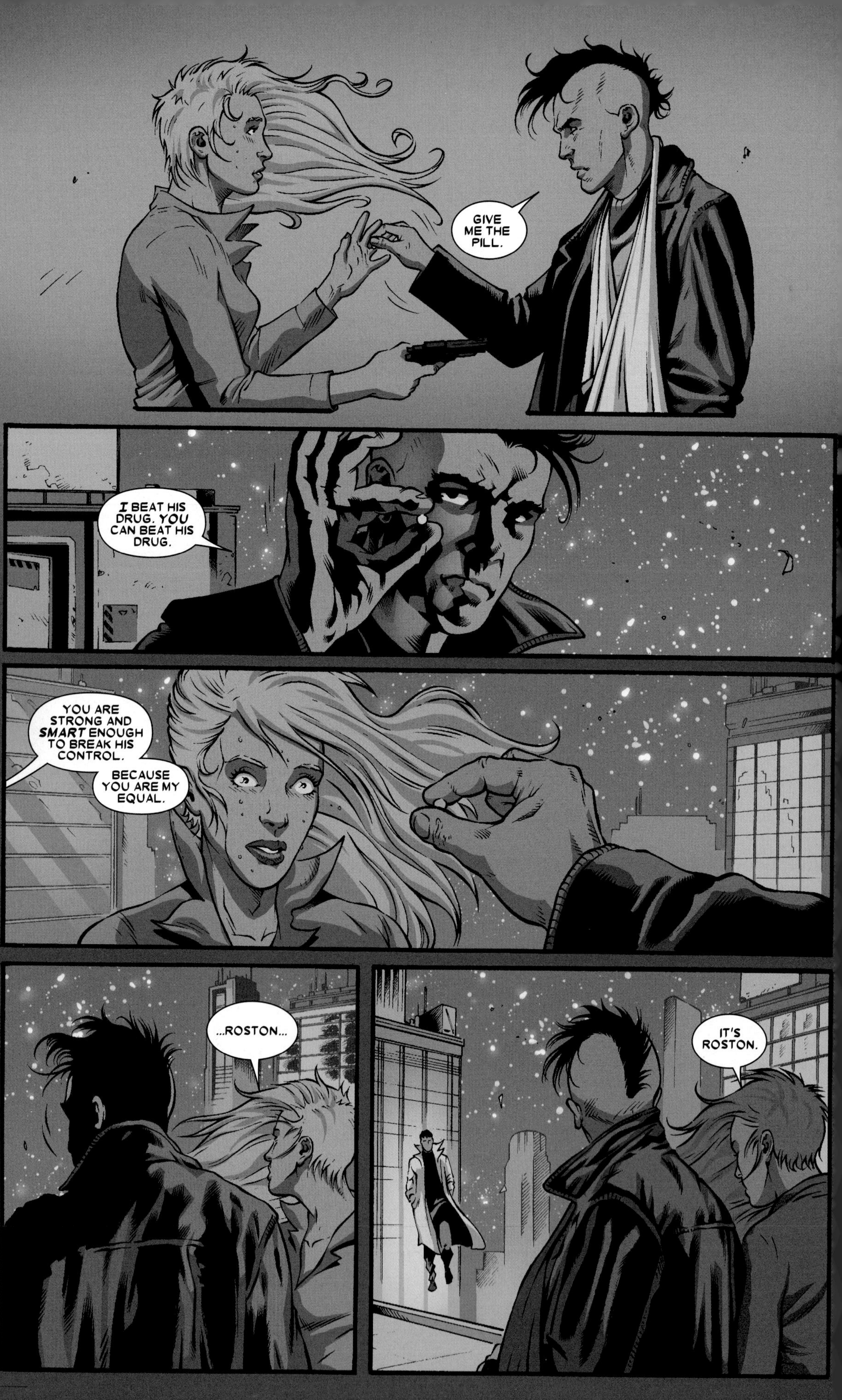
GIVE ME THE PILL.
I BEAT HIS DRUG. YOU CAN BEAT HIS DRUG.
YOU ARE STRONG AND SMART ENOUGH TO BREAK HIS CONTROL.
BECAUSE YOU ARE MY EQUAL.
...ROSTON...
IT'S ROSTON.

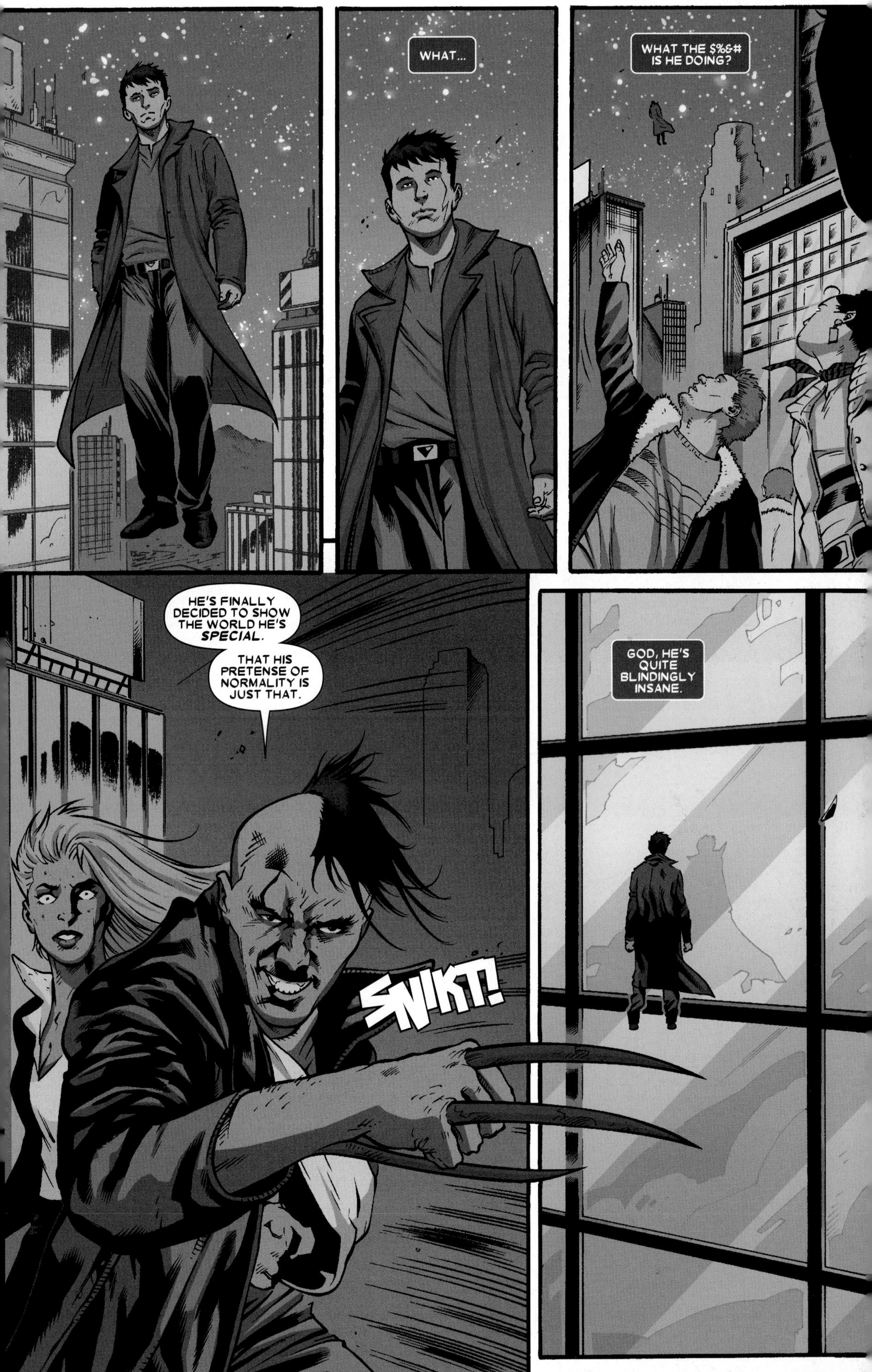
WHAT...
WHAT THE $%&# IS HE DOING?
HE'S FINALLY DECIDED TO SHOW THE WORLD HE'S SPECIAL.
THAT HIS PRETENSE OF NORMALITY IS JUST THAT.
SNIKT!
GOD, HE'S QUITE BLINDINGLY INSANE.

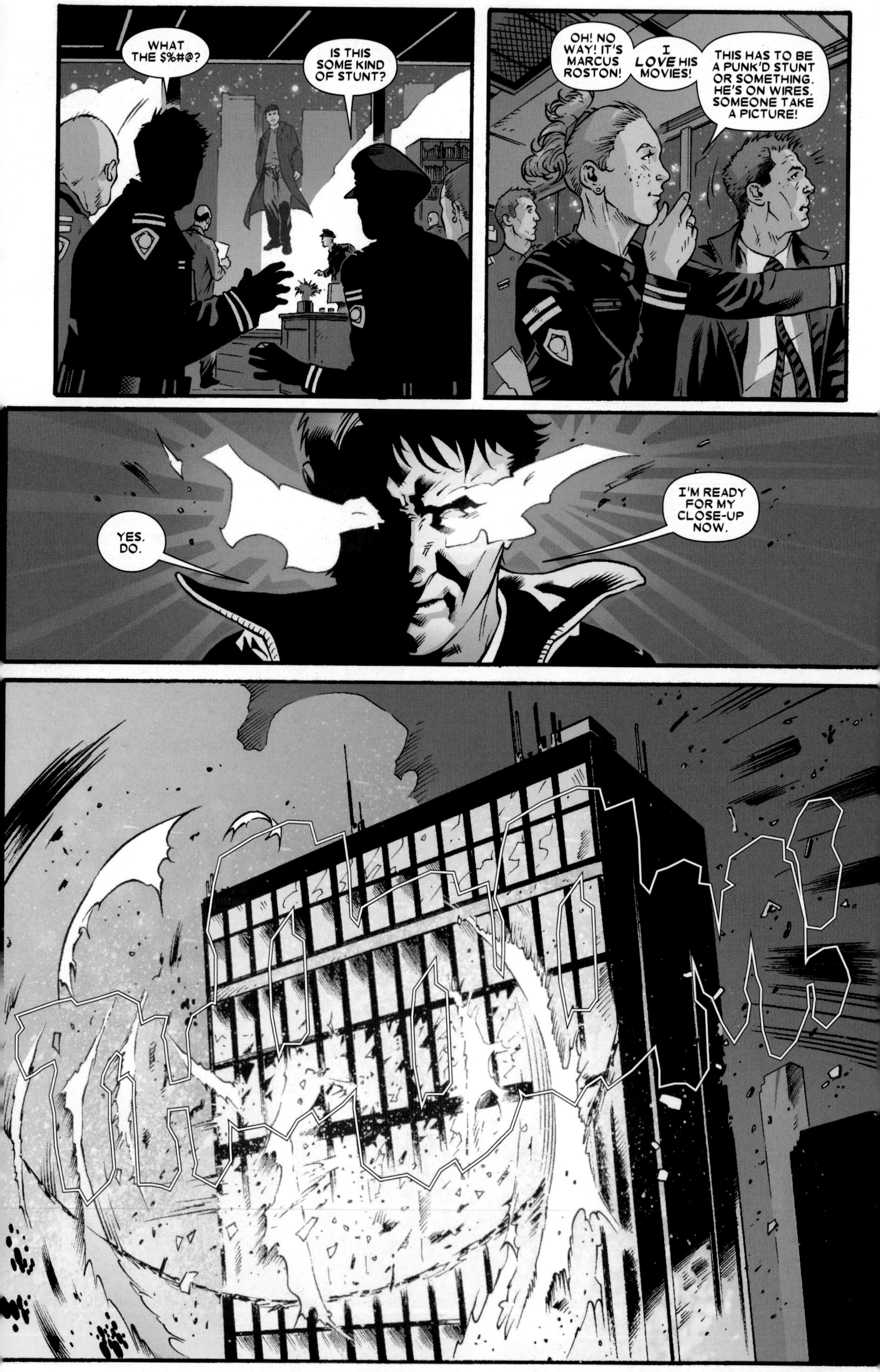
WHAT THE $%#@?
IS THIS SOME KIND OF STUNT?
OH! NO WAY! IT'S MARCUS ROSTON!
I *LOVE* HIS MOVIES!
THIS HAS TO BE A PUNK'D STUNT OR SOMETHING. HE'S ON WIRES. SOMEONE TAKE A PICTURE!
YES. DO.
I'M READY FOR MY CLOSE-UP NOW.

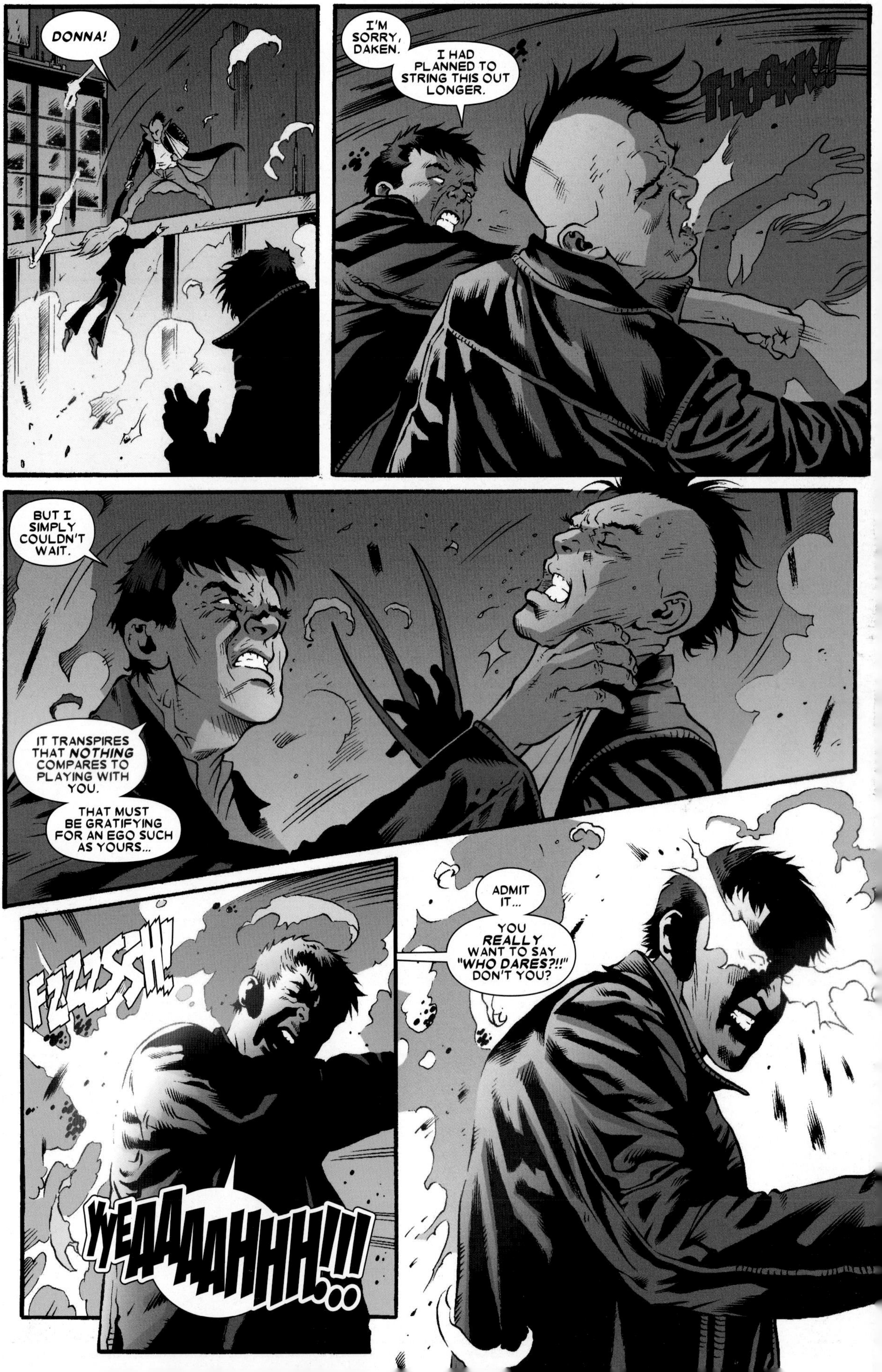
DONNA!
I'M SORRY, DAKEN.
I HAD PLANNED TO STRING THIS OUT LONGER.
THOOKK!!
BUT I SIMPLY COULDN'T WAIT.
IT TRANSPIRES THAT NOTHING COMPARES TO PLAYING WITH YOU.
THAT MUST BE GRATIFYING FOR AN EGO SUCH AS YOURS...
FZZZSH!
ADMIT IT...
YOU REALLY WANT TO SAY "WHO DARES?!!" DON'T YOU?
YYEAAAAAHHHH!!!

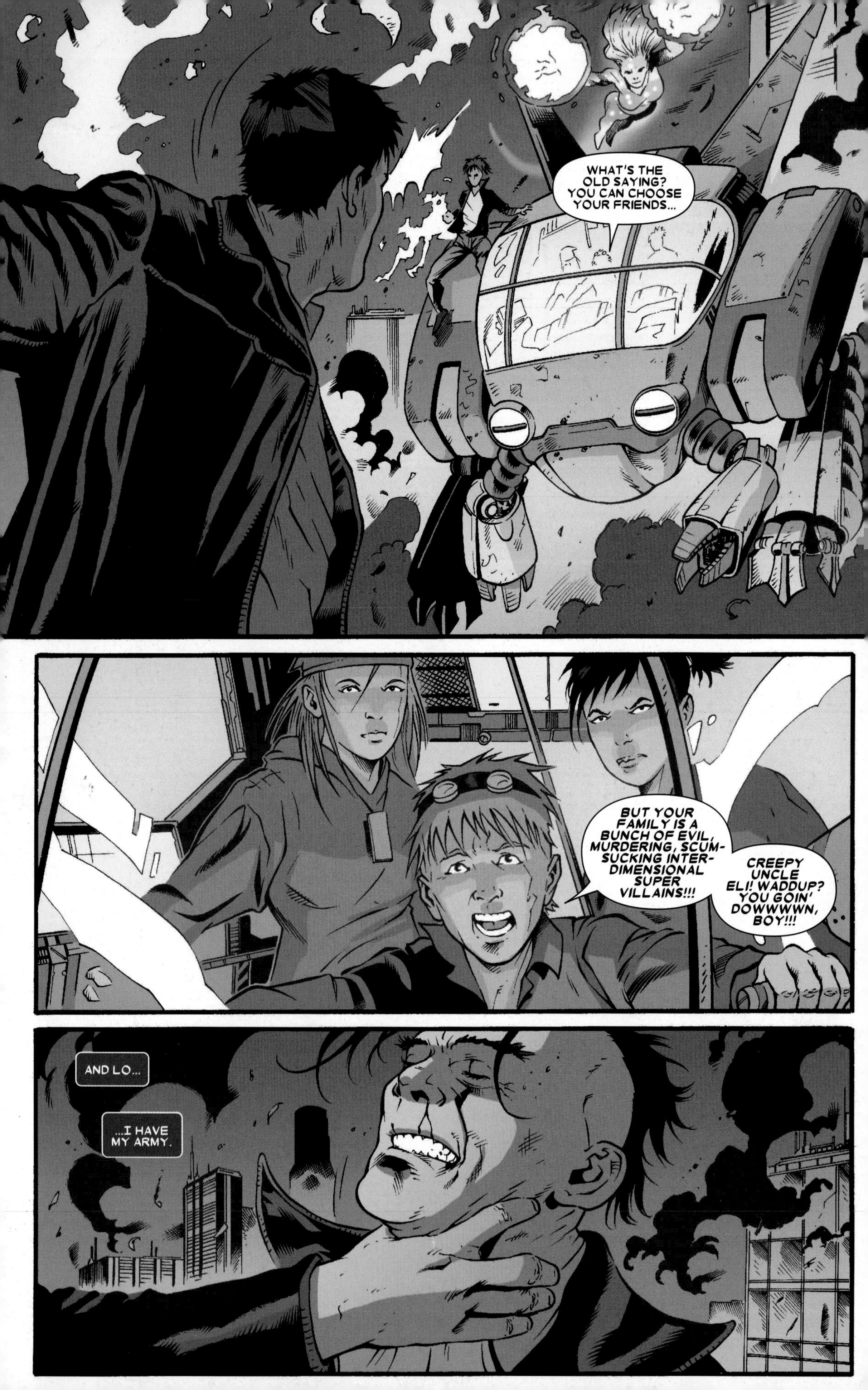
WHAT'S THE OLD SAYING? YOU CAN CHOOSE YOUR FRIENDS...
BUT YOUR FAMILY IS A BUNCH OF EVIL, MURDERING, SCUM-SUCKING INTER-DIMENSIONAL SUPER VILLAINS!!!
CREEPY UNCLE ELI! WADDUP? YOU GOIN' DOWWWWN, BOY!!!
AND LO...
...I HAVE MY ARMY.

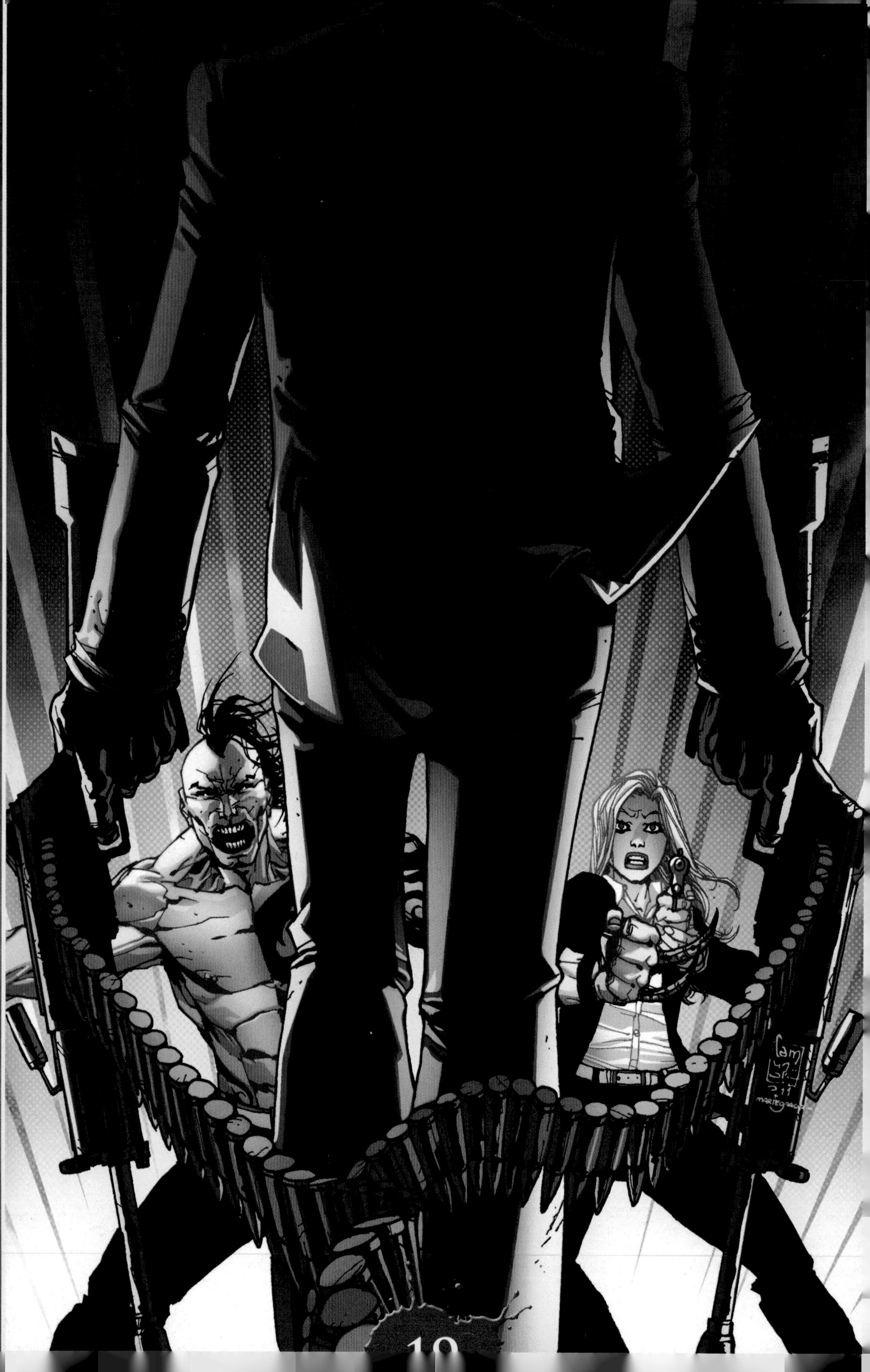

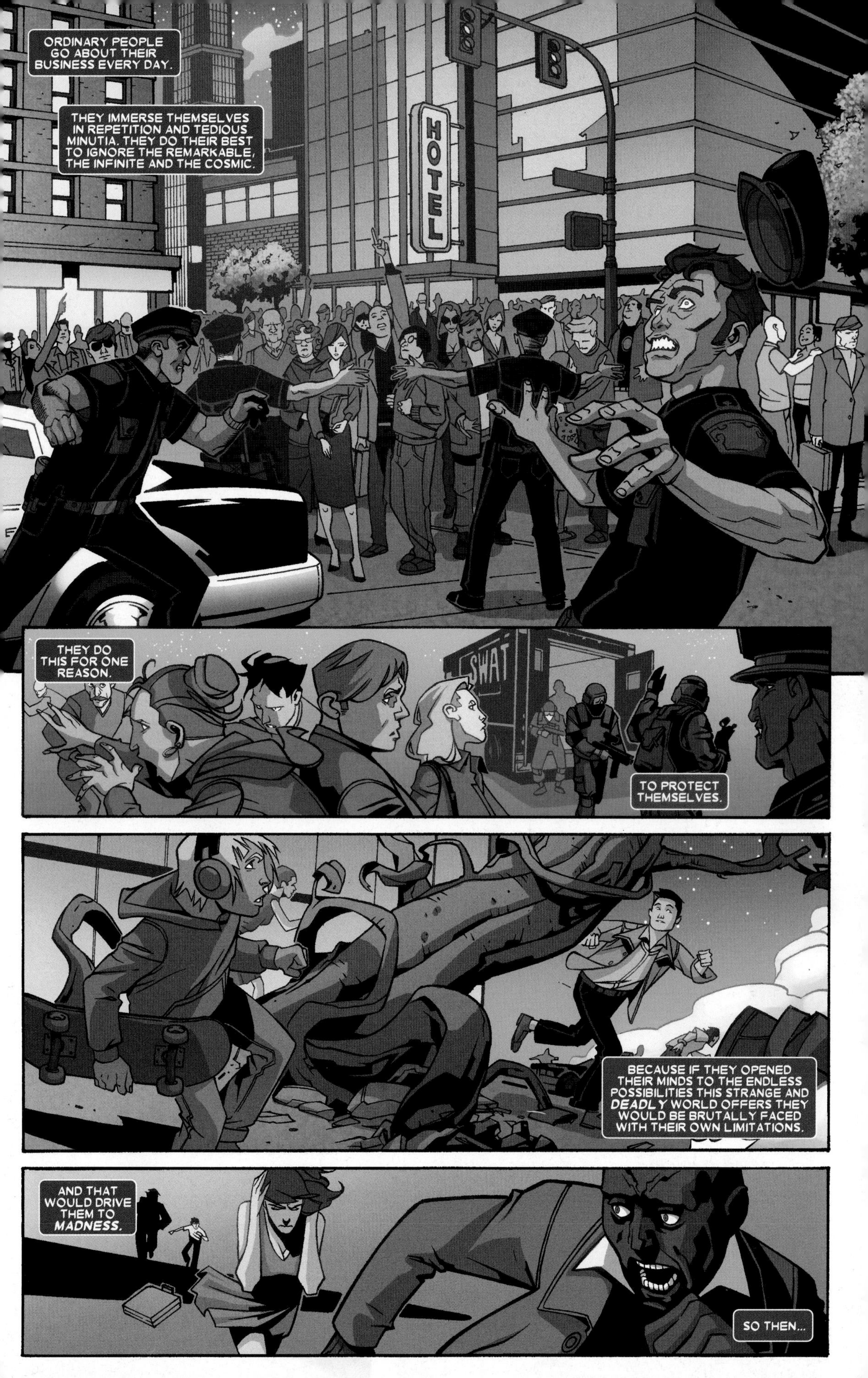
ORDINARY PEOPLE GO ABOUT THEIR BUSINESS EVERY DAY.
THEY IMMERSE THEMSELVES IN REPETITION AND TEDIOUS MINUTIA. THEY DO THEIR BEST TO IGNORE THE REMARKABLE, THE INFINITE AND THE COSMIC.
HOTEL
THEY DO THIS FOR ONE REASON.
SWAT
TO PROTECT THEMSELVES.
BECAUSE IF THEY OPENED THEIR MINDS TO THE ENDLESS POSSIBILITIES THIS STRANGE AND *DEADLY* WORLD OFFERS THEY WOULD BE BRUTALLY FACED WITH THEIR OWN LIMITATIONS.
AND THAT WOULD DRIVE THEM TO *MADNESS.*
SO THEN...

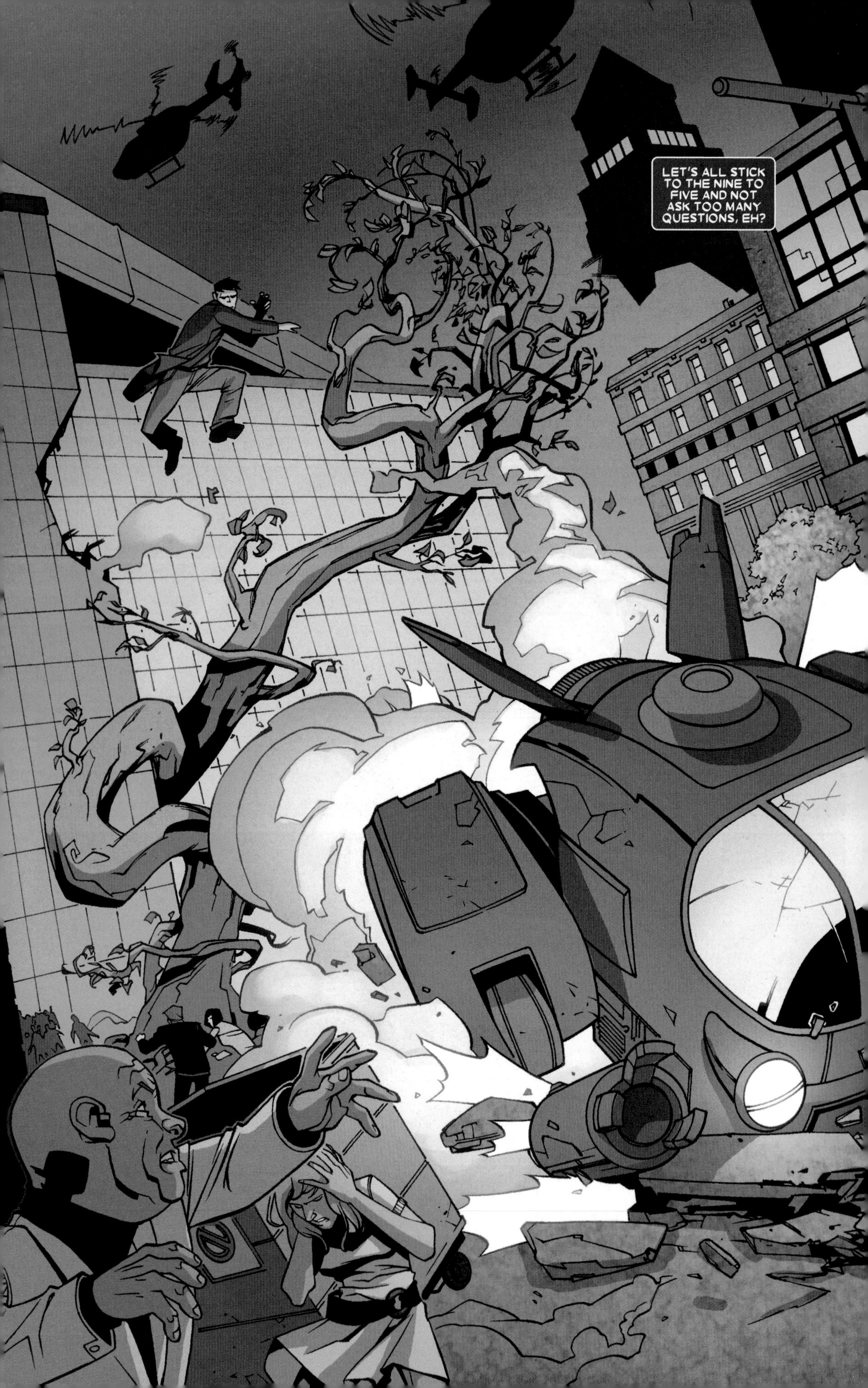
LET'S ALL STICK TO THE NINE TO FIVE AND NOT ASK TOO MANY QUESTIONS, EH?

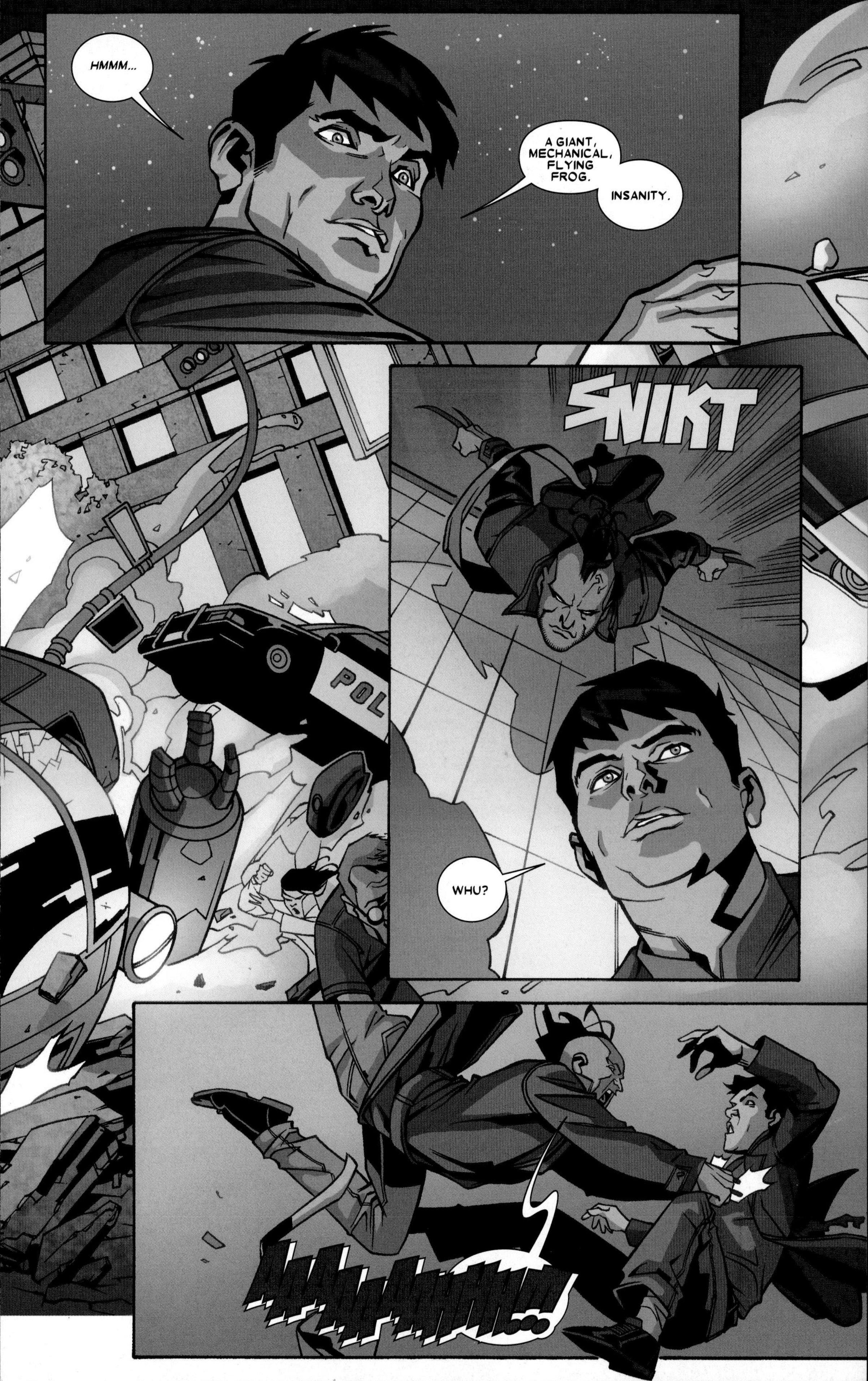
HMMM...
A GIANT, MECHANICAL, FLYING FROG.
INSANITY.
SNIKT
WHU?

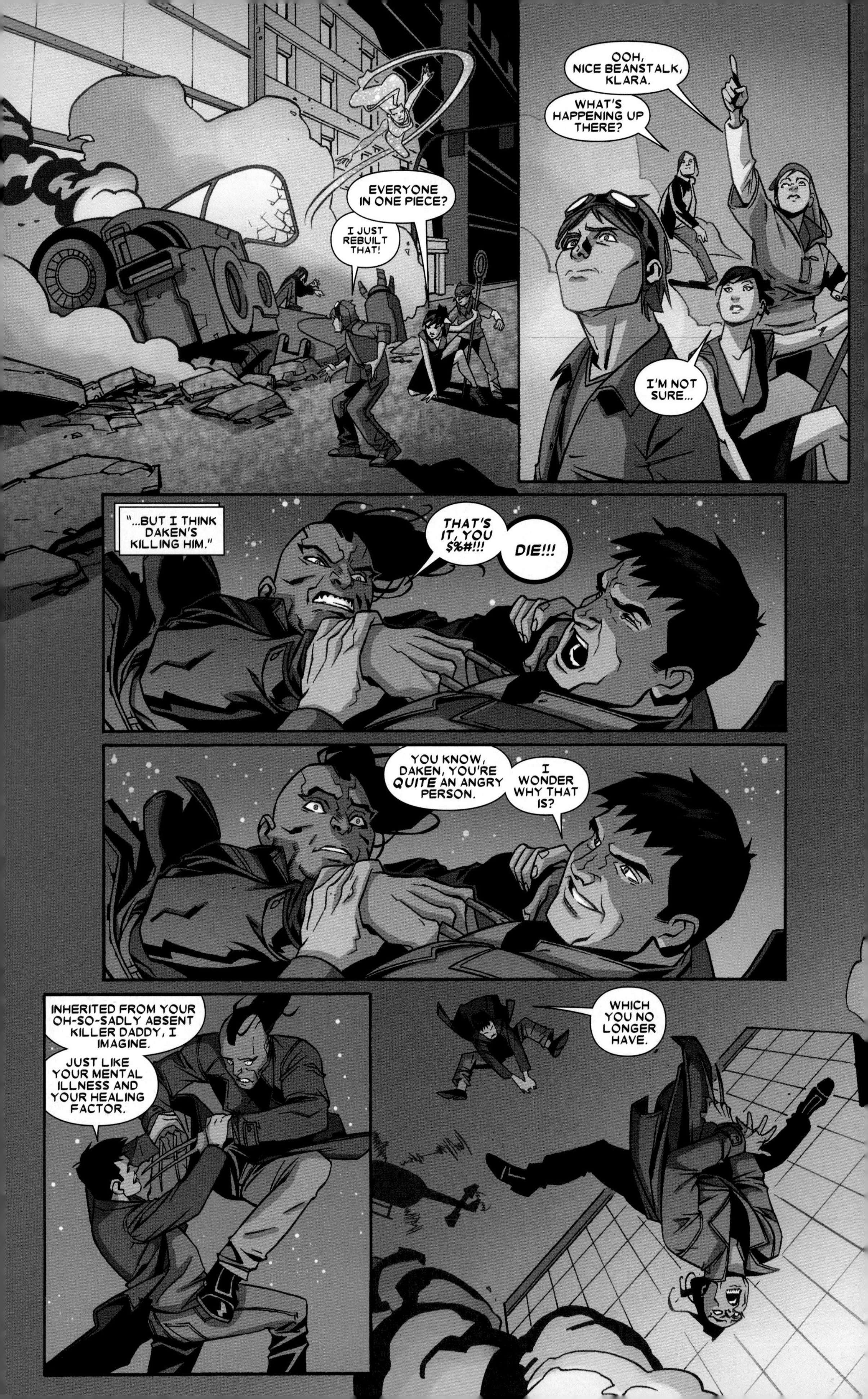
EVERYONE IN ONE PIECE?
I JUST REBUILT THAT!
OOH, NICE BEANSTALK, KLARA.
WHAT'S HAPPENING UP THERE?
I'M NOT SURE...
"...BUT I THINK DAKEN'S KILLING HIM."
THAT'S IT, YOU $%#!!!
DIE!!!
YOU KNOW, DAKEN, YOU'RE QUITE AN ANGRY PERSON.
I WONDER WHY THAT IS?
INHERITED FROM YOUR OH-SO-SADLY ABSENT KILLER DADDY, I IMAGINE.
JUST LIKE YOUR MENTAL ILLNESS AND YOUR HEALING FACTOR.
WHICH YOU NO LONGER HAVE.

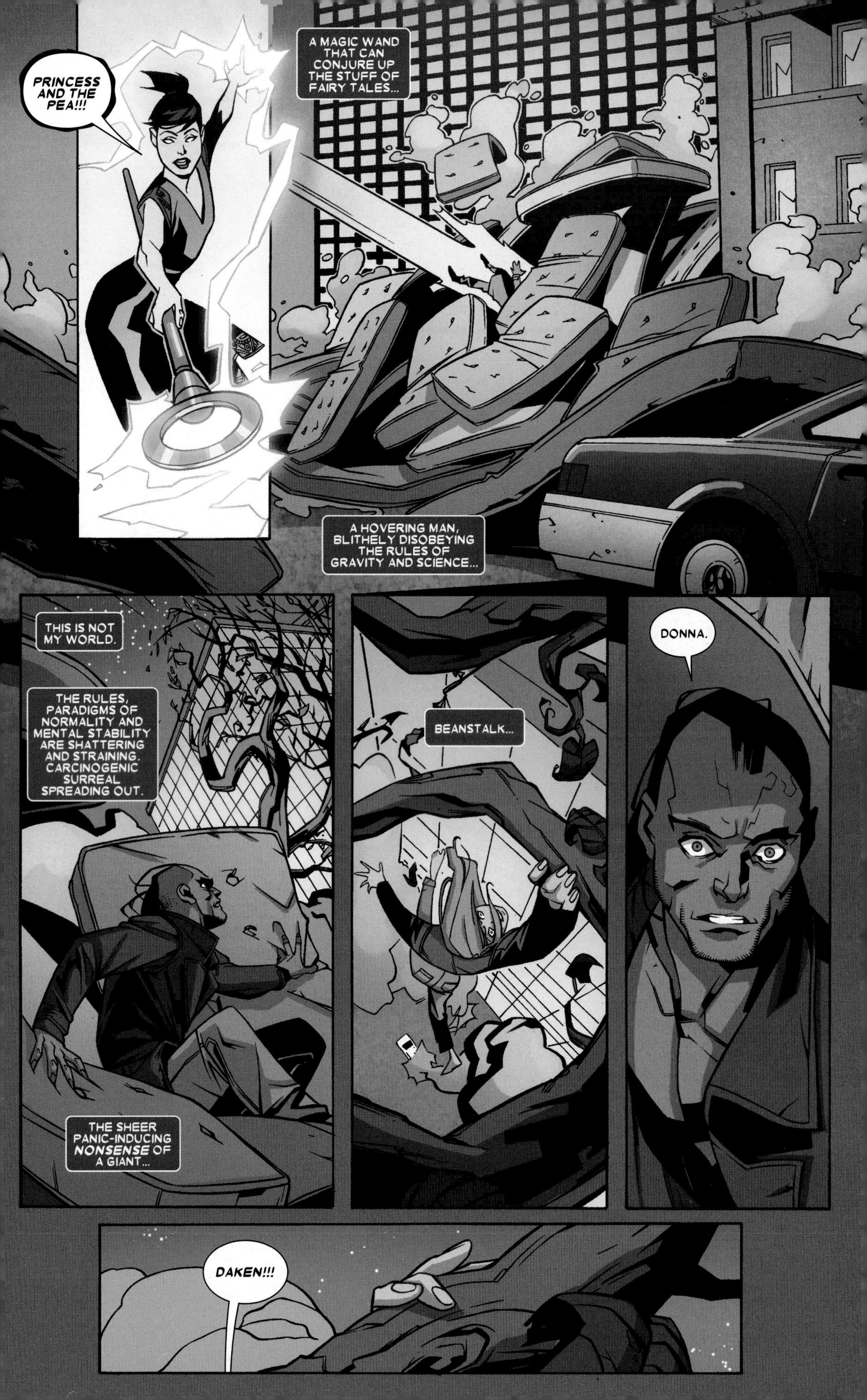
PRINCESS AND THE PEA!!!
A MAGIC WAND THAT CAN CONJURE UP THE STUFF OF FAIRY TALES...
A HOVERING MAN, BLITHELY DISOBEYING THE RULES OF GRAVITY AND SCIENCE...
THIS IS NOT MY WORLD.
THE RULES, PARADIGMS OF NORMALITY AND MENTAL STABILITY ARE SHATTERING AND STRAINING. CARCINOGENIC SURREAL SPREADING OUT.
THE SHEER PANIC-INDUCING NONSENSE OF A GIANT...
BEANSTALK...
DONNA.
DAKEN!!!

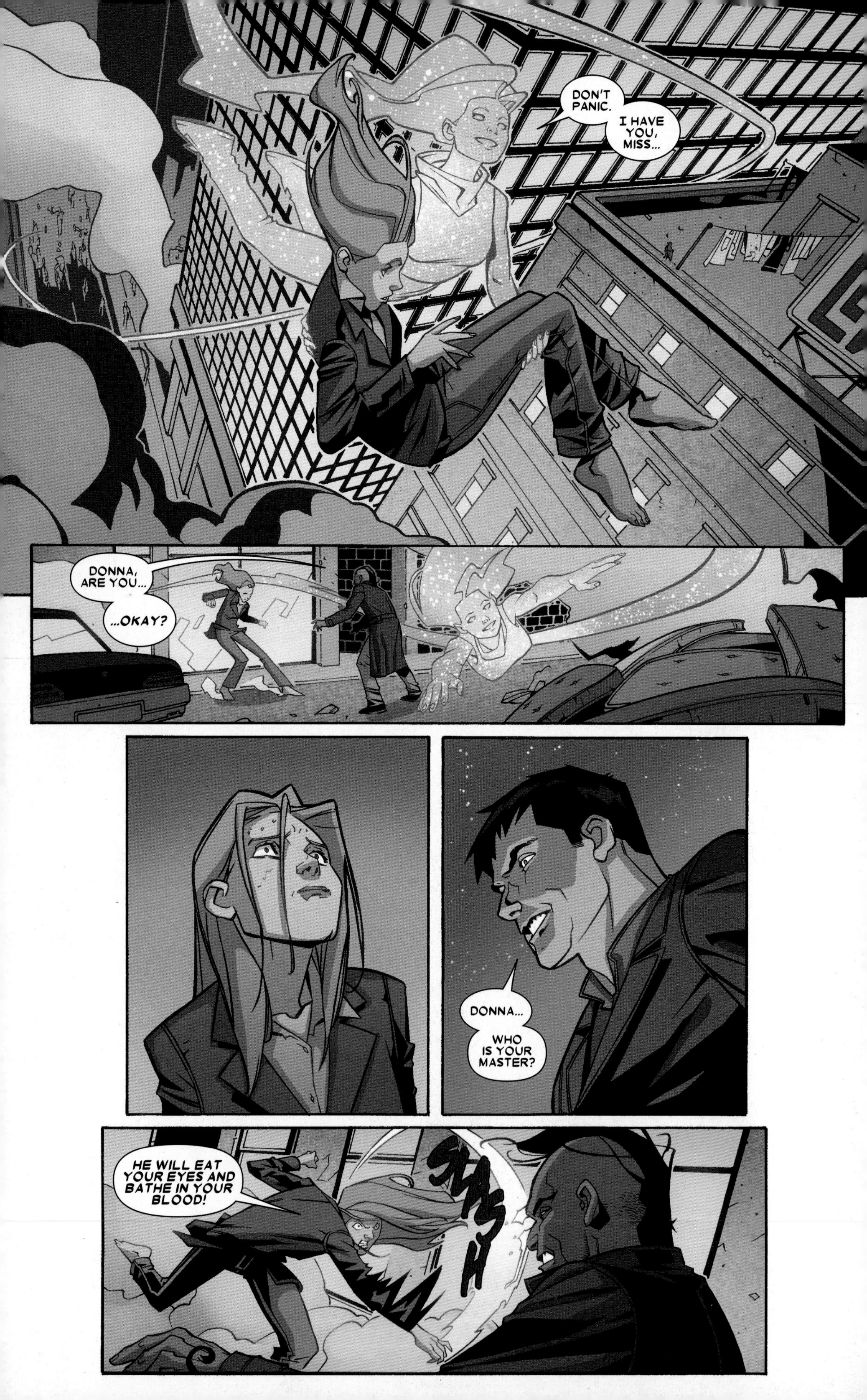
DON'T PANIC.
I HAVE YOU, MISS...
DONNA, ARE YOU...
...OKAY?
DONNA...
WHO IS YOUR MASTER?
HE WILL EAT YOUR EYES AND BATHE IN YOUR BLOOD!
SMASH

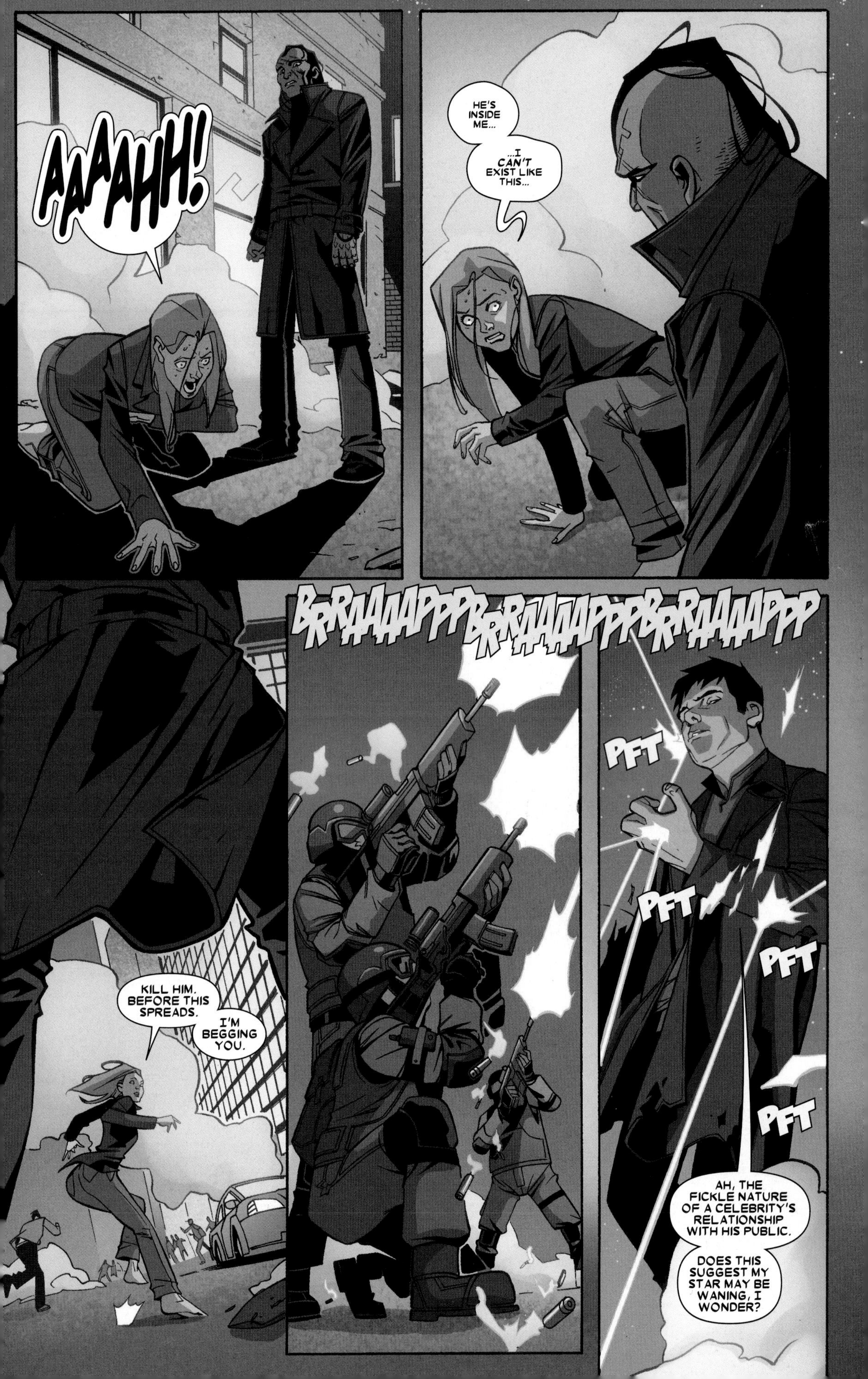
AAAAHH!
HE'S INSIDE ME...
...I CAN'T EXIST LIKE THIS...
BRRAAAAAPPP BRRAAAAAPPP BRRAAAAAPPP
KILL HIM. BEFORE THIS SPREADS.
I'M BEGGING YOU.
PFT
PFT
PFT
PFT
AH, THE FICKLE NATURE OF A CELEBRITY'S RELATIONSHIP WITH HIS PUBLIC.
DOES THIS SUGGEST MY STAR MAY BE WANING, I WONDER?

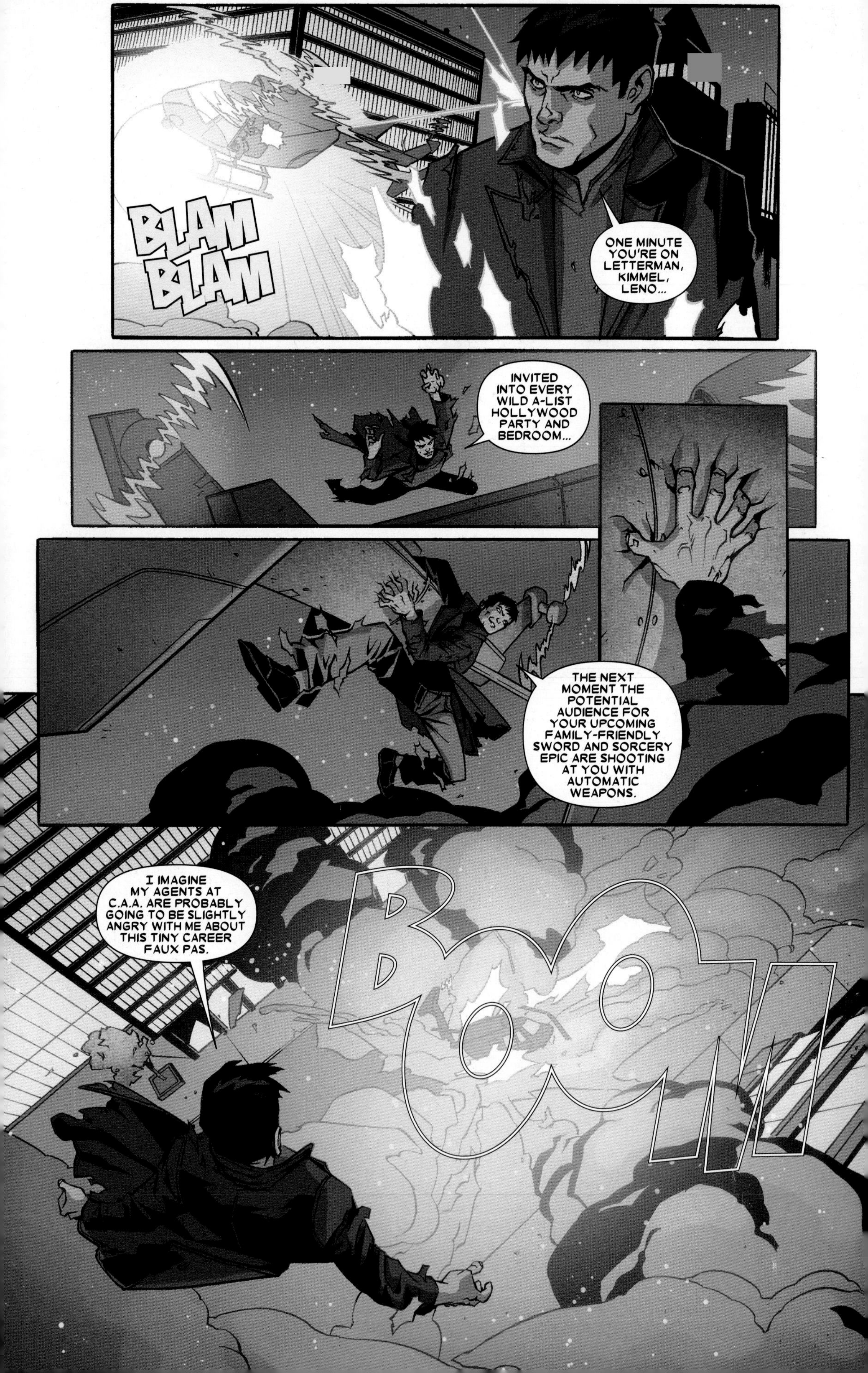
BLAM BLAM
ONE MINUTE YOU'RE ON LETTERMAN, KIMMEL, LENO...
INVITED INTO EVERY WILD A-LIST HOLLYWOOD PARTY AND BEDROOM...
THE NEXT MOMENT THE POTENTIAL AUDIENCE FOR YOUR UPCOMING FAMILY-FRIENDLY SWORD AND SORCERY EPIC ARE SHOOTING AT YOU WITH AUTOMATIC WEAPONS.
I IMAGINE MY AGENTS AT C.A.A. ARE PROBABLY GOING TO BE SLIGHTLY ANGRY WITH ME ABOUT THIS TINY CAREER FAUX PAS.
BOOM

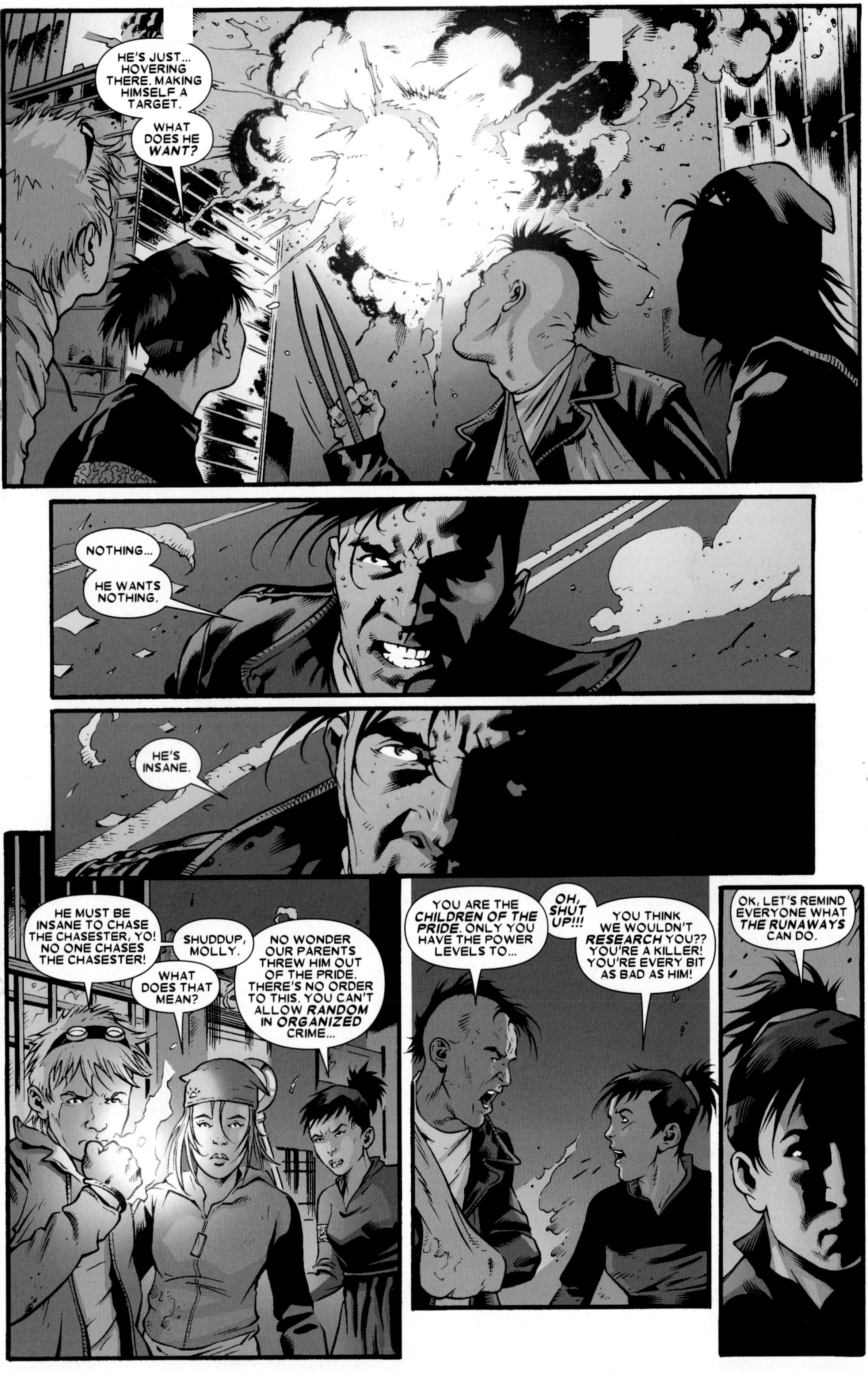
HE'S JUST... HOVERING THERE. MAKING HIMSELF A TARGET.
WHAT DOES HE WANT?
NOTHING...
HE WANTS NOTHING.
HE'S INSANE.
HE MUST BE INSANE TO CHASE THE CHASESTER, YO! NO ONE CHASES THE CHASESTER!
SHUDDUP, MOLLY.
WHAT DOES THAT MEAN?
NO WONDER OUR PARENTS THREW HIM OUT OF THE PRIDE. THERE'S NO ORDER TO THIS. YOU CAN'T ALLOW RANDOM IN ORGANIZED CRIME...
YOU ARE THE CHILDREN OF THE PRIDE. ONLY YOU HAVE THE POWER LEVELS TO...
OH, SHUT UP!!!
YOU THINK WE WOULDN'T RESEARCH YOU?? YOU'RE A KILLER! YOU'RE EVERY BIT AS BAD AS HIM!
OK, LET'S REMIND EVERYONE WHAT THE RUNAWAYS CAN DO.

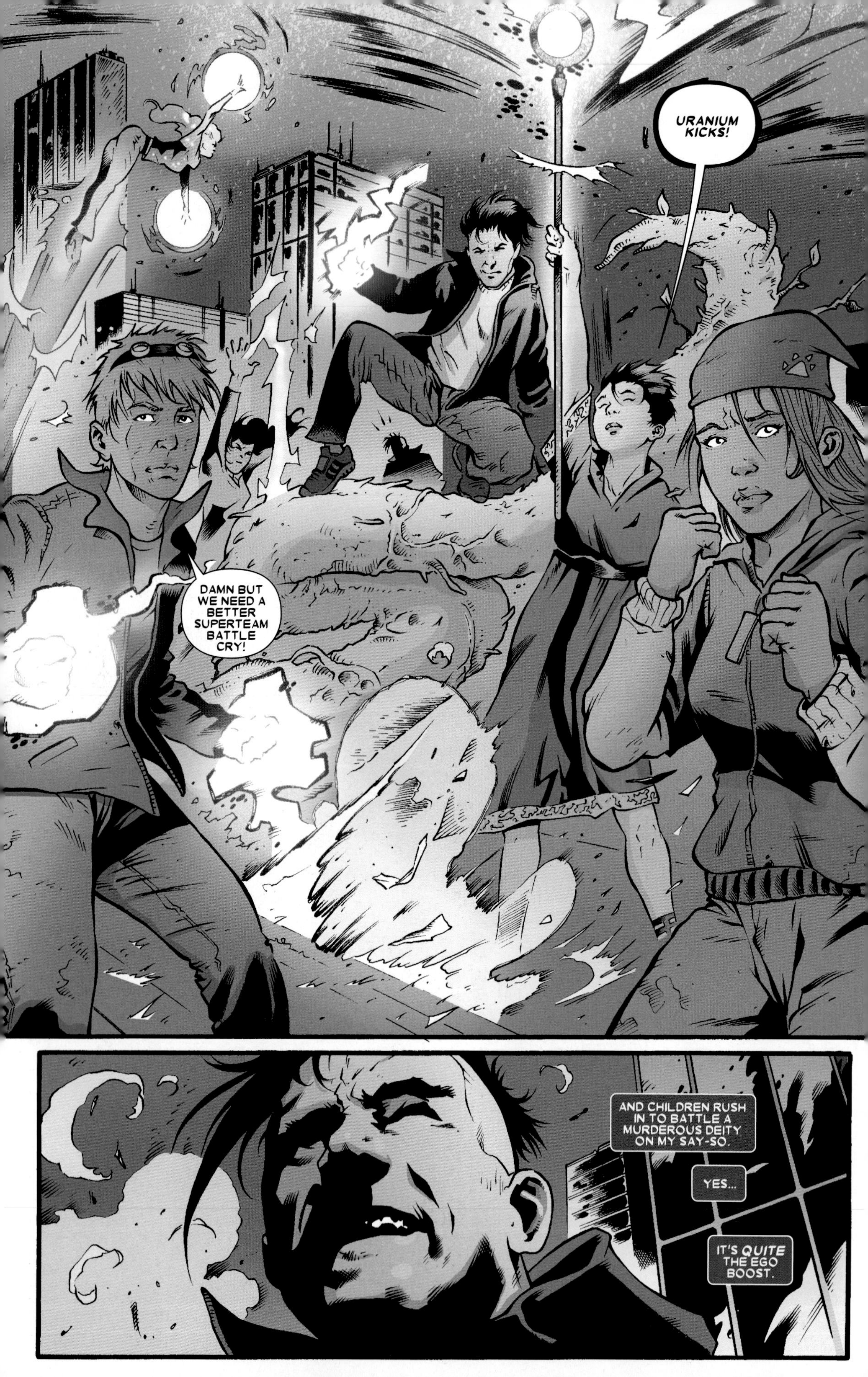
URANIUM KICKS!
DAMN BUT WE NEED A BETTER SUPERTEAM BATTLE CRY!
AND CHILDREN RUSH IN TO BATTLE A MURDEROUS DEITY ON MY SAY-SO.
YES...
IT'S *QUITE* THE EGO BOOST.

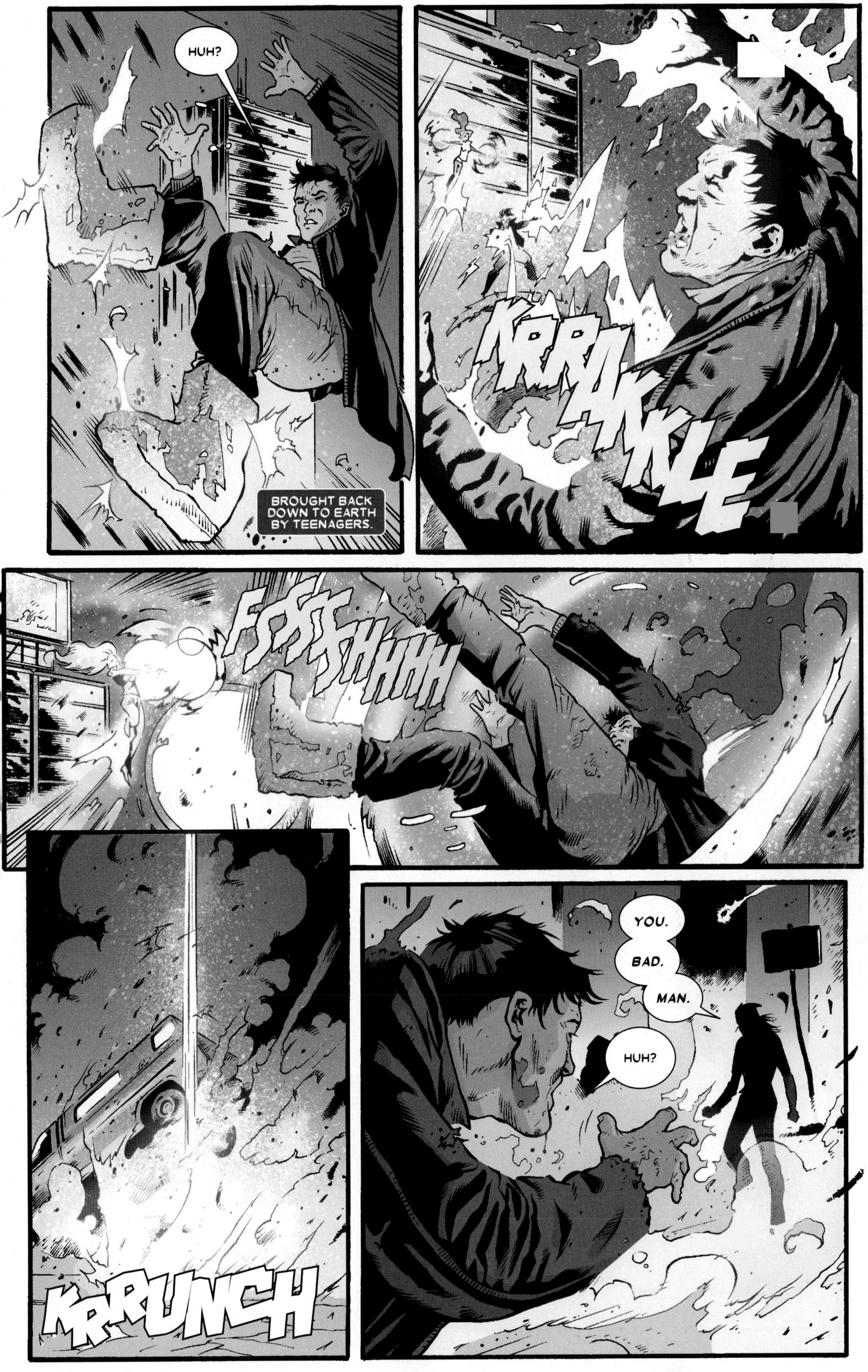
HUH?
BROUGHT BACK DOWN TO EARTH BY TEENAGERS.
KRRAKKLE
FSSSSHHHH
KRRUNCH
YOU.
BAD.
MAN.
HUH?

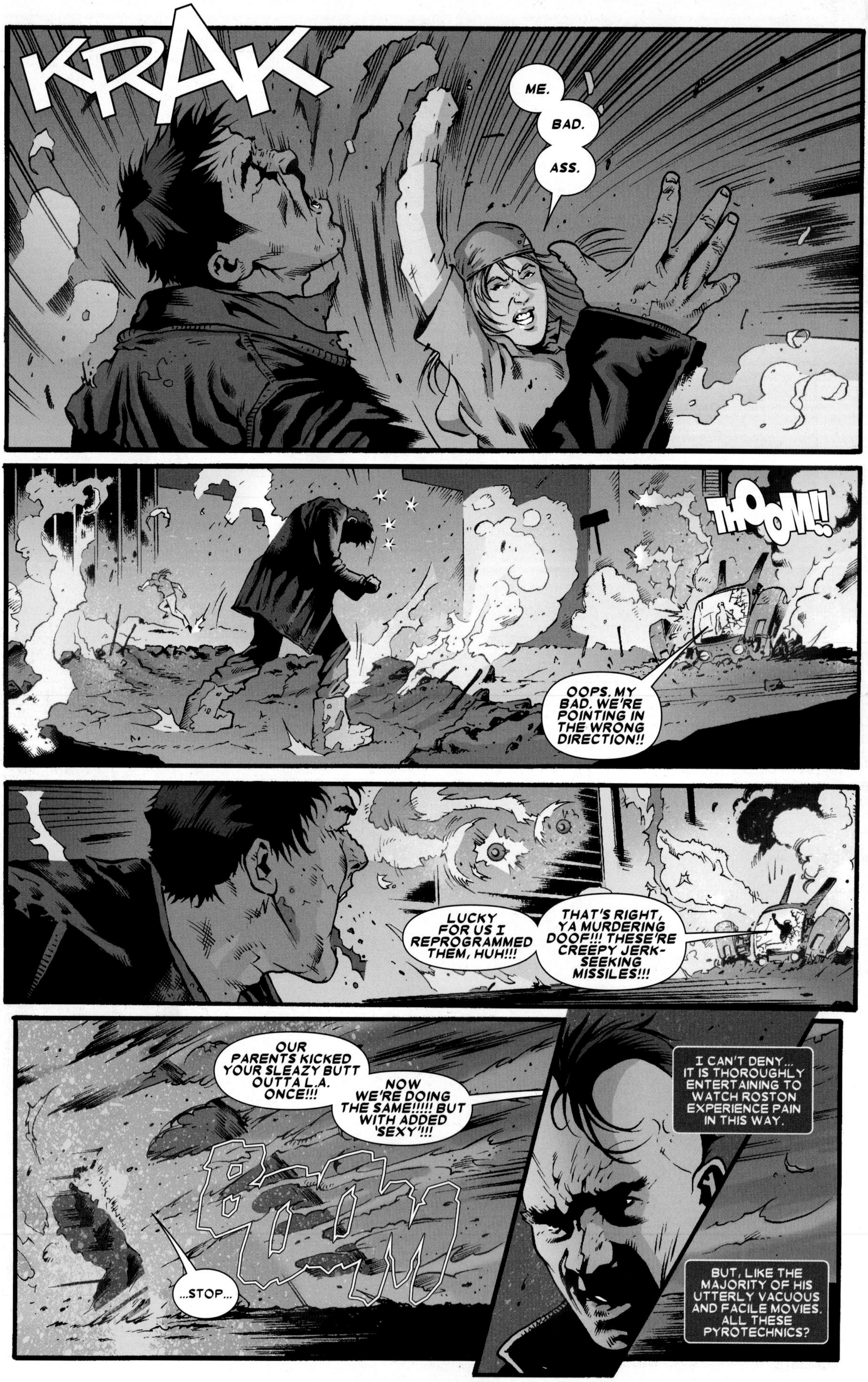
KRAK
ME.
BAD.
ASS.
THOOM!!
OOPS. MY BAD. WE'RE POINTING IN THE WRONG DIRECTION!!
LUCKY FOR US I REPROGRAMMED THEM, HUH!!!
THAT'S RIGHT, YA MURDERING DOOF!!! THESE'RE CREEPY JERK-SEEKING MISSILES!!!
OUR PARENTS KICKED YOUR SLEAZY BUTT OUTTA L.A. ONCE!!!
NOW WE'RE DOING THE SAME!!!!! BUT WITH ADDED 'SEXY'!!!
I CAN'T DENY... IT IS THOROUGHLY ENTERTAINING TO WATCH ROSTON EXPERIENCE PAIN IN THIS WAY.
BOOM
...STOP...
BUT, LIKE THE MAJORITY OF HIS UTTERLY VACUOUS AND FACILE MOVIES. ALL THESE PYROTECHNICS?

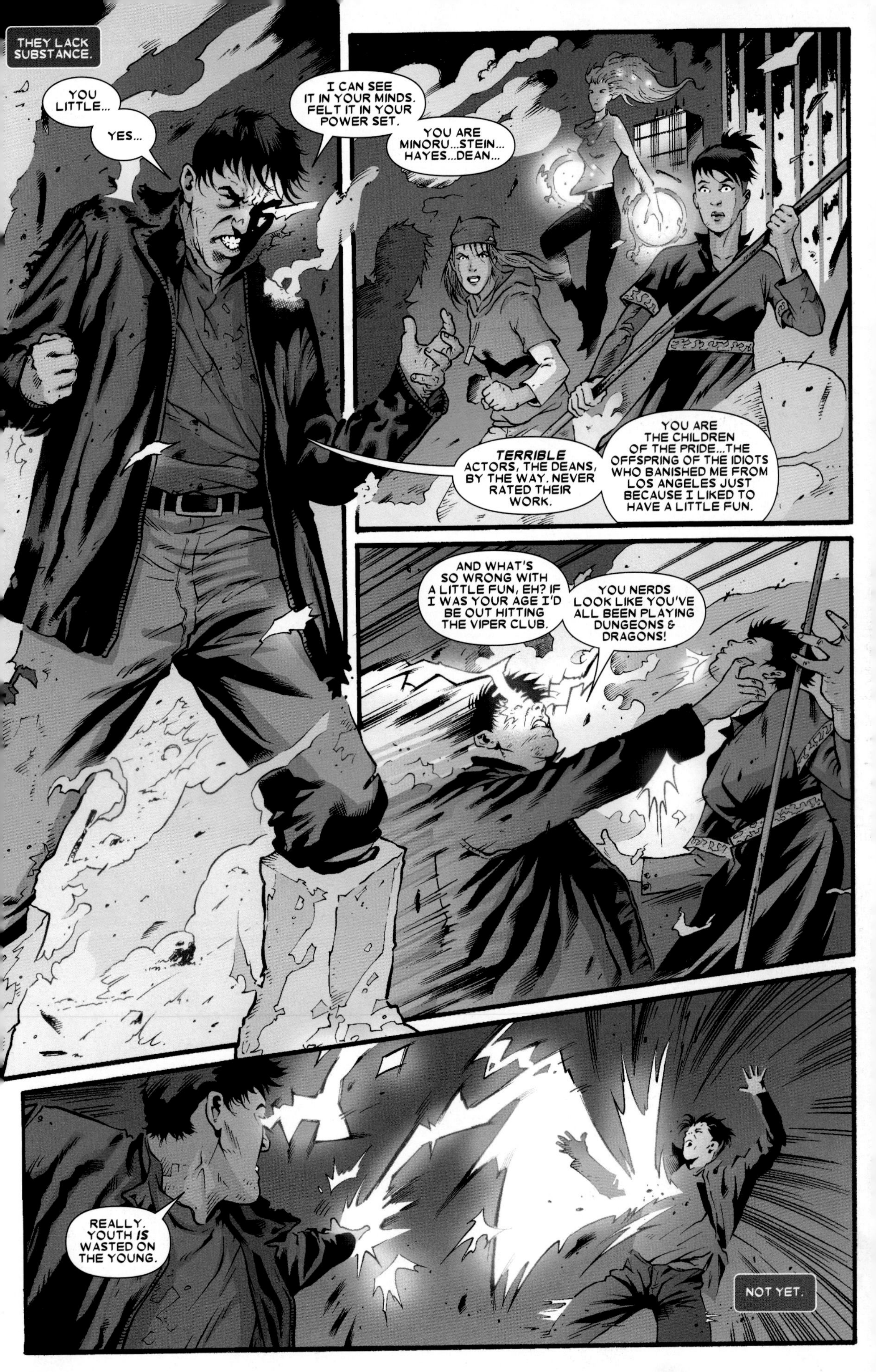
THEY LACK SUBSTANCE.
YOU LITTLE...
YES...
I CAN SEE IT IN YOUR MINDS. FELT IT IN YOUR POWER SET.
YOU ARE MINORU...STEIN... HAYES...DEAN...
YOU ARE THE CHILDREN OF THE PRIDE...THE OFFSPRING OF THE IDIOTS WHO BANISHED ME FROM LOS ANGELES JUST BECAUSE I LIKED TO HAVE A LITTLE FUN.
TERRIBLE ACTORS, THE DEANS, BY THE WAY. NEVER RATED THEIR WORK.
AND WHAT'S SO WRONG WITH A LITTLE FUN, EH? IF I WAS YOUR AGE I'D BE OUT HITTING THE VIPER CLUB.
YOU NERDS LOOK LIKE YOU'VE ALL BEEN PLAYING DUNGEONS & DRAGONS!
REALLY. YOUTH IS WASTED ON THE YOUNG.
NOT YET.

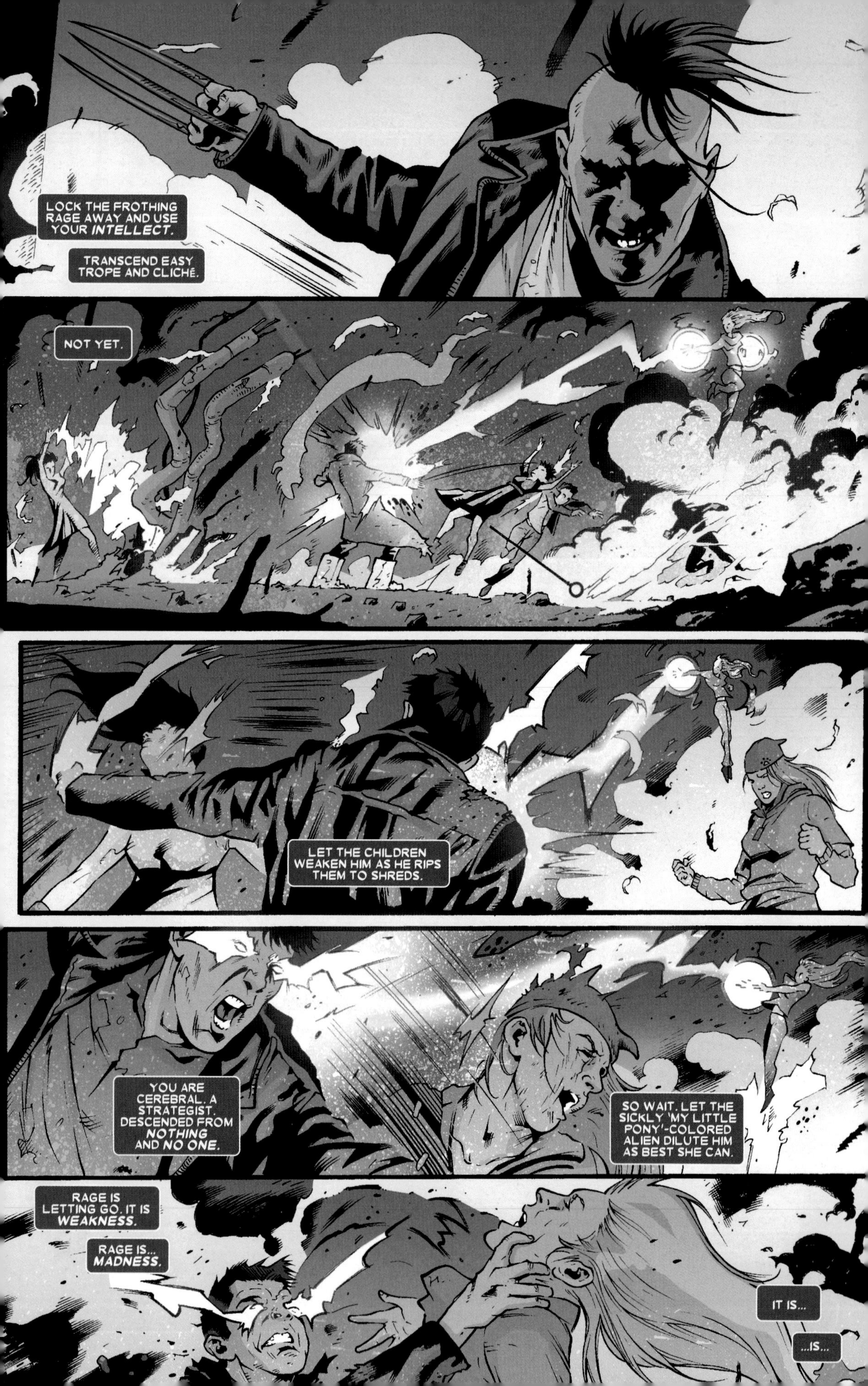
LOCK THE FROTHING RAGE AWAY AND USE YOUR *INTELLECT*.
TRANSCEND EASY TROPE AND CLICHÉ.
NOT YET.
LET THE CHILDREN WEAKEN HIM AS HE RIPS THEM TO SHREDS.
YOU ARE CEREBRAL, A STRATEGIST, DESCENDED FROM *NOTHING* AND *NO ONE*.
SO WAIT. LET THE SICKLY 'MY LITTLE PONY'-COLORED ALIEN DILUTE HIM AS BEST SHE CAN.
RAGE IS LETTING GO. IT IS *WEAKNESS*.
RAGE IS... *MADNESS*.
IT IS...
...IS...

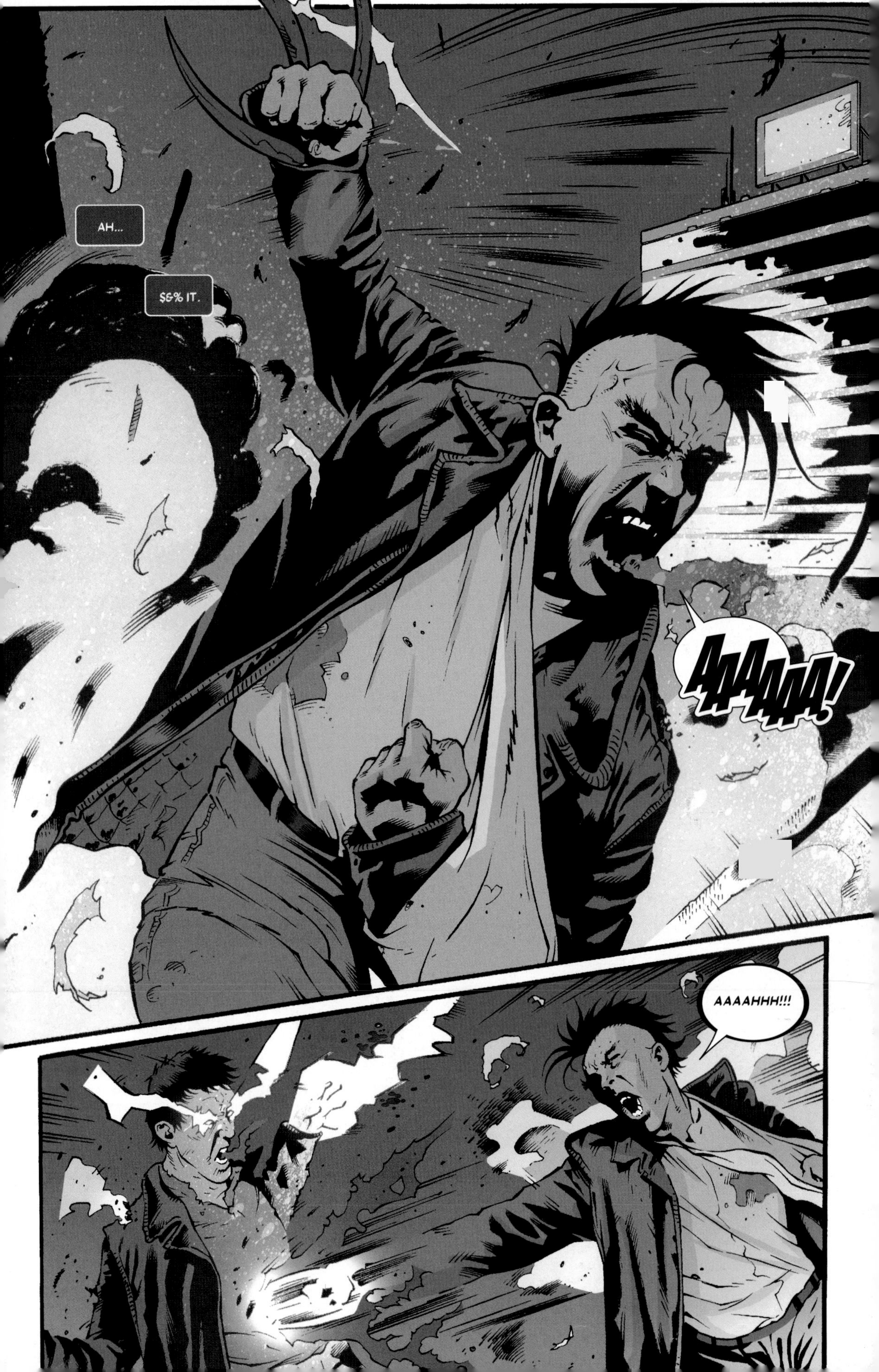
AH...
$&% IT.
AAAAAA!
AAAAHHH!!!

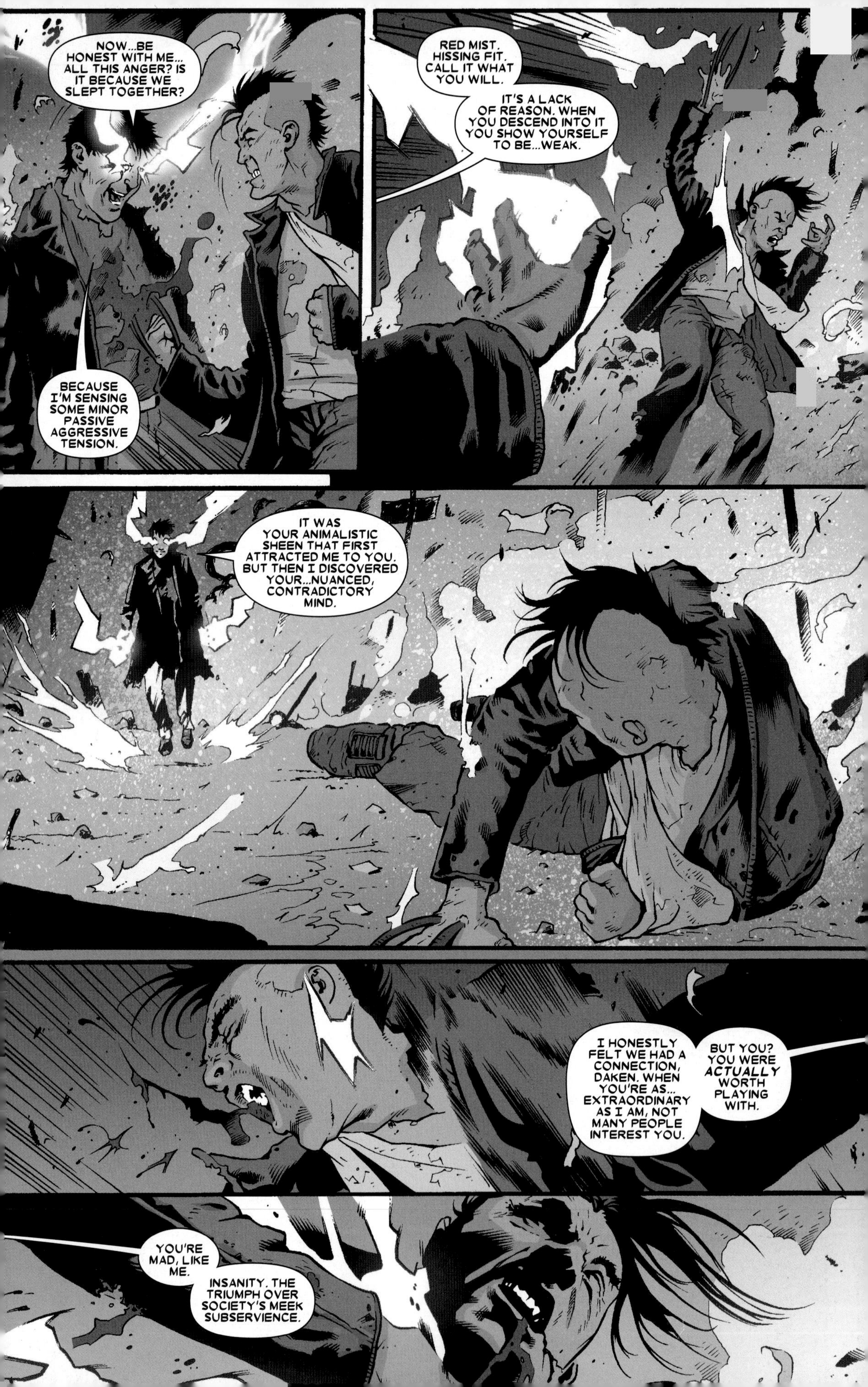
NOW...BE HONEST WITH ME... ALL THIS ANGER? IS IT BECAUSE WE SLEPT TOGETHER?
BECAUSE I'M SENSING SOME MINOR PASSIVE AGGRESSIVE TENSION.
RED MIST. HISSING FIT. CALL IT WHAT YOU WILL.
IT'S A LACK OF REASON. WHEN YOU DESCEND INTO IT YOU SHOW YOURSELF TO BE...WEAK.
IT WAS YOUR ANIMALISTIC SHEEN THAT FIRST ATTRACTED ME TO YOU. BUT THEN I DISCOVERED YOUR...NUANCED, CONTRADICTORY MIND.
I HONESTLY FELT WE HAD A CONNECTION, DAKEN. WHEN YOU'RE AS... EXTRAORDINARY AS I AM, NOT MANY PEOPLE INTEREST YOU.
BUT YOU? YOU WERE *ACTUALLY* WORTH PLAYING WITH.
YOU'RE MAD, LIKE ME.
INSANITY. THE TRIUMPH OVER SOCIETY'S MEEK SUBSERVIENCE.

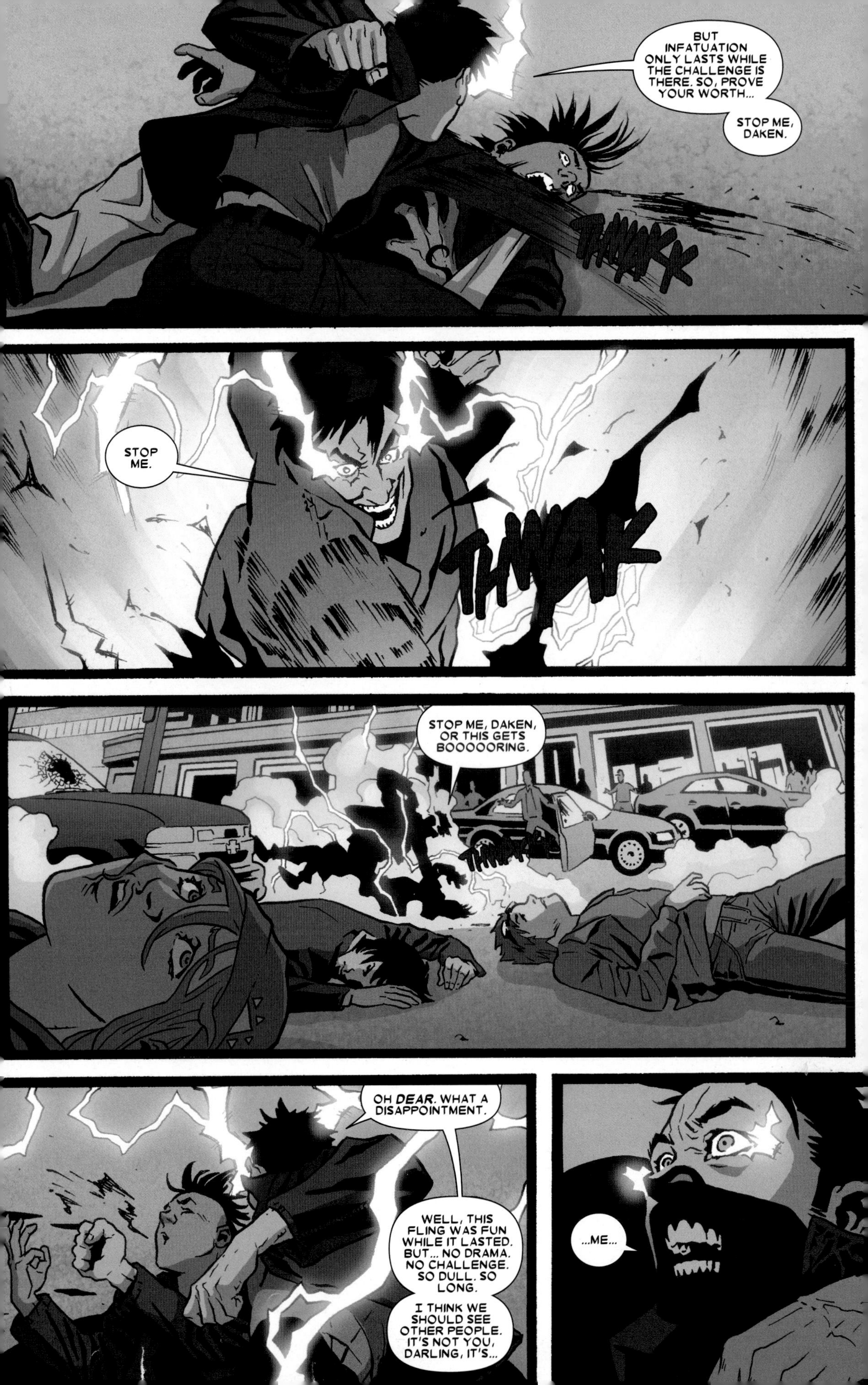
BUT INFATUATION ONLY LASTS WHILE THE CHALLENGE IS THERE. SO, PROVE YOUR WORTH...
STOP ME, DAKEN.
THWAKK
STOP ME.
THWAK
STOP ME, DAKEN, OR THIS GETS BOOOOORING.
OH DEAR. WHAT A DISAPPOINTMENT.
WELL, THIS FLING WAS FUN WHILE IT LASTED. BUT... NO DRAMA. NO CHALLENGE. SO DULL. SO LONG.
I THINK WE SHOULD SEE OTHER PEOPLE. IT'S NOT YOU, DARLING, IT'S...
...ME...

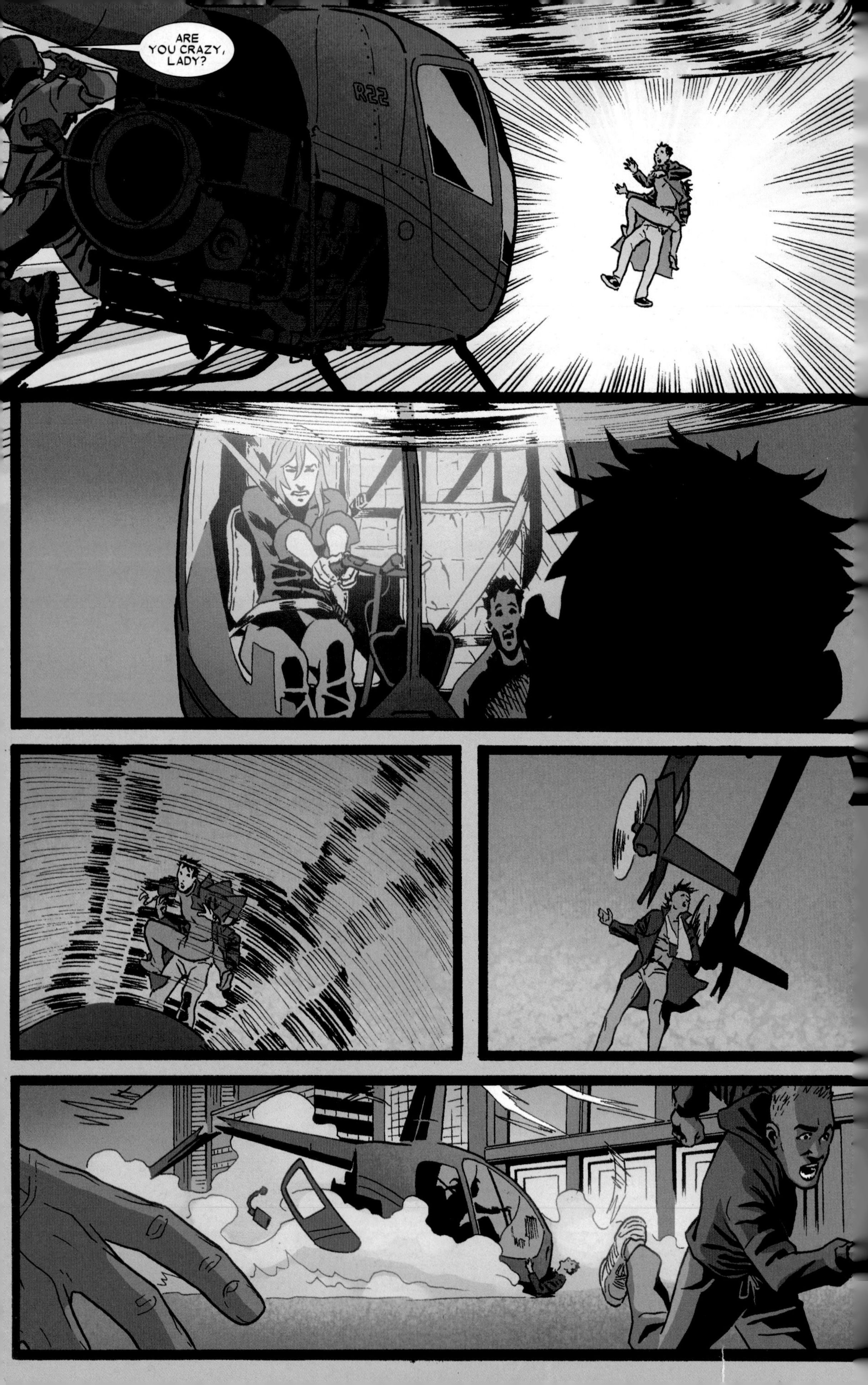
ARE YOU CRAZY, LADY?
R22

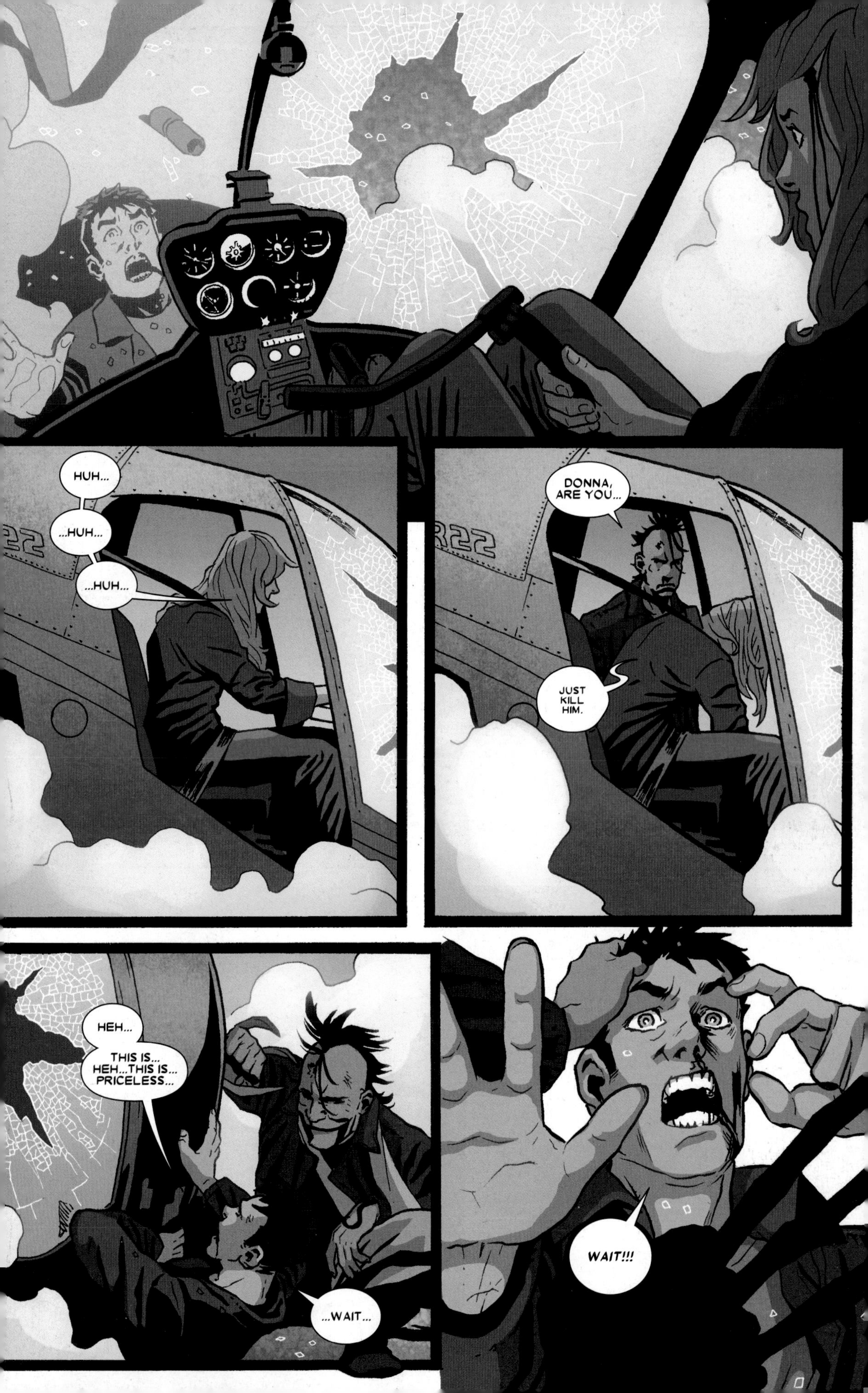
HUH...
...HUH...
...HUH...
DONNA, ARE YOU...
JUST KILL HIM.
HEH...
THIS IS... HEH...THIS IS... PRICELESS...
...WAIT...
WAIT!!!

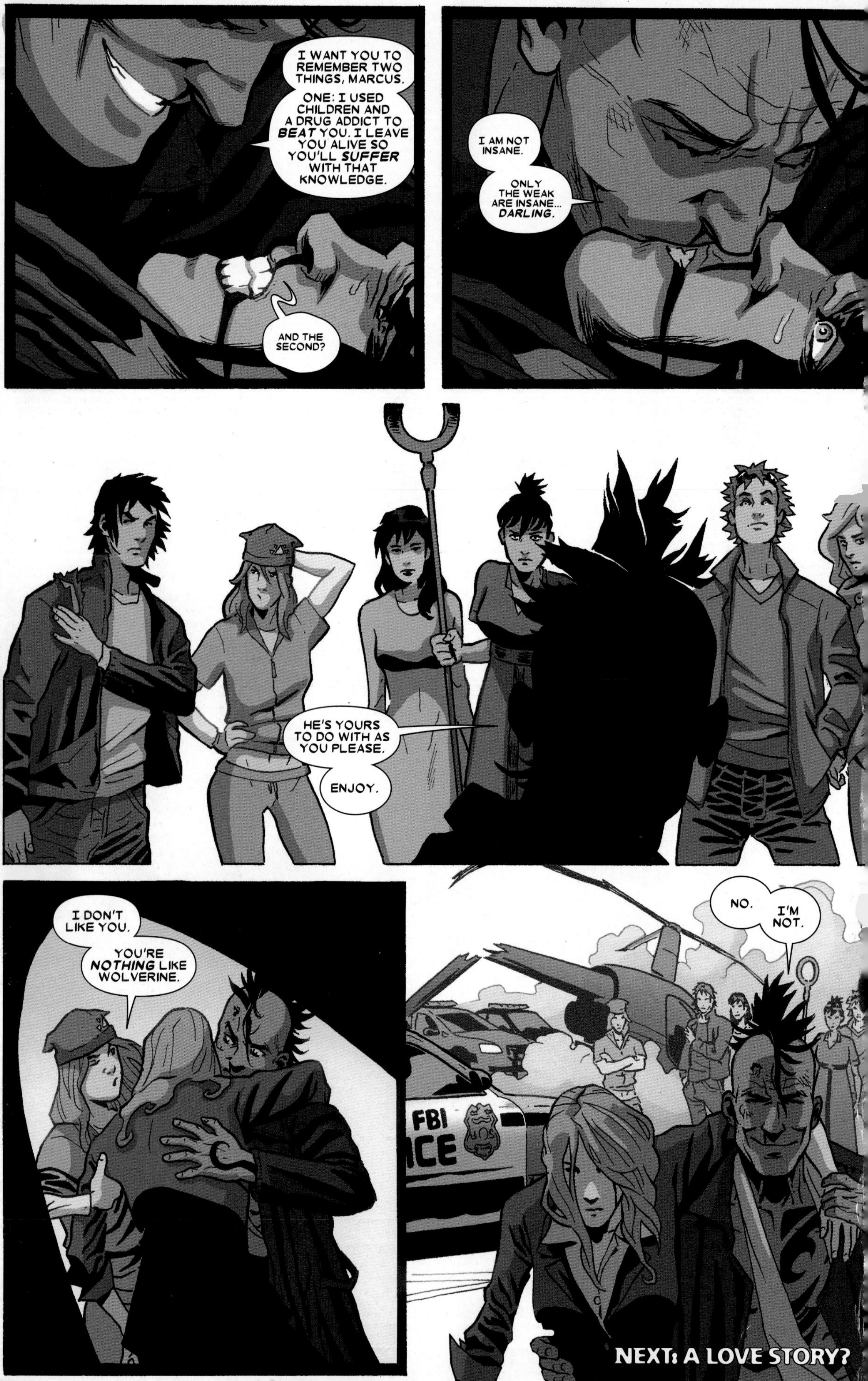
I WANT YOU TO REMEMBER TWO THINGS, MARCUS.
ONE: I USED CHILDREN AND A DRUG ADDICT TO BEAT YOU. I LEAVE YOU ALIVE SO YOU'LL SUFFER WITH THAT KNOWLEDGE.
AND THE SECOND?
I AM NOT INSANE.
ONLY THE WEAK ARE INSANE... DARLING.
HE'S YOURS TO DO WITH AS YOU PLEASE.
ENJOY.
I DON'T LIKE YOU.
YOU'RE NOTHING LIKE WOLVERINE.
NO.
I'M NOT.
FBI
NCE
NEXT: A LOVE STORY?